The American
Golfer
The Sport Pictorial

November 15, 1924   25 Cents

Edited by Grantland Rice

With which is combined "Sports Graphic"

JIM BARNES

The Five Most Important Tips - James M. Barnes

The American
GOLFER
THE SPORT PICTORIAL

March 10, 1923   Grantland Rice -- Editor   25 Cents

HEY- THAT'S MY BALL!

Bernard Darwin--Grantland Rice--O. B. Keeler--George A. Dixon, Jr.
E. Ellsworth Giles--J. S. Worthington

THE CLASSICS OF GOLF

Edition of

THE AMERICAN GOLFER

Edited by

Charles Price

Foreword by Herbert Warren Wind
Afterword by Robert Cromie

Charles Price, a good amateur golfer who began his career in writing as a reporter for Golf World *magazine in the late 1940s, has been a prominent part of the golf scene since those days. He was the first editor of* Golf, *the monthly magazine; he has written several entertaining books including, most recently,* "A Golf Story: Bobby Jones, Augusta National, and the Masters Tournament"; *and he is at present a regular contributor to* Golf Digest *magazine. However, I doubt if any of Charlie Price's accomplishments has surpassed his work as the editor of* "The American Golfer", *a really brilliant collection of some seventy-five pieces that appeared in the magazine of that name between 1920 and 1936. The magazine died in 1936, as so many good things did during the Great Depression. Price's anthology, published in 1964, captures both the words and the music of that remarkable publication: the elegant layout; the sophisticated covers and line drawings, and the attractive advertisements; the superb photographs of the great golfers and the great golf courses; and, along with them, the charming informal photographs of the stars of stage, screen, government, and business who were avid and happy golfers: for starters, Ty Cobb, Ruby Keeler, Charles Schwab, Crown Prince Hirohito, Katharine Hepburn, John McCormack, Marshall Field, Lady Astor and Harold Lloyd. Last but not least, it projects the impression that, in issue after issue,* The American Golfer *was loaded with bright, lively golf writing. Indeed it was.*

Some of the regular contributors to The American Golfer *included Grantland Rice, the nationally syndicated sports columnist, who was the magazine's editor; Ring Lardner; Bernard Darwin, the golf correspondent of the* Times *of London; William D. Richardson, of the New York* Times; *O.B. Keeler, of the Atlanta* Journal; *and Robert T. Jones, Jr., the well-known golfer, who, after his retirement from competition, wrote many extremely perceptive articles for the magazine. Champions like Walter Hagen, Ted Ray, Chick Evans, Jock Hutchison, Tommy Armour, Jim Barnes, and Joyce Wethered provided intelligent instruction articles that had the sound of their own voice. Rice and his assistant editor, Innis Brown, were always on the look-out for good writers, and contributors as various as Clarence Budington Kelland, one of the venerable stars of* The Saturday Evening Post, *and James Reston, a young Scottish journalist who had come to this country, appeared in its pages.* The American Golfer *depicted a world of happy, able, and spirited men and women who made it clear they appreciated that golf was an important part of their lives.*

The American Golfer, *which came out monthly, was founded in 1908 by its first editor, Walter J. Travis, a truly exceptional man. Born in Australia, Travis came to the United States when he was still a boy. He did not take up golf until he was thirty-five. He taught himself how to play the game by setting aside two instruction books. One was the Badminton Library's volume on "Golf", edited by Horace Hutchinson and published in 1890. The other was Willie Park, Jr's*

"The Game of Golf", the first instruction book written by a golf professional. It came out in 1896. During the autumn of that year and the winter of the next, Travis, a man with a very disciplined mind, examined the theories and practical suggestions profferred by the two books and accepted those which he thought would best suit a man of his age and slight physique. He spent much of the spring and summer of 1897 practicing the movements of his swing rather than playing the course of the club he had joined, the Oakland Golf Club, on Long Island. In 1898, Travis entered the United States Amateur championship and actually reached the semifinals. In 1900, four years after he had started to learn the game, he won the U.S. Amateur, which was held that year at the Garden City Golf Club, on Long Island. He successfully defended his title in 1901 at the Country Club of Atlantic City, and in 1903 he won the Amateur for the third time at the Nassau Country Club, another Long Island course. In the final, playing crisp par golf, he took care of Eben M. Byers, of Pittsburgh, 5 and 4. The Old Man, as Travis came to be called, didn't hit the ball far, but he was always down the middle from tee to green. On the greens, with his body relaxed but perfectly still, and with his smooth putting stroke resembling the swing of a pendulum, he rolled in putt after putt. Although he went on winning tournaments until 1915, when he won the Metropolitan Amateur championship for the last time, his career really had reached its apex in 1904 when, at forty-three, he had the crust to enter the British Amateur, and, at Royal St. George's in Sandwich, he became the first foreign golfer to carry off that prized championship. On his undeterrable march to the title, Travis defeated seven tournament-seasoned golfers, including old Horace Hutchinson himself in the semifinals.

During Travis's years as its editor, The American Golfer was a fine magazine that covered the game handsomely and was very strong on instruction. In its first issue in 1908, Travis paid a great deal of attention to the country's U.S. Amateur champion, young Jerry Travers, stating in so many words that Travers had the finest golf swing he knew of. (Travers, after winning our Amateur in 1907 and 1908, came back to win it again in 1912 and 1913, and he then went on to add the United States Open in 1915.) Along with editing his magazine with a firm hand, Travis spent the latter years of his life designing golf courses in the summer and enjoying the companionship of his Old Guards group at Palm Beach during the winter. He was a painstaking and skillful golf-course architect. A typical Travis course, which puts a high premium on accuracy, is the Garden City Golf Club, where the Travis Memorial tournament is held each spring. Two other courses of his that I know fairly well and like immensely are in Manchester, Vermont—Equinox and Ekwanok. On the latter, Francis Ouimet won the U.S. Amateur championship in 1914.

When the new American Golfer arrived on the scene in 1920, it was published by Conde Nast, a firm situated in Greenwich, Connecticut, which specialized in such glossy, well-produced magazines as Vanity Fair and Vogue. Grantland Rice was its editor—the perfect choice. A pleasant, knowledgeable, high-principled man, Rice, a Tennessean who had gone to Vanderbilt University, was probably the most widely read sportswriter in the country, for his daily column was syndicated from coast to coast. Like most of the sportswriters of his era, Rice devoted a good deal of his attention to professional baseball, college football, championship boxing, and the Olympic Games. He was very much at home, though, in tennis and golf, and he had a lot to do with their escalating popularity in the 1920s. Of course, this was the decade when American tennis players finally came into their own at Wimbledon and when homegrown American golfers showed the world that times had changed by dominating the British Open. A low-handicap golfer, Rice was the first prominent American sportswriter who thought of golf as a major sport. He was a close friend of Bobby Jones's and one of the charter members of the Augusta National Golf Club. In 1936, when the Olympic Games were held in Berlin, The Rices and the Joneses went over together. Rice's informal, informed style set the tone for The American Golfer.

Since you have Charlie Price's "The American Golfer" handy, let me suggest that you turn to page thirteen and begin your reading with "The Most Common Faults", which was written by O.B. Keeler, Jones's longtime friend from the Atlanta Journal. This piece is fundamentally the account of a recent experience Keeler underwent when he attempted to interview Jones's mentor, Stewart Maiden, about the basic elements of the correct golf swing. Maiden, a taciturn Scot, was, predictably, in no

mind to expostulate on such a touchy and misunderstood subject. Keeler, however, stays valiantly with his task, and little by little, in a different way than you have ever heard a celebrated teacher talk about what makes for a sound golf swing, Maiden, over the course of nine-and-a-half pages, tells you much more about the golf swing than you had ever expected, and he tells you this in an eminently logical and lucid way. Keeler's interview is a fascinating tour de force.

A great many of the articles included in Price's collection are written with such skill and flavor that they remain fresh today. Here are a few examples. First, a paragraph by Bernard Darwin from his article "The Style of Harry Vardon", which appeared in The American Golfer in 1929:

> Well, now, what were the characteristics both of his [Vardon's] method and its results which made him so devastating a conquerer? Results are easier to tackle, and I will take them first. Vardon was first of all a magnificent driver. He was with the gutty ball uncommonly long, especially down the wind, and he was very straight. Taylor had been regarded as inhumanly accurate, and so he was. Now here came Vardon who rivalled his accuracy and added to it a little something more of freedom and power. He had a gift of hitting long carrying shots, and, because of his upright swing, the ball would sit down with but little run where it pitched. The gift was of enormous value through the green. The brassie was not atrophied then, there were lots of wooden shots to be played up to the pin, and Vardon, who often played them with his driver, could and did

put the ball nearer the hole than other men could with their mashies. It was his most overpowering stroke and, even if he had been a bad putter then (which he was not), it left him little putting to do.

Here is Rice gravitating to Bobby Jones in a piece called "They Can't Stop Jones Yet". He is writing about the 1929 U.S. Open at Winged Foot, a championship Jones had apparently thrown away by taking two 7s on the last eleven holes. In the third paragraph of this article, Rice tells us,

Jones came to Winged Foot in late spring for the National Open, feeling fit and ready, just coming into his game. He was a bit ragged on the first practice round, but after that he sent out warning that he was ready again with a series of sensational performances. Instead of being worn out after his playoff with Al Espinosa, he said the next day that he felt as if he had just started hitting the ball and could use a lot more golf.

Two paragraphs later, Rice returns to his theme:

It has been said before that golf is full of more astonishing twists and turns, squalls and upsets, swirls and eddies, than any game ever planned or played. This championship proved it. Al Espinosa spotted Bobby Jones six strokes at the sixty-sixth hole, and then caught him on the seventy-second. But a day later, after getting a two-stroke jump on Jones on the first hole of the playoff, Espinosa then lost twenty-five strokes on the next thirty-five holes. How could this happen? Easily enough when one is overgolfed and suddenly realizes that his timing is

gone against an opponent who is hammering every shot straight for the pin.

This naturalness and sense of immediacy was very much on hand in the magazine's instructional features. For example, consider the final paragraph of "My Angle of Putting" by Walter Hagen, one of the best putters of all time.

I keep my weight largely on my left foot, but such fine putters as Bobby Jones and Jerry Travers keep their weight almost evenly balanced. The matter of weight and stance doesn't matter so much, so long as you feel comfortable and natural, anything to cut down tension and the feeling of stiffness and tightness. Keep your body out of all short putts or fairly short ones, but that doesn't mean to turn your body into a stone post. There can be no feel when you are that way, all tightened up. I've seen a lot of good putters use a lot of different methods, but I never saw a good putter who looked stiff and uncomfortable. They simply don't go together.

The American Golfer's portals for articles on instruction were open not only to the famous champions. For example, Eddie Loos, a club professional who played excellent golf on his periodic visits to the P.G.A. tour, contributed some first-class instruction pieces to the magazine. Here is an excerpt from one of them called "The Eight-Inch Golf Course"—the player's head, naturally:

The oldest golf instruction extant in the early days of the paid professional coach was to take the beginner and make him swing a club without a ball for days before he actually hit one. Then, to make him hit shots with the various clubs various distances without actually playing a game—this for a month or so. This system, a wonderful one, was based—although I never heard it so explained—upon the building in the beginner's mind of proper mental patterns, free from the obstructing strain of actual play.

I learned to play golf with the flat swing of Willie Anderson, my idol. I created my mental patterns upon this method of play. When I changed to the "upright swing" and the "game through the air", I was forced to completely change my train of mental patterns, those relating to the arc of the swing, the stance, and the timing. Of course, my grip and my "club feel" patterns remained the same. My game went back. But once the new mental patterns were correctly established, by experiment and practice, my game became better than ever before.

Here is the way mental patterns evince themselves. I stand up with an iron. My usual shot would be a high, long ball to drop dead upon the green. But a strong wind is blowing against me. So I call to mind my mental pattern of a push shot, get my directions, and execute it.

I don't believe that there is an only ordinarily good article in this collection. I find it impossible to pick any one favorite, but, if pushed, I might say that O.B. Keeler's account of the 1930 British Amateur is far and away the best account of a match-play tournament I have ever read. I am very fond also of Keeler's report on the 1929 U.S. Amateur at Pebble Beach— the first course west of St. Louis on which an American national championship was held. Jones was expelled in the first round that year by Johnny Goodman, but Keeler adjusted to this, and his article is a perfect example of the feeling of the enjoyment, discovery, and appreciation of the game that was so characteristic of The American Golfer. Here is a brief paragraph, for example, that comes near the end of the article:

It's a tough course as well as a beautiful one, at Pebble Beach. Indeed, that is the impression I carry away with me from the 1929 National Amateur Championship. In the South, we have no courses suitable to compare with those architectural visions on the Monterey Peninsula, and with those I saw at Los Angeles. And even along the Eastern seaboard, and on the famed black turf of the Middle West, there seems to me nothing so fine and beautiful. I honestly believe that the California courses I have seen, at Los Angeles and near San Francisco, and especially Cypress Point and Pebble Beach, on the Monterey Peninsula, are the finest golf courses in the world today.

For no planned reason, most of the articles I have mentioned or quoted from were written in the 1920s. Let me assure you that there was no letdown in the quality of The American Golfer as it moved into the mid-1930s. Lawson Little's stunning "double double"—he won the British Amateur and the U.S. Amateur in both 1933–34 and 1934–35—is documented with suitable exuberance, and there are photographs of the youthful Byron Nelson and the strong, untrained swing of that future phenomenon, Babe Didrikson, which linger in the memory.

When The American Golfer *was forced to discontinue publication in 1936, it hit many people hard. Grantland Rice, however, remained the leading voice in American sportswriting for many years to come. The last time I saw him was at a luncheon at Toots Shor's restaurant in the summer of 1953 to welcome and honor Ben Hogan upon his return from winning the British Open at Carnoustie. Rice served as the master of ceremonies, and this sort of made things official.*

One thing more. Charlie Price's "The American Golfer" is a treasure trove. A word to the wise. Be smart and limit yourself to no more than two articles at one sitting.

The Afterword is the generous contribution of Robert Cromie, for years the celebrated literary critic of The Chicago Tribune. An inveterate golfer, Cromie has edited a superb golf anthology, "Par for the Course," published in 1964.

Herbert Warren Wind

THE AMERICAN GOLFER

BOOKS BY CHARLES PRICE: *The World of Golf*
The American Golfer (EDITOR)

The American Golfer

EDITED BY CHARLES PRICE

 RANDOM HOUSE · NEW YORK

The author wishes to thank the publishers and editors of *The American Golfer* magazine for making this book possible, and especially ROBERT T. JONES, JR. for permission to include his copyrighted articles.

I can think of no contributor to this book—living or dead—who would begrudge me the opportunity of dedicating it to

BOB JONES

the American Golfer

TABLE OF CONTENTS

The American Golfer BY CHARLES PRICE

Who——and What——He Was

THE AMERICAN GOLFER IS SUPPOSED TO HAVE been not so much a real person as an outrageous state of mind, like the era he lived in —the Roaring Twenties. It is typical of the distortion with which this period is often looked back upon by golfers that the Roaring Twenties sometime include the first half of the Thirties. It is an almost pardonable error. After all, people have been playing golf for three hundred years longer than they have been playing the piano.

The American golfer is supposed to have always dressed in knickers baggy enough to have concealed a dozen oranges at each knee and in argyles whose screams could be heard six fairways off. He smoked Melachrino cigarettes and drank instant gin. His wife was a flat-chested, gum-chewing nincompoop who spent half her nights dancing the Charleston to saxophones and snare drums. Together, they tooled their way in a roadster to the country club, their clubs tossed into the rumble seat. He spent a casual day intentionally losing a match to his tyranical boss (probably his father-in-law) and she spent the day taking lessons from some tweedy Scottish professional with a theatrical burr in his voice and a habit of discussing in painful detail how he had won the Caledonia Open somewhere back around the Boer War.

The husband shot consistently in the 90's over a course no more hazardous than a pool table. He sported approximately twenty-six hickory-shafted clubs, only four of which he actually used: a brassie, a mashie, a niblick and a putter that he took home to bed with him because his wife at the time was secretly in love with Rudolph Valentino. She—well, she couldn't shoot 110 in the shade, mainly because she spent most of her time on the course flirting, applying lipstick, or deciding which end of the caddie to hit the ball with.

That's what the American golfer is supposed to have been.

For a reason that altogether misses its mark with the golfer of that period, this version of the American golfer is always painted by Americans who never hit their first golf shot until after the last World War. It's worth noting that *they* play golf in short pants instead of knickers, colored sweat socks instead of argyles, smoke Salems instead of Melachrinos, and drink instant vodka instead of gin. Their wives, to continue, are flat-chested without trying to be, chew tranquilizers instead of gum, and spend half the night dancing some form of the Twist rather than the Charleston. But let's not go into all that here. The point is that each of us has a pompous tendency to regard the youthful ways of our antecedents as slightly ridiculous.

The American golfer may have been peculiar, even humorous, but he was never ridiculous. He just seems that way today because he had as marvelous a capacity for laughing at himself as we sickly do today at others. He did this through H. T. Webster and Rube Goldberg and Gluyas Williams and Clare Briggs and Fontaine Fox, using pen and ink, and through George Ade and Irvin S. Cobb and Don Marquis and Ring Lardner, using the typewriter. (If you can't laugh at Lardner, you really are sick.)

In many respects, the American golfer as he is portrayed here could only have prevailed during those uninhibited years which invariably follow a major war. Until 1920— when this anthology begins its selections— golf was played almost exclusively at golf clubs, as distinct from country clubs. Clubhouses were built on the scale of bungalows then, not motels. Golf shops had not yet become haberdasheries but, rather, were little more than shacks, redolent with the intoxicating odors of shellac, pitch and old leather and dirty from lampblack, hickory shavings, and bits of twine, "Whipping," it was called.

Then, in the space of the dozen years during which the American golfer came into his own, golf clubs became country clubs in every sense of the word, with clubhouses built on the order of Grand Central Terminal. No, come to think of it, Grand Central must have been built on the order of them. One, Olympia Fields, near Chicago, had four eighteen-hole courses, a hundred houses, a hospital, a fire department, two thousand caddies, dining halls that could feed fourteen hundred people simultaneously, a dancing pavilion large enough to have accommodated a Democratic Convention, and a veranda that wasn't quite as long as the back stretch at Arlington Park. You weren't a "member" at Olympia Fields; you were a citizen.

At the beginning of those twelve years, there probably were no more than 500,000 golfers in America. At the end, there were easily ten times that number. And the country

clubs that were built to handle them reached a figure that was not surpassed until 1963, many of the originals having gone bankrupt during the depression or having been used as the sites for housing projects soon thereafter.

The American golfer was also peculiar in that he bought gold-plated putters, elbow girdles, practice nets, and lessons that were given by phonograph records. There was nothing ridiculous about this extravagance. It only seems ridiculous when you see golfers buying them forty years later, now that we know how worthless they are.

But make no mistake! The American golfer knew how to play golf, his extravagant ways notwithstanding. Indeed, with his wooden shafts, his mismatched irons, his slick grips, his balloon ball, his lofted putters for skimming the ball over peanut-brittle greens—and no "sand wedge" mind you, but using instead a delicate pitch out of a bunker with a niblick— he played an introspective brand of golf that we might never see again, developing an individualistic style that flew in the face of almost everything academic we had known about playing the game, and winning championships with a competitive spirit that sometimes bordered on genius.

In the space of nine years Walter Hagen, who had already won two National Opens, won nine more major national championships here and in Great Britain, successfully defending one of his titles an unprecedented three successive times. In eight years Bobby Jones played in twenty-one major championships and finished either first or no worse than second in seventeen of them. During that period he won more than sixty per cent of the championships he entered. After he had won them all—each of the four big ones in a single cataclysmic season—he quit because he was twenty-eight and civilized enough to realize that there should be a limit to any man's share.

The scores they won by? Well, there are dozens and dozens of courses all over the world where Hagen set unofficial records, often on his first and only tour of the layout, which have yet to be broken. And Jones set course records that often didn't last more than twenty-four hours because he broke *those* records the day afterwards.

But they were Jones and Hagen, whose molds somebody threw away. Of the others, there was, well, Glenna Collett, for one. In 1925 she played against Joyce Wethered in the wind at Troon in the third round for the title of the Ladies Golfing Union, which comprises the women's amateur championship of Great Britain. The match lasted fifteen holes. Glenna was one over par, but she lost. Miss Wethered had played a stretch of ten holes in four pars and six birdies. They met again four years later for the same title at St. Andrews, this time in the final, at thirty-six holes. Glenna went out in 34 during the first round but eventually lost again—three and one—because Miss Wethered played the next eighteen holes in 73. I don't know whether you have ever played St. Andrews in the wind, but it has been known to make scratch players switch to tennis.

Then there was old Mac Smith, a tweedy Scottish-American pro who won sixty-odd tournaments—not one of them, incredibly, a major championship—and who never once stooped to bragging about how he had won any of them. Mac Smith had a swing that was as graceful as the leap of a cat. He had a peculiarity of never taking divots. He just sort of brushed the ball off the turf, treating it, in the words of Tommy Armour, "as though it were an altar cloth."

Back in 1910 Mac tied for first in the National Open, but lost the play-off to his brother Alex. Twenty-three years later he won the Western Open at Olympia Fields—coincidentally while using steel shafts for one of the first times. He missed only one green in regulation figures and was off the fairway only once in the entire seventy-two holes. One thing you can say for those American golfers, they were durable.

Oddly enough, the American golfer was almost as much British as he was American. Nearly half his ranks on the professional tournament scene were born either in England or Scotland, and no American golfer, professional or amateur, was considered a bona fide competitor unless he played at least part of his golf on the British Isles. He did this almost as a gesture of courtesy toward Harry Vardon, J. H. Taylor, Harold Hilton, Ted Ray and the others for having come over here an era before to show us how the game ought to be played. As things turned out, it was an odd way of thanking them. For during the years which this anthology chronicles, Americans won twelve of the sixteen British Opens played, becoming thereby the unquestioned leaders of the game throughout the world. Not even the most ardent Anglophile tried to make an argument of that.

The American Golfer—the magazine—was born in 1908, and it perhaps could not have been fathered by anyone other than the man who did, Walter J. Travis. At that time, Travis probably knew as much about golf as anybody else in the world. His obsession with the game has perhaps since been matched only by Ben Hogan. As with Hogan, golf to Travis wasn't just a way of fulfilling his life. To Travis, golf *was* life. Everything else was distracting or, at best, analogous to the game. He could, and once did, write a 7000-word essay on the Versailles Conference almost entirely in golf terms. He could theorize about the swing, discuss the process of hitting the ball, spiel the game's history, and argue the fine points of architecture with anyone. Not even Bernard Darwin, the brilliant grandson of the famous evolutionist, who turned out to be the game's most eloquent spokesman, could match the length and breadth of Travis' knowledge of golf. Travis could also play, superbly. But that is a subject Grantland Rice got to, next in this book, in a way I won't try to match.

It may also be that *The American Golfer* could not have been edited when it was by anyone other than Grantland Rice. He took over the reins from Travis after the Great War and steered it right into the middle of the depression, maybe through it if the public had been able to afford the rich sort of wares his publication was selling. Those years were not only years of great golfers but of great magazines, such as *The Century* and *Vanity Fair,* both of which became, beginning in 1919 and 1929 respectively, sister publications of *The American Golfer.* Granny loved golf more than any other game, and he loved every game: baseball, polo, marbles, life itself. More importantly, maybe, everybody loved Granny —indeed, he may well have been the most beloved American since George Washington —and he seemed to know everybody: the political, the artistic, the lettered, the athletic, the elect, the disestablished. They were all represented in his magazine, whether rich or poor, famous or infamous, from Al Smith to Al Jolson, from Aga Khan to Otto Kahn, from Gene Tunney to Jean Harlow—from Walter Hagen to the most thoroughly unknown, underpaid pro at the most ignominious club. All he asked was that you be a golfer with something to say to those in America who had found in golf, as writer Herbert Warren Wind was later to say of their species, that game which best gave them what they hoped to find in a game.

Rice took over a shoestring operation and made it into a paying publication to which attention had to be paid. In one issue—an issue not particularly better than any other—he printed articles by, among others, Ring Lardner, Marc Connelly, Don Marquis, O. B. Keeler, Bernard Darwin, John Kieran, himself, and every current major champion in the United States and Great Britain. All this was done during the peak of a career in which he also wrote hundreds of movie scripts, a thousand magazine articles, twenty-two thousand newspaper columns, and seven thousand pieces of verse—he never referred to any of them as a poem—for a total output of sixty-seven million words, the equivalent of 670 average novels.

Under Travis and then Rice, *The American Golfer* was a golf magazine which took for granted that you played golf, not at it, even though that playing might not have been very good. They assumed that you, as they did, dedicated a little part of your everyday thinking to studying, contemplating, or worrying over this jarringly close imitation of life. As a result, you felt while reading the magazine that if there were a Rosetta Stone to golf—and who doubts even now there isn't?—it would be found among these pages.

That was a lot to expect merely of a magazine. But, as its subscribers came to swear, *The American Golfer* was not a mere magazine. Even today, nearly thirty years after it last went through the mails, you run into golfers who never expect to see its like again. During the British Open at St. Andrews this past year, a competitor in that event recalled that he had taught himself to play, as a boy, by practicing everything he had studiously absorbed from its pages, especially the meticulously phrased, utterly logical instructional pieces by Bobby Jones. But then, he may have been unduly impressed as a boy, particularly since he and Jones have the same first name. His last name is Locke and as a whole later generation of American golfers were to find out, he too could play—like crazy.

New York City

THE AMERICAN GOLFER

Walter J. Travis, first of the great international champions to come from the United States. He founded *The American Golfer* in 1908.

The Old Man BY GRANTLAND RICE

There Will Never Be Another Player Like the
Founder of The American Golfer

IN MANY RESPECTS WALTER J. TRAVIS WILL stand as the most remarkable golfer that ever lived. Just consider, as a starter, these two facts. He won the first tournament he ever entered at the age of thirty-five, a month or so after he had hit his first golf ball. He won the last tournament he ever entered, the Metropolitan Championship, at the age of fifty-four, in 1915, and on his way through he beat Jerry Travers, the United States Open champion of the same year.

Here was a man who started golf at middle age, or well beyond the competitive prime of life. He began a difficult game, a game demanding the imitative power of youth, at the age where most men leave off as champions. He was of slight physique, with rather slight hands and slender wrists. He weighed no more than one hundred and forty pounds. Yet against all these handicaps he wrested four national championships from the best golfers of America and Great Britain.

Few learn golf in a lifetime. Championship golf is usually a matter of many years of struggle from a young start. Travis picked up his first golf in October, 1896, when he was nearly thirty-five years old. Two years later he had reached the semi-final round of the Amateur Championship. Within four years of his golfing debut he was the amateur champion of his country—and for four years—1900, 1901, 1903 and 1904 he was champion of either America or Great Britain.

He was forty-four years old when he invaded Great Britain and brought back the famous cup from Sandwich. After that invasion such American stars as Chick Evans, Jerry Travers, Francis Ouimet, Fred Herreshoff, Bob Gardner, Bobby Jones, Bill Fownes and many others were to try for the same height in vain for the next twenty-two years. It was not until 1926 that Jess Sweetser duplicated the Travis achievement, and Sweetser at the time was twenty years younger than his famous predecessor had been.

Many years ago, when Walter J. was in his prime, the late George W. Adair, who played with him often, made this comment on his game: "Travis can beat any golfer that ever lived on a golf course only ten yards wide with a keen wind blowing."

Some of his forgotten achievements are remarkable. In one match at the old Westchester course he hit the flagstick three times and missed it only by inches on other occasions.

In a thirty-six-hole match with "Snake" Ames at Garden City he had 36—36——72 in the forenoon and 36—36——72 in the afternoon. He had exactly par on thirty-four of the thirty-six holes played. On one of the most testing of all golf courses this must stand a record for deadly consistency.

Mr. Travis in 1897, one year after he first took up golf. He was then thirty-six.

Jerome D. Travers, the brilliant young American amateur who was Mr. Travis' chief rival in the United States.

On another occasion at Garden City he had six consecutive 2's in one week on the difficult and elusive second hole. At the age of sixty he had 66 and a 68 in one of the Florida championships and at the age of sixty-four he played Garden City in 73, even par, and just two strokes above the record of the course.

It must be remembered that such great golfers as Bobby Jones, Jess Sweetser, Walter Hagen, Johnny Farrell, Tommy Armour and Gene Sarazen started golf when they were seven, eight or ten years old, under good instruction, when it was possible to develop a fine swing instinctively. They also had surpassing physical powers.

But consider the case of a rather slight, slender middle-aged man who started at thirty-five to build up his own game without any outside help, and who, within a short while, stood as the amateur champion of the two greatest golfing nations in the world.

Walter J. Travis could do more with a putter than any golfer in history. He was probably no better than Jerry Travers upon the green itself. But he could also use the putter effectively off the green and from bunkers where the ball was lying well.

He devised the scheme of smaller holes on the practice course at Garden City, holes only a trifle larger than the ball. He practiced here for hours. When you can drop them steadily in a two-inch cup, one double the size looks like a keg.

One of his main angles in regard to putting was to imagine you were driving a tack into the back of the ball and let the putting blade go on through. He considered putting largely a right-handed affair and the right hand predominated in his grip. The left was merely a steadying aid.

But he was something more than a magnificent putter. He was straight down the course from the tee and almost every type of iron usually left the ball fairly close to the cup. He had a peculiar grip, no overlapping or interlocking, with the right hand well under, but he understood the value of flexible wrists that were firm but never tight or tense.

One of Travis' greatest contributions to American golf was a detail which frequently made him enemies. This was an insistence on playing the game in the letter and spirit of the rules. He would tolerate no deviation from the correct path, even in a friendly round. In the early days of the game, when there was an even greater laxity in playing by the rules than anyone can know today, he set a standard which gradually took effect.

There was still another feature to his play—he never played a careless, indifferent shot. No matter how unimportant the match, he played every stroke as if he were in a championship test. He made careful, accurate golf a habit. He thought too much of the game to desecrate it with any indifferent effort. Every shot was a problem to be worked out and worked out in the right way. His rank as a course architect was high, for he knew the value of holes and how they should be arranged to call for skill and to keep up sustained interest.

He was fifty-four years old when he faced Jerry Travers, his leading rival for many years, for the last time, at Apawamis in 1915. Travers had been his hardest barricade. He had checked Travis out of many championships. In this last meeting they came to the final hole all square with the Metropolitan Championship at stake, and for old time's sake, Travis sank a thirty-foot putt to win, one-up. He knew this was his last chance to beat a victorious opponent from many years gone by and yet no one ever swung the blade of a putter with a smoother, steadier stroke as he sent the ball spinning across the green into the cup.

It was always a treat to play with the Old Man. Even though his conversation was scarce, one could learn more from him in a few words than from almost anyone else in a long day's talk.

He had the courage of an unbroken will and an unbreakable determination. There was no faltering in any crisis, where he was usually at his best.

There has been only one Bobby Jones in golf. And there, also, has been only one Walter J. Travis.

Granny BY RED SMITH

The Sort of Man the Editor Was

GRANTLAND RICE WAS THE GREATEST MAN I have known, the greatest talent, the greatest gentleman. The most treasured privilege I have had in this world was knowing him and going about with him as his friend. I shall be grateful all my life.

Years ago Granny wrote a verse upon the death of a friend. Addressed to Charon, the ferryman of the Styx, it began:

"Why do you always look my way?
Why do you take my friends?"

Now, I do not mourn for him, who welcomed peace. I mourn for us.

Granny was a restless sleeper. Sometimes he threshed about and muttered in his sleep and sometimes he cried out in the dark. "No!" he would shout. "No, dammit, no! Frankie, help me! No, I say!"

Does that seem a curious thing to tell about him now? It isn't, really, because it was so characteristic. It required no dream book by Freud to help interpret those cries. All through his waking hours, Granny was saying yes, surely, glad to, of course, no trouble at all, certainly, don't mention it. Not only to his friends, but to all the others who imposed on his limitless generosity. And so, when he slept . . .

The only thing greater than his talent was

his heart—his gentle courtesy, his all-embracing kindness. And as great as that was his humility.

Once, his working press ticket for the Army-Notre Dame football game went astray in the mail. This was Grantland Rice, who did as much for American football as any other man who ever lived; who practically invented the Army-Notre Dame game; who made it a part of the literature with his "Four Horsemen" story of 1924.

He went down Broadway and bought a ticket from a scalper and watched the game from the stands, with his typewriter between his knees. When it was over he made his way apologetically to the pressbox to do his work.

A friend who heard of this was aghast. "Why didn't you throw some weight around?" he demanded.

"Tell you the truth," Granny said, "I don't weigh much."

In 1944 when the whole World Series was played in St. Louis, the working press had one ticket for the Cardinals' home games and another for the Browns'. On the day of the last game Granny arrived at Sportsman's Park with the wrong ticket.

Nobody crashes the World Series. Granny was going to catch another cab, fight the traffic three or four miles to the Chase Hotel and return with his proper credentials. "You'd miss the first six innings," Frank Graham said. "Come with me."

Leading his reluctant friend through the press gate, Frank whispered to the man at the turnstile: "This is Grantland Rice behind me. He has the wrong ticket."

"Where?" the gateman said, his face lighting. "Come in, Mr. Rice, come in!"

Now they were inside but at the entrance to the pressbox proper another guard held the pass. Again the conspirational whisper, the thumb gesturing back over the shoulder.

"Grantland Rice!" the guard said. "Mr. Rice, how are you, sir? I've always wanted to meet you."

"Frankie, you are marvelous," Granny said as they took their seats. "How did you manage that?"

Perhaps it is not literally true that Grantland Rice put a white collar upon the men of his profession, for not all sports writers before him were cap-and-sweater guys. He was, however, the sports writer whose company was sought by presidents and kings.

When Warren Harding was President he asked Granny down to Washington for a round of golf and Granny invited his friend Ring Lardner.

"This is an unexpected pleasure, Mr. Lardner," Harding said as they hacked around. "I only knew Granny was coming. How did you happen to make it, too?"

"I want to be ambassador to Greece," Lardner said.

"Greece?" said the President. "Why Greece?"

"Because," Lardner said, "my wife doesn't like Great Neck."

Granny and several friends were leaving Toots Shor's a few weeks before his death. There was some confusion just inside the revolving door and one of the group was aware, without looking back, of strangers hesitating behind them, uncertain whether to push through or wait for the way to clear. He heard a woman say:

"A lovely man. Let them go."

The small sounds of departure covered the question that must have been asked, but the woman's reply came clearly to the sidewalk:

"Mr. Grantland Rice."

She spoke quietly, but her tone was like banners.

Grantland Rice, editor of *The American Golfer* from 1919 to 1936.

How to Look at the Ball BY JOCK HUTCHISON

An Enlightening Discussion of One of the

Fundamental Essentials of the Game

IT IS EASY ENOUGH TO TELL A GOLFER TO KEEP his eye on the ball. It is much easier to tell him than it is for him to follow your advice.

In the first place, 99 golfers out of every hundred understand well enough that they must look at the ball if they expect to hit it. But this one thing alone won't keep them from looking up just before the clubhead gets around.

I have seen any number of experienced golfers lift their heads on one stroke after another when they knew just what the fault was and were trying their best to correct this fault.

How, then, can a golfer follow the old advice to keep his eye on the ball when his head won't let him? This, I know, is what the average golfer would like to find out.

I believe most golfers hold their necks and heads too rigidly fixed as they start the club back. How can anyone set his neck as if it were in a steel brace, keep it that way, and then still have a free, natural swing?

I don't believe it is necessary for a golfer to keep his head still as so many advise. I believe his neck and his head should be allowed a certain amount of play or of freedom.

Those who have seen Jerome D. Travers play can get a good tip from him. Just as his club starts on the backswing he shifts his chin to the right so that only his left eye covers the ball. This makes it a hard matter to look up. As the clubhead starts through, his head tilts to the left again, but he has finished his stroke before any damage is done.

I shift my head a good deal as Travers does. Only my shift is much more pronounced. To keep my neck from being held in any one fixed place on the backswing, I move my chin several inches to the right, almost as if I was trying to see someone standing back of me. Then as my clubhead starts down I let my head follow the swing and direction of the club. I find this gives a lot more freedom to my swing and that it also keeps me from suddenly looking up.

There are two sides to this matter of looking at a ball. One is mental; the other is physical.

If you are thinking about where the ball is going to drop or about some bunker just beyond you that must be carried, you are almost certain to look up quickly to see where the ball has started. The result, of course, means a missed shot.

But if you will only think about your swing, about hitting the ball, regardless of where it may go, you are not very likely to look up.

Make a practice of thinking only about hitting the ball as if you were playing it into a net. It will be hard at first, but it will work out before very long.

This is the mental side of the matter.

The physical side is the point that I have made about moving your head at least a trifle in the same direction that the club starts on the backswing. And then as the club starts forward again let your head move gradually in the same direction.

It isn't so necessary that you look at the ball as it is that you don't lift your head suddenly. For this movement draws your body up and breaks up the swing completely. And you are much more likely to look up suddenly if you try to keep your head and neck rigidly fixed than you are if you allow them a certain amount of freedom.

There is no good system that makes a player uncomfortable or that takes away any of the freedom of his swing. Too many golfers keep their heads fixed in a vise and this has the tendency to make the head fly up all the quicker when it is finally released.

It is not necessary to keep both eyes on the ball. By focussing your left eye only you will probably get better results, for then your right eye will be well away from the line of flight and therefore from the line of temptation.

The more a golfer worries about lifting his head or looking up, the more certain he is to look up. And if he starts this very bad fault he is pretty sure to keep it up most of the round, especially at any place where he has a hard stroke to make or where there is a bunker to be carried.

Just remember that the head and neck are not fixed to any one place. That they have just as much right to freedom as the arms have. But in moving the head on the backswing, always let it come to the right as if you were looking at something back of the ball rather than to the left. You will find that most of the fine golf players adopt this system of looking at a ball. It is a common habit among the leading professionals and among many of the better amateurs. Travers is a notable example in this respect. He makes it physically hard to look up and by doing this he manages to keep his eye on the ball about as well as any man I know. No advice that is given you can be adopted and put into effect at once. It will take some time and practice. But don't let anyone tell you that the head and neck should be held rigidly in one place without being moved through the course of the swing.

There is no surer way to break up all rhythm in the swing and to destroy the freedom of the stroke, no matter what club you use.

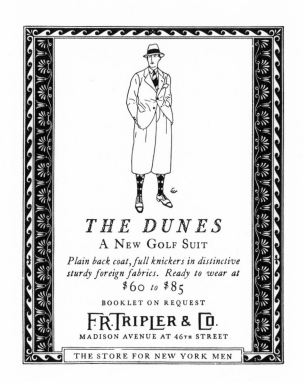

Shush!!! 1921 BY RING LARDNER

An Authority on Athaletics
Makes a Suggestion

To the Editor: I want to call your tension to something about golf that has been ranking in my bosom for a long wile and I would have said something about it yrs. ago only I thought a man of your brains and intelligents would take steps, but I suppose you are afraid of the Old Guard amist your readers and scared of offending them, but where they's a principal involved I never fail to speak out my mind and my friends say I have done it so often that it is what you might call spoken out.

Well, it looks to me like they was room for improvement in the game and when I say the game I don't mean my game but the game itself as gotten up by St. Andrew and Simon Peter his brother and the next time the rules committee gets together I wished they would make a change in the code witch looks to me to be a whole lot more important than takeing the endearing terms out of tennis or makeing a pitcher keep his finger nails pared so as he can't scratch baseball or self.

According to what I have read golf is suppose to be the most sociable game in the world and in my $1.50 dictionary one of the definitions of sociable is "suited for, or characterized by, much conversation." Well, then, why and the he-ll don't they mend the golf rules so as a man can talk wile they're playing?

Instead of witch, if you say a word to a regular golfer wile he is makeing a shot, why the first thing he will do is suffer a nervous break down and then he will give you a dirty look and likely as not he will pick up his toys and walk off the links, as I have nicknamed them. And when you ask somebody what was the idear they will tell you that your ethics is rancid and you must be scum, because how can a man concentrate on their shot when somebody is makeing remarks at them. And if you was in the gallery at the national amateur and even wispered wile Bobby Ouimet was trying to run down a millimeter put, why the head linesman would reach in his hip pocket for a sawed off niblick and knock you for a safety.

Well, gents, I have seen a good many different kinds of athaletics and took a small part in a few of them and I ask you as man to man what other event is they where comments is barred?

"Yes," you will say, "but they's no other sport where a man has got to concentrate on what they are doing. If your mind is distracted wile you are playing golf you're gone."

How true.

And now leave us suppose that Ty Cobb is up in the ninth inning of a ball game with 2 out and the score 7 to 4 vs. Detroit like it usually is and Young and Bush on base. Well, the bench warmers on the other club is yelling "Pop up, Ty! You been a good old wagon but you done broke down." And the catcher is wispering "What shall I have him throw up here, Ty? Do you want a slow ball?" And the boys in the stands is hollering "Strike the big cheese out, Lefty. He's through."

But all this don't worry Ty because he is thinking to himself "I mustn't forget to send my laundry out when I get back to the hotel." His mind ain't on the game at all and when Lefty throws one up there, why it's just from force of habit that he swings and next thing you know Felsch is beating it back to the left center field fence and Jackson is getting set to make the relay. But suppose Ty had been thinking about that next pitch instead of his shirts, why the uproar would of give him neurasthenia and they'd of had to send the trainer up to hit for him.

Or suppose for inst. they's a horse race and they are comeing down the strech and Vagabond the favorite is out in front and the second horse is Willie the Wisp that's 20 to 1 and a lot of waiters has a bet down on him and they all begin screaming "Come on Willie" so loud that Vagabond can't help from hearing

President Warren G. Harding, Grantland Rice, Ring Lardner, and Secretary of State Henry Fletcher pose on the portico of the White House before a round of golf at nearby Chevy Chase.

them, but he don't even look up as he is thinking about a couple of library books that he promised to bring home to his mare.

Or you take what happened down to Toledo last 4 of July. Dempsey lept up and crowned Jessica in the left eye and Jessica suddenly set down but he got up again and 60 thousand and no hundreds larnyxs was shreeking "Kill the big dog, Jack!" and as I recall it, instead of the remarks bothering Dempsey, why he hit Jessica again with the same Gen. results and I would of swore he was concentrateing, but I found out afterwards that he was trying to figure out weather he would have veal chops or a steak for supper. Otherwise he would of raised his hand unlocked and told the referee that he wouldn't go on unlest the fans shut up their d-m noise.

Or leave us consider that extra inning game that wound up in Europe a couple yrs. ago and they was a guy name Frank Foch or something that was suppose to be figureing out how to put on the finishing touchs to it and he was setting down with a map in front of him, but the Germans kept on shooting Big Bertha and Little Eva with the loud pedal on, so finely a orderly come in and asked Mr. Foch if the noise bothered him. And Mr. Foch says "Oh no. It might if I was rapped up in what I am doing. But I was just wondering if I would look better with my mustache off or on, so let them keep on shooting." So it looks like if Mr. Foch had of been really forced to think about the job they had wished on him the Germans would probably be in Harrisburg by this time, changeing engines.

And then they's examples in the more intimate sports like shooting craps or driveing a car. For inst. you have made four passes and you've left it all ride and you come out with a deuce and a four and all the boys that's fadeing you begins yelping "Billy Hicks can't six" and "How many wonders in the world?" and etc. and you might get rattled and seven only that you ain't concentrated on the crap game a-tall, but you're thinking what a good time you might of had in Yellowstone Park last summer if you hadn't went to the 1000 Islands.

Or let's say you're driveing up Fifth Ave. at 4 P.M. and your wife keeps pinching one of your arms and the gals in the back seat screek every little wile and say "Look out be careful!" why you might bump somebody if your mind was on the traffic instead of Dr. C. Roach Straton's latest sermon.

Now in regards to golf itself leave me give you a couple of incidence that happened to me personly witch will show that the boys who crabs against a little sociability is makeing a mountain climber out of a mole trap. Well, once I was playing out to Riverside near Chi with Albert Seckel and he was giveing me seven and no hundreds strokes per hole and when we came to the last tee we was even up. Well, the last hole was about 260 yds. but you had to drive over the Blue Ridge Mts. of Virginia and you couldn't see the green from the tee and if you didn't get your drive over the Mts. you was utterly lost. Well, for some reason another Seck had the honor and just as he was going to drive, I says "I hope you don't miss the ball entirely" so he drove onto the green and went down in two.

And down to Toledo last July, a few days before Willard became an acrobat, I and Rube Goldberg met in a match game out to Inverness and we was playing for a buck a hole and my caddy was Harry Witwer and he had broughten along a alarm clock and when we would get on the green, witch was seldom, why just as Rube was going to put, Harry would set off the alarm, and Rube got so nervous that on the 15th. hole Harry throwed my towel into the ring and I was seven down.

So all and all, Mr. Editor, I say pass a rule makeing it legal to open your clam when you feel like it and leave us forget this old obsleet law of silent golf witch was gotten up in Scotland where they wouldn't no more talk for nothing than Harry Lauder would sing for the same price. But weather the rule is past or no, when I am playing at golf I am going to say what I want to when I want to and if my oppts. don't like my ethics, why they's showers in the locker room.

Yours Truely,

The Most Common Faults BY O. B. KEELER

Sounding Out Stewart Maiden on Certain Difficulties

UNDERTAKING TO INTERVIEW STEWART MAIDEN is something of an undertaking. Few Scots are loquacious. This particularly applies to golfing Scots. Jock Hutchison, now, will talk on occasion. There is a certain Caledonian poem concerning one Jock McLean, a Hieland mon, which The Hutch will recite with rare unction, properly approached. George Duncan also will talk fluently on practically every subject from a socketed mashie shot to the Theory of Evolution—and George has sound and substantial ideas on both. But in the main Scots are reticent, and Stewart Maiden of East Lake, mentor unto Bobby Jones, Alexa Stirling and Perry Adair, is one of the most consistently and thoroughly reticent Scots your correspondent ever has encountered.

Once upon a time I went out to East Lake—this was many years ago—seeking an interview with Stewart regarding an approaching Southern Amateur Golf Championship shortly to be played at his course; it was in 1915, I believe.

The interview was to be about the state of the course; the prospective entrants and their prospective chances; the incumbent champion —that sort of thing.

As eventually printed, the interview extended a column and a quarter in a local newspaper; about a thousand words. Of these thousand words Stewart had said three, accurately counted and carefully verified.

The rest of the words were—well, interview. I forgot what Stewart said they were. It was some expression he must have learned as a lad in Carnoustie.

So it was not without trepidation that I undertook to get from this celebrated golf instructor some of the ideas on which he proceeds with the instruction of his pupils. Here was an interview not like the first. In that it was all right (though Stewart never has so agreed) for me to go ahead and set out at length my own ideas, with Stewart saying "Yes," or in a sudden and effusive burst of confidential exuberance, "No."

Not now. Any golf instructor of the caliber of Stewart Maiden is bound to have sharply defined ideas and his own peculiar method in golf teaching. And if Stewart, whose aversion to publicity is nothing short of proverbial, elected to restrict himself to yes and no, why, there was nothing to be done about it.

I had a line of approach figured out and it looked like a foozle at the very start. I said: "Stewart, what fault do you find most prevalent in golf beginners?"

He said: "I don't know."

I said: "Well, in duffers who have played the game a while and want some coaching?"

He said: "I don't know."

This was distinctly unpromising. "Kiltie" was as noncommittal as usual, which is fearfully noncommittal. I tried another tack.

"Well, they all have some faults, don't they?"

"Yes, or they would be playing good golf and not coming to me for lessons."

This was a sort of start, anyway. I tried again.

"They bend the left arm, don't they?"

"Yes. So does Harry Vardon."

"But he gets away with it and they don't—isn't that true?"

"Yes."

"You don't bend your left arm at the top of the swing."

"No."

"You don't teach your pupils to bend the left arm at the top of the swing?"

"No."

Then Stewart, possibly being goaded, actually opened up on the topic of the straight left arm.

"I'll tell you why it is. It is possible to swing correctly and bend the left arm at the top of the swing. Vardon does it, and eases the swing a little by it. But Vardon's left arm straightens out before the club is brought on the ball. This is a delicate part of timing the stroke which none but a master should try. When the beginner or the duffer, or what you are fond of calling the average golfer, bends his left arm at the top of the swing or at any part of the upward swing, he invariably converts the swing into a chop. The arc of the club's head descends on a radius only so long as from the left elbow to the clubhead, working on a moving axis, which is the left elbow. If the axis were still, the swing would be too short and too much up-and-down. With the moving axis the swing becomes a chop. The clubhead either comes down behind the ball, or on top of the ball, or, if it happens to hit the ball squarely by accident, sends it away in a feeble and uncertain manner. That bent left arm is one of the main reasons you see duffers chopping up turf and scalping the ball all over the place."

"Then you consider the bending of the left arm the principal fault in the beginner or the duffer?"

"I didn't say so. I don't believe it is. But it is a big fault and a general fault."

"How do you cure it?"

"Sometimes I don't. I can't hold a man's left arm straight for him, any more than I can keep his head down. It's *his* arm. I tell him he must not bend it, and I show him how to get the club back without bending it. Then if he won't keep it straight, I can't help it."

"There's a harness made to make him keep his left arm straight, isn't there?"

Stewart grinned. "I believe so," he said. "I never have used it on a pupil. Probably it would keep his left arm straight in the up-swing, but if it did that it also would keep his arm straight through the finish, and that would not work on many styles of swing, I should say. Not on mine."

Stewart still seemed inclined to communication on the straight left arm, and I was glad enough to let him proceed.

"Keeping the left arm straight automatically prevents overswinging, which is another serious fault, especially with irons, and most especially with lofted irons. With the straight left arm, the player can hardly get the club back too far for a full shot, unless he lefts his hands higher than his head, which he is not likely to do. The straight left arm promotes correct wrist-work, if not positively, at least negatively. Maybe it would be better to say it permits or favors correct wrist-work, which is next to impossible and certainly useless with the choppy stroke resulting from the bent left arm."

"Do you teach wrist-work?"

"I certainly do not. I do not tell a pupil anything about using his wrists in the shot."

"But the wrists have a great part in the stroke, don't they?"

"Of course they do. They have so much to do with the stroke that as soon as the average golfer begins thinking about using them, he begins scattering golf balls all over the county."

"Well, if the use of the wrists is part of the mechanics of the stroke——"

"I don't like that word, mechanics," objected Stewart. "The best swing is the one with the least mechanics. When you see George Duncan or Harry Vardon or Bobby Jones swing, do you notice any mechanics? I don't want my pupils to bother their heads about mechanics, or which hand takes the club up, and which hand sends it down. Both hands, I tell them, take the club back, and then hit the ball. Leave out the mechanics. As to the wrists and their part in the stroke, I try to settle most of that in fitting the pupils with a grip—by the way he takes hold of the club in addressing the ball. If he holds the club properly, keeps his left arm straight, and swings, the chances are good that the wrists being wound up unconsciously in the backswing, will unwind unconsciously in the forward swing. That is better for him and better for the results. Too much bother about mechanics in the golf swing, anyway. Too many maxims."

"I suppose you wouldn't even tell a pupil to keep his eye on the ball and his head down?" I suggested.

Stewart suddenly came out as an astounding radical. "Well, I wouldn't—much," he said abruptly. "As to keeping his eye on the ball, that means looking at it. I would give almost any pupil credit for having enough intelligence to look at something he was going to hit with an implement, whether it was a shingle nail or a golf ball. As to keeping his head down, I don't know whether I keep my own head down or not."

"I know," I said. "You do."

"Well, it's part of the swing, then, and no mechanical effort," asserted Stewart. "I believe a man's head flying up or his eye flying off the ball is more a result than a cause. He's doing something wrong in the swing—that's all."

"So much for the straight left arm," I said. "You teach a pupil that it is essential, and that the bending of the left arm in the backswing is the worst fault—"

"One of the worst faults in execution. There is another one worse than that. And then there is the fault resulting from various causes, known as the slice, and there is the hook——"

"The slice is popularly supposed to be the hardest to cure, isn't it?"

"I don't know. But it isn't the hardest. It's about the easiest. The hook, now—that's something else."

"Well, how do you cure the slice? And what's this other vice that's worse than bending the left arm or anything else?"

Stewart shook his head.

"The average slice can be corrected by putting the left hand more on top of the shaft and turning the right hand farther under."

"Pronation," I assumed.

"What the devil is pronation?" asked Stewart peevishly. "Talk English. Swinging from the outside in, falling back, pulling in the hands—anything that will draw the club across the ball at impact also will give you a fine slice. If you are standing up to the shot and hitting it, and slicing, put the left hand farther over and the right hand farther under."

"So you will pronate unconsciously?"

"Listen," said Stewart earnestly. "If you want a lecture on pronatal influences in golf go to Woods, Hutchison or Dr. Brady."

"Well, if you are falling away, or pulling in the hands, or otherwise dragging the club across the ball, how do you stop it?"

"Just don't do it. A lot of pupils seem to think a teacher can give them a formula that will hypnotize them into doing things or not doing things. It can't be done. A teacher can change a pupil's grip so he *can* swing properly, so far as the grip is concerned. If he *won't* do it, it's his business."

"Business for the teacher, too."

"Yes. Blamed stupid business. If you think there's any fun struggling with a 200-pound man built like a prizefighter and rigid and quivering with horror in the presence of an ounce and a half of rubber, you ought to try it."

"No, thanks! There's trouble enough struggling with the ounce and a half of rubber deviltry. But we were looking for the commonest fault of golfers. A fault usually hinges on something—what does the commonest fault in golf turn on? Where is the chief trouble?"

"I suppose you'd say it turns on the pivot," replied Stewart. "And you wouldn't be far wrong."

"What if you don't pivot?"

"Then you don't shoot golf. Everybody pivots—everybody that shoots golf. There is no other way."

"But some golfers pivot more than others, don't they?"

"I don't think so. A golfer playing from an open stance has to do a bit more pivoting than a man playing from a square or a closed stance, simply because he is facing a little more away from the position he must reach at the top of the swing."

"Doesn't a flat swinger pivot more than an upright swinger?"

"Not so you can notice it. I keep telling you that all good golfers hit the ball practically the same way. And they all pivot."

"Well, Ted Ray sways along with the pivot, doesn't he? And Tommy Armour has a hip-sway along the line of flight; and so does Max Marston and Alec Smith, and it looks as if they don't twist the hips as much as some others."

"The hip-sway goes with the pivot, and a golfer can't twist his shoulders without twisting his hips."

"You mean Harry Vardon and Bob Jones swing the hips along the line of flight?"

"You bet they do! Where do you think all that kick in the big shots comes from? If you want to cultivate a *real* fault, try to swing without swaying the hips, or twisting them. If you can get to doing that—and a whole lot of golfers do—then you'll have a fine case for the golf doctor. That's one of the first things a beginner tries to do. After you get him impressed with the idea that he mustn't sway his whole body back and forth, he almost always tries to get the club back with his arms alone. That's a whale of a fault."

"How do you tell a pupil to turn his hips properly?"

I regret greatly that I cannot quote Mr. Maiden's instruction verbatim on this point. It was couched in four short words and was the very essence of pith and plainness. From it the veriest duffer could understand readily that he was to pivot at the hips.

"Well, that brings us back to the start of the backswing. How do you start it, anyway?"

"There's a little difference among good players there. Ted Ray and Harry Vardon both start the hands first. They carry the hands back almost a foot before anything else moves, even the clubhead. That may possibly be their way of getting the arc of the swing flat at the time the ball is taken, or it may be a mannerism. I don't know. Others start the clubhead back first. They say they shove it back with the left hand in control. Maybe they do."

"What's the best way?"

"The way that gets the best results for the player. I tell my pupils to start everything at once—hands, club, hips and shoulders."

"That is, push with the left and pull with the right?"

"There you go again! There's too much stuff written and taught about 'left' and 'right,' and about all it does is mix up the player. How can you start twisting or pivoting with the left hip or the left shoulder without doing the same thing at the same time with the right? Take the club back with an easy pivot and don't bother about it. When the club is back, bring it down the same way."

"I've heard some good players say they started the downward swing with the left hip."

"Maybe they do. I never watched one with a microscope. It looks to me as if they start everything at once. Others say the left shoulder leads the forward swing. I suppose it does —it's in front, and it can't very well be helped."

"Then you are not conscious of 'throwing down' the club with the right hand, or 'starting' it with the left?"

"I am not conscious of any part of the swing after I start the club back, and I don't believe anybody else is, no matter how much they talk about it."

Now a resident of New York, Miss Alexa Stirling, the former national champion from Atlanta, plans to enter several events during the coming season.

Walter Hagen, the current British Open Champion, starts his backswing with a driver. Observe the compactness of his stance and the air of full concentration on the task of hitting the ball.

Recognized as one of the best putters among the professionals of the country, Peter O'Hara believes in addressing short putts with the blade of his putter four or five inches behind the ball as an antidote to stabbing the ball.

"You don't mean to say you hit the ball with a blank mind?"

"Yes, I do. That is, so far as any part of the stroke is concerned. If I am hitting the ball with a blank mind and a driver, I am conscious of thinking how far I want it to go. If I am swinging a mashie, I think about how far I want the ball to go and what I want it to do when it gets there—roll a bit, or stop short. But as to the stroke, I don't think about it, section by section, and I don't believe anybody else does, or can. Certainly I never try to teach a pupil to do this or that at a certain part of the swing. Swing right, and keep your blank mind as much as you can on the shot."

"But if you're playing different kinds of shots—the push shot; the pitch-and-run; the intentional slice?"

"Do your thinking before you start the swing. You won't be likely to do it afterward. That's a common fault, too—trying to think after the stroke is started."

It occurs to your correspondent just here that this is a singularly fine explanation of that somewhat broad term, concentration. Stewart says to do your thinking before you start the stroke. While making the stroke, *think of nothing but the shot*. I believe this canny Scot has said something. I wonder if this can be the commonest fault—trying to think of some part or parts of the stroke after it has started?

Certainly Stewart explains unconsciously the well-known advantage possessed by the golfer who started as a child and plays the game naturally over the most thoughtful and intelligent golfer who took up the game as an adult and learned by precept and instruction. The former, taking his stance for a shot, is able to make it with a mind free of all considerations or worries except the range and the necessity for stopping the ball, if any.

As to making the stroke, that is as easy for him as wielding a knife and fork to the average civilized man—he simply doesn't think about that part of it. The latter as a rule must concern himself also about what Stewart dislikes so emphatically—the mechanics of the swing. And few golfers who learned the game as adults—Walter Travis, a paragon of concentration, being a notable exception—have conquered the impulse to diffuse their concentration on various phases of the swing.

Perhaps, too, this explains the importance of constant and patient practice; making a shot over and over. For by doing this even the man who takes up golf comparatively late in life may acquire sufficient muscular habit, or "muscular memory" as somebody terms it, to enable him to swing "with a blank mind" so far as the swing is concerned.

I rather fancy that correct, smooth pivoting has more than anything else to do with a golfer's position as what is called a "stylist." Surely no feature of Harry Vardon's style, or George Duncan's, or Bob Jones', is more admired than the pivoting. It means a tremendous deal to the shot, too.

Ted Ray, not rated much of a stylist, combines a body sway with a full pivot. Ted says himself that the sway enables him to get his heft into the shot. Unquestionably he gets something into it; and his pivoting, while not as graceful as Vardon's or Jones', is perhaps more pronounced than either, as he plays from a notably open stance, and has to turn more to get the club back to the same position.

Stewart modestly was reticent about Bob Jones' style in this regard, because Bob acquired it from Stewart when Bob was about seven years old. You may not have heard Stewart Maiden heralded as a stylist, but the fact remains that this little Scotsman has one of the smoothest and most perfectly balanced swings in the golfing world today. I know of at least one time when Bob Jones, playing a shot at a distance, was mistaken for Stewart by a man who knew Stewart before he came to this country; and I know of one critic who identified him as Alexa Stirling's teacher the first time he saw Miss Stirling swing, without knowing who she was.

It is perfect pivoting and the consequent perfect balance that enables Bob Jones to hit his hardest—which is exceedingly hard—and complete the stroke with all the ease and grace of a posed finish. I never once have seen the boy swing himself the least bit off balance, and I have seen him clip more than one 300-yard drive.

"So you think that trying to pivot in sections, or failing to pivot enough, is the commonest fault?" I asked Stewart.

"I didn't say so," he replied cautiously. "At that, I think the pivot is the turning point of what may be the commonest fault."

"Now about this matter of timing?" I suggested.

Stewart Maiden reflected.

"Well, they seem to have a pretty hard time timing," he said. "I should say that the majority of golfers never get it, except once in a while; sort of accidentally."

"Then there must be a secret about it."

"Yes. That's just it. It's a secret."

"All right. You can't keep a secret like that. So let's have it."

"It's not my secret. I wish it was."

"You can time a swing, can't you?"

"Yes. At least I used to. And I can look at a swing and see that it is well timed, or not well timed—that is, usually."

"Well, then, isn't that all there is to it?"

"Not by a whole lot. The timing device is inside a player. What I see of his swing is the outside. That's merely the result of the way his timer is functioning, or not functioning. I can tell him that he is hitting too soon, or getting his hands ahead of the club, or any one of a lot of other things he may be doing wrong. And sometimes that will help him 'set' his timer. And then, again, it won't."

"Why won't it?"

"Timing is instinctive, when you get right down to it. There's an open window. You are about forty feet from it. Can I tell you *how* to throw a ball through it? If you happen to be a baseball pitcher, it would be a cinch for you to throw a peck of balls through it, one after the other. If you missed it would be an accident— an error of timing. You didn't cut the ball loose at the right place, or the final snap in the wrist was a bit off. A pitcher's speed and accuracy both are a matter of timing. So is a country boy's ability to sting another with a green ap-

ple. It's an instinct, cultivated by practice."

"A woman would have a skinny chance to hit anybody with a green apple, wouldn't she?"

"Exactly. And it is much harder to get a woman to time a golf swing than it is a man, as a rule. Men have been throwing things around for several hundred thousand years, I suppose. The throwing instinct probably is pretty much hereditary. Some people have it more than others."

"But about hitting?"

"Same thing. I should say the golfing swing is a good deal more complex than the throwing swing; using an implement and striking the ball instead of holding it and letting it fly from the hand. A lot more complex. But the instinct is the same. And in a general way the action is very similar. Without being any great baseball fan I have seen a number of games, and I always noticed that the pitcher had a backswing and a forward swing and a follow-through and a finish that, allowing for the different plane of action, were substantially the same as in a stylish golfer. And I noticed that the pitcher with the greatest speed and accuracy seemed to be timing his swing as near perfectly as is humanly possible. It is very pretty to watch."

"So you don't believe Walter Johnson could tell me *how* to throw a ball through that window?"

"No. But he might give you a bit of advice as to how to draw your arm back, and tell you to throw overhand instead of sidearm; something like that. But if you ever get to throwing at all as he can, you'd have to develop timing."

"And then some! In other words, he couldn't tell me just when to cut the ball loose and just how to snap the wrist—that would have to be a developed instinct?"

"Yes. And don't bear down so on that snap. I'll bet Johnson is not conscious of any snap when he's shooting a fast one. He's just throwing."

"And the expert golfer is just swinging? Good enough. But you *do* tell 'em something about timing, don't you? Say a fellow is lunging at the start and getting the kick into the swing about a yard before the club reaches the ball. Don't you tell him to keep his body back?"

Stewart grinned. "No. On the other hand, I tell him to start his body first."

This was just about the most unorthodox thing, apparently, I ever heard a Scottish Presbyterian say. Stewart knew he was administering a shock. He went on to explain:

"I want the pupil to start the downswing with his left shoulder and his left hip. As near as I can figure it, they move together. The point is, I want him to begin drawing his arms down with his hands in practically the same position as at the top of the swing. I want him to get his hands pretty well along on the swing, somewhere around the hip level, before the real *hit* starts. And as near as I can tell you, *that* is timing; holding back the *hit* until the body has turned and the hips are shot along the line of play so as to produce all the tension possible."

The cautious Caledonian paused, considered, and then qualified somewhat.

"I should say, that is the way timing looks to me on the outside. Remember, I am not trying to tell you any secret of timing from the inside."

I sought to recapitulate on the outside.

"Start the downswing with the left shoulder and hip. Keep the hands as at the top of the swing until the greatest tension is gained by the body-turn and shooting the hips. Then add to that the sudden unwinding of the wrists—the turn-over. Get all the spring in your system out at one time. Is that it?"

"Something like it. Then if you hit the ball on the nose you may get a golf shot."

"That's hopeful. And how many chances do you suppose there are for part of the combination to go wrong?"

"I don't know. About seven thousand. Especially if you try to think about it in parts. I don't like this business of taking a swing to pieces. And it's blue ruin to try to make a swing by sections. A teacher has to correct the outward faults that will prevent proper timing, if he can. As to the timing instinct——"

Stewart shook his head, the gesture carrying a strong inference that the timing instinct, if not inherent, must be a matter of fasting, meditation and prayer.

"When did you become conscious of a timing instinct?" I asked.

"Not yet. I suppose a man trying to play golf would sooner be conscious of not having it."

"When did you start playing golf?"

"When I was about five years old. Maybe four. I don't remember when I wasn't playing, as a youngster."

"Did you play by note or by ear?"

"By ear. And, say—that may be a sort of explanation of timing. You know some people can't learn to dance or keep time in music. Rhythm, I think they call it. Well, maybe there's a good bit of rhythm in timing. Certainly there is in a proper swing."

"Now about clubs. Some people say a heavy club helps in timing, because you can feel the head through the swing better."

"That's rot. A club should be so balanced that the head may be felt. But that doesn't mean it has to be heavy. Most real hitters prefer light clubs. The slow swingers like heavy clubs as a rule. Bob McDonald doesn't seem to have much trouble timing his big shots, and the last time I saw him he was using wood clubs that weighed 12¼ or 12½ ounces: looked rather like child's clubs. And how he does crack 'em! Not many can drive with Bob."

"I have heard that some people advocate trying to time the swing so that the maximum velocity is reached at a point just beyond the place where the ball lies, on the idea that the ball rides the club some distance and the speed of the club should be increasing after impact—that is, during the follow-through—so that the ball in rebounding from the club would get more of a shove."

Stewart shook his head again.

"Too fine a point for me," he admitted. "I think that's drawing it too fine, even if you could do it. And I don't believe one of the high-tension balls would stick on the club while it moved more than two inches at the most. One inch seems more like it. Better not bother about that. Hit the ball! If you can time

John McCormack, the famous Irish tenor, finishes a shot at Brae Burn, near Boston, after a recent round.

Mrs. Ronald H. Barlow, popular Philadelphia matron, is looking forward to another season on the Quaker City courses.

Eugene Grace, president of Bethlehem Steel, was caught by the camera at the Palmetto Club, in Aiken, South Carolina, while straightening out the kinks for what looks like a busy golf season ahead.

your swing to deliver all the kick on that ball, you can feel you've done your duty. The ball will get away so fast it won't have time to debate with the club about whether it could get an extra yard of ride if the kick was an inch farther on. Timing is enough trouble when you are trying to fasten it right on the ball, and not some place ahead of the ball."

"So you think the commonest fault in golf has to do with timing."

"I didn't say so, and if I did, you would have what Ring Lardner calls a he-ll of a time sorting out the faults that affect timing. You might say that about seven thousand of the ten thousand or more golf faults have to do with timing. But there *is* one special fault, now . . ."

"This sounds interesting—tell me more!"

"It'll keep. It's been going on a long time."

As well as I can make out, the correct swing is located approximately in the left hip pocket, but it cannot be had in half-pint sizes at a purchase-price.

This conclusion is reached by an inverse process of ratiocination, a word I always have wanted to employ, but had a long struggle finding a job for it. I mean, if you locate the most common and ruinous fault in the swing, the thing that most surely will eliminate it logically must be somewhere in the vicinity of the secret of correct play.

Of course, I did not get Stewart to come right out and say what was the secret of the correct swing, or where it was. I may even have got an inference slightly on the bias. Stewart is perhaps the most noncommittal golf professional that ever was brought up on oatmeal. I will detail the dialogue and you can form your own conclusion.

"Do we get to it this time?"

"I should say it's time we were getting somewhere."

"Good. The commonest fault in golf, then, is——?"

"Hitting too soon."

"Just what does that mean?"

"Hitting too soon."

"Of course. I mean, hitting before what?"

"Hitting before several things. Hitting before the club has got back to the intended limit of the backswing. Hitting before the body has pivoted. Hitting before the hips are advanced. There are a dozen ways of hitting before you are ready to hit. Maybe more than a dozen. I never counted them."

"How do you stop your pupils from hitting too soon?"

"I don't always stop them."

"Well, how do you go about trying to stop them?"

"Depends on the way they are hitting too soon. I was just telling you there are several ways of hitting too soon."

"Is a player with a full swing more likely to hit too soon than one with a short swing?"

"Yes."

"Why?"

"Well, he has more room in which to make the mistake. I have seen players with a very full swing start hitting upwards."

"Where would the ball have to be to get the full benefit of that kind of a hit?"

"About waist-high, I should say. And he would knock it almost straight down."

"Then the main trouble with starting to hit too soon is that it discharges the kick before the ball is reached?"

"Yes. All the ball gets is a hang-over."

"What happens then?"

"One or more of several things. The ball may be hit square, but it gets no kick; it is merely knocked away weakly, though it may go straight. Some players never understand why they don't get decent distance when they seem to be hitting the ball pretty well. That usually is why."

"What else?"

"The ball may be smothered, topped, pushed out, swung, sliced, hooked or schlaffed."

"That seems to be about all that can happen to one ball at one time—and all from hitting too soon?"

"Of course, hitting too soon may be combined with one or more other faults. But I imagine that by itself it could produce practically any kind of a bad shot in golf."

"That is to say, a player really talented in the art of hitting too soon could be just about as bad a golfer as possible?" "Yes."

"Then it would appear that *not* hitting too soon is absolutely essential to playing good golf."

"It is."

"Well, what's the remedy?"

"Don't hit too soon."

"I mean, haven't you any method of teaching a pupil how to hold back the hit for the right juncture? What about pausing at the top of the swing? Is there anything against that?"

"Nothing in the world. Twenty years ago it was the fashion in Great Britain. Harry Vardon in his prime had a distinct pause at the top of his swing. Practically every good golfer did. The fashion has changed. Nowadays most golfers do not pause so you can notice it."

"Did they play as well twenty years ago?"

"Sometimes I think they played better, considering the limitations of the ball then in use. They played as well, at any rate."

"Well, what I was getting at was this: Wouldn't a distinct pause at the top of the swing tend to prevent hitting too soon?"

"Not necessarily."

"Seems to me it would. For one thing, the player couldn't begin swinging down before the club had finished swinging up."

"No. But he could begin hitting with his body stationary. Seems to me I told you the hit should not start until the body was pivoting and the hips moving along the line of play. It is possible that a decided pause at the top of the swing would encourage the player to start hitting before the pivot began."

"Then hitting too quick is another name for faulty timing?"

"Not exactly. It depends on the individual. I should think timing was the art of getting the right part of the *hit* at the ball. A player might start the *hit* properly and not *time* it right. But he couldn't possibly get the *timing* right if he started the *hit* at the wrong time."

"So the fundamental principle is starting the hit at the right time?"

"Yes."

This, for Stewart, was pretty dogmatic. Coupled with his opinion, in a previous interview, that the initiatory movement in the downswing seems to be with the left side of the body—the left shoulder and hip leading—we appear to be running the secret of the golfing swing steadily in the direction of the left hip pocket. Please understand that this is my own inference. I would not think of committing Stewart to any such incautious or undignified epigram.

Stewart added, under pressure, that pressing probably was another name for hitting too soon—"in the main." So this prominent defect also is mixed up with our commonest fault.

"Is there also a tendency in short play to hit too quickly, the same as in long play?"

"More so, if anything."

"And in putting?"

"Yes. It sometimes is called 'stabbing' the putt."

"Well, once again, now—how do we go about correcting the trouble? Isn't that fine old admonition, 'slow back,' a pretty good remedy?"

"No. Some players swing back slowly naturally and some swing back rapidly."

"There's such a thing as swinging back too fast, isn't there?"

"Certainly."

"Davy Herron swings back awfully fast."

"Not for him. That's his style. He doesn't swing back as fast as Gil Nicholls or Alec Smith. George Duncan swings back very fast, too. He's a pretty fair golfer, with a pretty fair style. At that, it might be better for a beginner to be on the deliberate side in the backswing, and not snatch the club back out of control."

"Is there anything you always tell your pupils, to help them get the club back smoothly and start the hit at the right time?"

"Yes. I always tell them to count. One-Two. Like a dance-step. 'One' for the backswing; 'Two' for the downswing. In cadence, like the manual-of-arms, with the little pause between counts. That tends to smooth out the whole action and give the pupil a chance to hold the hit back until the proper time."

"Chick Evans seems to swing in three counts," I suggested. "With Chick, 'One' is the 'press forward' of the hands and hips; 'Two' is the backswing; 'Three' the downswing. It looks that way to me."

"Possibly so. You can do it in three counts, all right. There is a little press forward right at the beginning by all good players, I suspect. The main thing is to get into a regular rhythm for the whole stroke. All along I have been trying to keep you from picking the golf-swing to pieces, and you have kept asking about this part and that part."

"Well, you said yourself that the hit was the thing, and that it could be started too soon, so it must be a part——"

"Don't split whiskers. If you swing right the hit will take care of itself. Remember that."

With this warning, I will have to take the responsibility for the summing up of Stewart Maiden's ideas on the Commonest Fault in golf, and the correction thereof.

As I get it, it is hitting too soon. Even timing is dependent on the proper starting of the hit; for while a player may start the hit right and not time it correctly, he cannot possibly time the stroke correctly if he starts the hit wrong. And if he starts the hit at the right juncture, correct timing will be most likely to follow automatically.

Also it seems to me that some distinction must be made in the terms "downswing" and "hit," in that the hit does not begin until the downswing is under way, the body pivoting, and the hips moving along the line of play, so as to produce the requisite tension and afford the anatomical position necessary for whipping the stroke well through.

And as to the crucial point—the starting-point of the hit—it more and more seems to me, after exhaustive cross-examinations of Stewart Maiden, a really remarkable teacher of golf, that the hit starts as the left hip is shot forward to its extreme position along the line of play. The downswing may be started by the left shoulder; but it seems the hit is started by that little twitch of the hips which the older school of golf writers (mistakenly, I am convinced) considered as the transference of weight from the right to the left leg.

Rather, it is the winding up of the tension that then unwinds with the requisite snap at the ball.

And where there is winding, you may look for a key—in this instance in, or near, the left hip pocket.

Chick Evans playing from a pile of stones along the roadway which lies behind the seventeenth green at St. Andrews during last year's British Open.

In the Rough BY BERNARD DARWIN

A Plea for a Little Variety
in Our Architecture

THERE ARE NO TWO EXPRESSIONS MORE FRE-
quently in the mouths of golfers than "fairway"
and "rough" and there always seems something
surprising about the fact that neither of them
is to be found in the Rules of Golf. That most
dreadful enemy, the rough, which probably
slays its tens of thousands while bunkers only
slay their thousands, has no legal existence. In
law it is exactly on a footing with the smoothest and most beautiful piece of turf in the very
middle of the course.

This seems today surprising and yet, without being too terribly old, I can remember the
time when "the rough" was neither a regular
expression nor a regular thing. In the eighties
and early nineties it was quite the exception to
find clear-cut areas of rough grass or other
destructive vegetation on either side to catch
the erring ball. I recollect that when I played
at Woking, which was the first of British
courses to be carved out of heathery country,
those parallel and menacing lines seemed
decidedly novel.

That was only twenty-five years ago. Seaside links had clumps of gorse or bushes here
and there and there was of course plenty of
bent grass on the sandhills, but there was no
hard and fast middle way; if there were bents

on the right there was open country on the
left. As to inland courses, certainly I played, in
the University match, on Wimbledon Common, where there were some terribly narrow
drives between gorse bushes, but the three
courses with which I was perhaps most familiar had no rough of any kind. Two were on the
Downs; the lovely springy turf stretched for
miles on either hand and apart from a chalk
pit or two and a few hurdles, you could drive
where you pleased under the vast dome of
Heaven.

The third was of a type fortunately rarer. It
was a flat, muddy Common, where the
wretched golfers of Cambridge were con-
demned to play. We were not allowed to put
up even hurdles and the only trouble consisted
in a few black and ill-scented ditches. Here
lurked troops of black, ill-scented little boys
who either recovered your ball from the water
for a penny or, if they deemed it a more
profitable speculation, stamped the ball into
the oozy mud and then, when you had passed
on, stole it at their leisure.

I am not holding up these latter courses for
admiration—far from it. I only use them as
illustrations of the fact that clear-cut lines of
rough have not been since immemorial. Now

they have certainly come to stay. My experience is far too small for me to generalize but I did not see a course in America that had not got them at any rate to some extent. Nearly all our inland courses today have them. Only on some of the seaside courses does the old, more varied state of things exist. At St. Andrews, for instance, there is certainly a rather broken line of rough country to catch a slice on the way out but that is all. For the most part you are trying to avoid a particular bunker from the tee or to obtain a certain strategic position for your next shot, not trying to go down a groove.

The same thing is true of Westward Ho! There are indeed plenty of tall and spiky rushes, but they are not, as it were, formed up in regular battalions but dotted irregularly here and there about the battlefield. It would be possible to give other instances but I think, even on sensible courses, there is more definite rough than there used to be. Muirfield, for instance, might in this respect be a typical inland course and at Sandwich, you have this feeling of hitting down an alley, though in a less degree, and the alley is a broader one.

It seems to me that golf architects might sometimes with advantage compromise between the two systems more than they do at present. There is, I suppose, not much doubt that the parallel lines of rough make the better educational school because they insist on rigidly straight play. Indeed, if St. Andrews does not turn out so many good golfers as it used, it may be because the young golfers there, having too much license in the matter of erratic driving, do not sufficiently curb their traditional, loose, slashing style. On the other hand, the sensation of being perpetually set in a framework of rough is a monotonous one and the golf tends to become monotonous.

It may be immoral, from the highest golfing point of view, that at St. Andrews a very wild hook may go scot free and a nearly perfect shot be trapped, but it is the endless variety of possible lines to every hole, changing with every little change of the wind, that make the unique charm of that great course. People often get annoyed with St. Andrews but they do not get bored with playing there. Where there is a definite fairway and definite rough, there is far less variety. Bang, bang, bang—right down the middle: that is the only game. It is not easy to do, I admit, and personally I cannot say that I have ever done it so persistently as to grow very weary of it; essentially wearisome. There is little strategy of tactics: no flanking movements, only frontal attacks.

There are one or two suggestions that I venture to make, obvious perhaps but not always acted upon. There should as a rule be two degrees of rough, purgatory and hell. It seems unfair but it is often the case that the man who goes one foot off the course lies in the grass just as thick and tangled as' he who goes twenty or forty. The moderate sin should only entail purgatory—there should be some chance of a startling recovery. And apart from grounds of abstract justice, hunting for lost balls is a sad nuisance both to ourselves and those who play behind us. That is another reason for not having the rough one uniform "hell."

Indeed, I think, uniformity is a thing to be avoided. I would not have the moderate sinner always let off with moderate punishment, any more than I would have the arch criminal always "up to his neck." Let us have a little variety, even if we have to admit that it ought to be called luck. It is a dreary business to take the niblick out of the bag as a matter of course the moment our ball is off the fairway. In an article I wrote some months ago I dared to criticize that wonderful American course, the Lido, on the one ground that the punishment was too uniformly severe and I was glad to see afterwards that some people agreed with me. It seems to me one of the charms of the National Golf Links, on Long Island, that there the rough is not always in definite lines nor does it always "make the punishment fit the crime."

Another thing that I always like to see where possible is an oasis of turf in the rough desert. Let the fairway now and then belly out, if I may so express it, into the rough. A hole looks infinitely more attractive when the side lines are thus broken and wavy and the number of interesting angles from which we may approach the green is increased. It may be that sometimes a man gets a grassy lie who on the intrinsic merits of his shot, deserved a rough one, but the world will not come to an end on that account.

I think the hardest hole I ever knew was a three shotter in which the fairway ran abso-lutely straight from tee to hole. On each side of it was a ditch of uniform depth and beyond the ditch heather of a uniformly damnable character. There was one small bunker exactly in the middle of the course and just in front of the green and that was all. I think, as I said, that it was the hardest hole. And I am quite sure it was the dullest.

Movie hero Richard Barthelmess and Mrs. Barthelmess pause during a recent round in Hollywood.

Movie magnate William Fox, who plays one-handed, scored a hole-in-one on the ninth at Inwood, on Long Island, last fall.

How Is Your Slice? BY JIM BARNES

Suggestions That May Enable You
to Eliminate This Troublemaker

YOU CAN UNDERSTAND HOW THE AVERAGE GOLFER feels about the slice when he knows that any one of twenty things may be causing it. He is generally so helpless that he gives up in despair, aims the ball for the left of the course and hopes it doesn't go out of bounds to the right.

The mere fact that he is aiming way to the left and standing for a slice is going to make the slice certain. It is one of the surest ways in the world to slice, with the left foot well back and the shoulders lined up in a slanting direction. It is a fine thing to make a study of the slice, to learn how to play one deliberately, for then you have a much better chance to avoid slicing when you want a straight ball.

I am going to take up here only some of the most obvious faults, or the most common ones, that cause slicing. In every case the clubhead is pulled across the ball, but many things can cause this result. It may be that the left hand is not over far enough, or it may be that the right hand is gripping too tightly.

These are two faults that one sees almost every round. So I suggest that one of the first things to try out is to turn the left hand a trifle more over the shaft of the club and to ease up just a little with the grip of the right.

Another common fault is not turning the body and the left knee enough on the backswing. In place of this pivoting too many golfers pull away from the ball on the backswing. This nearly always forces them to pull across the ball on the downswing. It is necessary to correct slicing to see both the knee and the body turn far enough to prevent this pulling away.

Very often, also, slicing is caused by lifting the club in too upright a manner from the ball with the arms too stiff. To break up this fault start the clubhead back on a line inside the ball, on an arc inside the line running through the ball towards the green. Don't let the clubhead get outside of this line.

In addition to this, keep the clubhead nearer the ground as it starts back, swinging it in a circle around the right foot. Be sure that the elbows are not too far from the body, with the left arm straight and the right elbow held compactly in.

A big fault just here is the lifting of the left shoulder instead of turning it to the left, if anything a trifle dropped. That left shoulder must not come up. Let it come around and a trifle on the downward side.

Be sure here that the weight is not all on the

right foot. This is one of the most common of faults and almost forces a slice. The left foot must carry its share of the weight, not quite half of it, but at least a distinct pressure from the inside of the left big toe.

Then we come to the fault of standing too far back of the ball. When this happens it is hard to get the clubhead in at the right time and the hands are generally too far ahead of the swing. When the hands get in front of the swing as the ball is being struck, you can look for a big slice nineteen times out of twenty.

If you are slicing I would suggest that you try a square stance, possibly with the left foot just a little in advance of the right, and be sure not to throw the clubhead out too soon on the downswing. Let it come around with the turn of the body.

Another common cause for slicing is not breaking the wrists as the ball is being hit. The right wrist snapping in here with the left wrist firm gets the clubhead in at the right time. In the same manner, many players make the mistake of pulling away just as they hit the ball. Let the clubhead go through.

If these remedies fail to work, be careful to see that you are not straightening up and looking up. Many golfers get down to the ball in the right way and then straighten up just as they are swinging through. If the head is lifted, the body is almost sure to be lifted with it, and when the body comes up a bad slice or a topped ball is a certainty.

If the left arm is bent too soon, in the act of straightening out as the ball is being hit, there is a strong tendency to pull across the ball in order to get the clubhead back in place. Golfers who bend their left arms badly on the backswing are invariably chronic slicers. With the left arm bent the hands and club are drawn in and then, when the downswing starts, both are thrown too far out.

The new United States Open Champion, Eugene Sarazen, displays the trophy for Tony Dominick, the sturdy urchin who carried the winner's bag at Skokie. There is a difference of only eight years in their ages.

Four Blisters in One Hand—
Fifth in Partner's BY RING LARDNER

Mr. Lardner Accounts for One of the Few Defeats
Suffered on His Southern Trip

WELL, FRIENDS, HERE I AM IN THE SUNNY SOUTH land and would not brag about same only that I seen a N. Y. paper the other day where it was said that I was beat 4 up and 3 to play in a golf tournament at Belleair and I suppose the same report was wired to every paper in the country as a man like I is bound to have enemies and any way I feel like I owe it to myself and friends to deny the report in totem and to tell what really come off and will therefore ask the kind indulgents of my readers wile I exclaim the raw deal of which I was made a innocent victim.

Well friends, the day after I reached here there was a man come up to me in the hotel and says would I like to enter in a golf tournament which was just going to begin and I says yes as I thought he was joking but the next thing you know he introduced me to a young man name Mr. Daniels who he said that I and he was pared together in the qualifying rd.

Well, as my readers probably knows there is a rule vs. a man playing a qualifying rd. alone without nobody to help him count his score, so rather than leave Mr. Daniels without nobody

to play with why I got out my golf sticks and played with him and will say at this pt. that Mr. Daniels use to be the champion swimmer of the U. S., but as far as golf is concerned I showed him some new strokes.

Well, I will not waste the reader's time describeing the qualifying rd. only to say that Mr. Daniels turned in a 84 which was next to the low score and personly I got a eagle 118 to say nothing about 4 blisters in one hand and 5th in partner's and naturally I thought the incidents was clothes, so you can imagine my surprise when I am setting in the hotel again that night and a friend of mine comes up and tells me I have qualified in the 2d flight and my 1st match game would be the following A. M. with a Mr. Oakford who seemed to of been named after 2 automobiles.

"Well," I says, "you can go and write the word defaulter in capital letters opp. my name as I haven't got no time for golf tournaments which if you get licked everybody gives you the bird and if you win they give you a prize that even your wife don't know if it's meant to be a umbrella holder or cuspidor."

But my friends said not to be a spoiled sport and maybe that was the very reason this Mr. Oakford had came south was on the bear chance of getting acquainted with some one like I, and so and so and this in that and finely I give in for no reason only as a favor to Mr. Oakford and how does he treat me in return?

1. He calls me Mr. Lauder.

2. When I stick my blisters right in front of his face he don't give them a rumble though when I showed them around the hotel men turned pail and women screemed.

3. The only chance I have got to beat anybody is have them get nervous watching me shoot, but Mr. Oakford looks the other way.

4. On the 3d hole he slices his tee shot and the ball goes to he-ll and gone and he says to his caddy you go and find that ball and I will give you a quarter, the net results of which generous offer is that we don't see no more of his caddy and my caddy has to carry both bags and I can't keep my mind on my game on acct' of feeling so sorry for my caddy.

Last but not lease, Mr. Oakford must of read an article by Jock Hutchison or somebody adviseing golfers to not pay no tension to anything that is said to them but keep their mind on their own game.

So far as listening to my funny cracks, why he might as well of been my wife. And not only that but he played dear when I mentioned something about concedeing putts, but the worst of all was when we come to the 9th hole and he was 5 up and it begin to rain pitchforks and I said I would concede the match as I had on new white pants and he said

yes but he kept right on playing and I had to play along with him and I conceded him the match on the 10th hole and again on the 11th and he says yes both times but kept right on playing and finally I just walked off the course though it was too late as far as my pants was conserned but when I quit he was only 6 up and we still had 6 or 7 to play so no telling how we would of came out if I had of forced him to go through with it but at lease my readers can see of themselves that I was not beat by no such score as 4 up and only 3 to play like the paper had it.

However I am not the kind that makes excuses when they get beat and as far as getting beat is conserned will say that the best man win though if they had give my blisters time to heel I would of made a sucker out of him and even with my blisters I would beat the life out of him on any other course, but on this course when you go in the rough, why you lay the ball out and count a stroke because the most of the rough is forests of palmettos which they's no chance to make a shot out of same and my best shot in golf is a mashie shot out of trouble. In fact on most courses over 50 per cent of my shots is those kind of shots.

That is as much as I care to say in regards to my showing in the tournament as reported in the papers, only I might add that Mr. Oakford himself was beat the next day by 4 up and 3 to play by a man who I never heard of him before but at lease it shows what kind of a golf player Mr. Oakford must be to get a trimming like that the idea of him beating me by any such score as 4 up and 3 to play is silly.

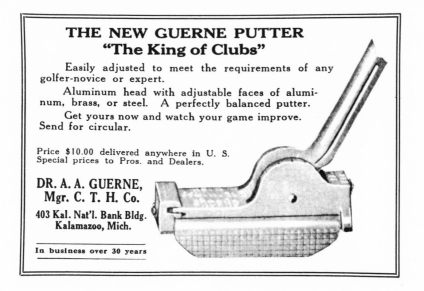

A Tale of Two Visits BY ROBERT E. HARLOW

Hagen's Victory at Sandwich Was a Fine
Vindication of His Failure at Deal

HOSTS OF PEOPLE WILL SAY THAT THE CROWNING moment of the successful golfing career of Walter Hagen was at Sandwich, England, when he became the first American-born golfer to win the British Open Championship. That was a big moment, and one which will live always in the history of American golf. No other man can ever claim the honor of being first to do this thing, although they may duplicate the feat of winning.

There is a little group of golf lovers in America who think they know of a greater moment in the career of Hagen than when he had won at Sandwich. These were in England, in 1920, when Hagen, then the United States Open Champion, played in his first British championship. It was held that year at Deal, in the same section as Sandwich.

Nearly everybody believes that Hagen failed at Deal, and so he did if the merit of a golfer is to be judged alone by the figures on his score card. Hagen finished in fifty-fifth position that year, but to those few Americans who were there, Hagen can never inspire more admiration than he did as he trudged over the last round at Deal, a beaten golfer.

It is easy to take the applause of victory. It is easy to play the game when you are up in front, fighting with the leaders for the title; followed by the crowds and respected by all. It is great to be alive then and to walk with confidence from tee to green. That has often been the joyful lot of Hagen.

But it is different to be the American champion, representing American golf in Great Britain, and to be playing badly in the British Open Championship—so badly that there is no chance of winning—no chance of finishing in the money—no chance of finishing among the first twenty-five. At such a time as that the courage of a golfer is put to its severest test.

That was the way of it at Deal for Walter Hagen. Heralded as the "great" American homebred professional, the mark of columns of comment in the British press upon his arrival in England in 1920, Hagen went to Deal determined to represent American golf as he knew it should be represented.

In his qualifying round he had played well; so well that he had gained the respect of the British critics, and when he arrived at the sand dunes of Deal all were curious to see "the American." He carried the largest gallery of the day as he started away on his first round.

On the first green in two, he ran his long approach putt up within three feet of the hole.

He missed the putt and took a five against the par of four. On the second green in two, again he took three putts and missed the par. So it went; shots slipped away; Hagen could not get going.

A golfer, in order to win, or finish among the leaders, when he is opposed by the world's greatest, must be playing well within himself, hitting the ball without great effort. He must have the touch. Hagen simply did not have the touch at Deal. He had to fight the ball, and never in a single round did he fall into his real golfing stride.

He was never a factor for the championship, or for a place among the money winners. After a day which must have been a nightmare for him, Hagen finished the first two rounds with a score which left him far down the list—too far behind to have any hope of being able to catch the leaders. His third round, played on Friday morning, was no better. The big gallery which had followed him on Thursday, satisfied that the title was not in danger by the American homebred, turned their attention to the leaders, and on his third round the American had but few spectators behind him.

It was with a very heavy heart that Hagen went out for his final round Friday afternoon. British newspapers had already told of his failure and he knew that the cables had carried the news back to America. The American champion certainly had no heart for the game when he trudged out, a late starter for that last eighteen holes of the championship. The leaders were playing ahead of him, and the crowds were following them.

There was George Duncan, who was making a remarkable comeback that was to win him the title; Jim Barnes, the American, who was up among the leaders; Abe Mitchell, who had "cracked" and was no longer setting the pace; the veteran Sandy Herd, who was playing a great game and in a position to win when he had five holes to play.

The American champion looked out over the Deal course and saw these great galleries following the leaders. He had often been in their place, for he is known as a great finisher and in more than one championship has taken out the gallery on the final round. But on that damp, cold, gray day at Deal, the American champion could be seen trudging along with none but his partner and their caddies.

There was Walter Hagen, American champion, pounding his shots into a terrific headwind on that wickedly long home nine at Deal, alone and discouraged, but game and finishing. At that moment he was a glorious sight for those who put the sport above the winning.

He realized before he set out on that unhappy and unpleasant journey that he could not finish inside the first forty players. It was the greatest disappointment of his golfing career. He was a beaten man, but to the everlasting credit of American golf and sportsmanship, the American Open Champion did not quit under the severest golfing fire ever heaped upon a player's head.

He demonstrated that he could take a beating, and see it to the bitter end, and certainly no golfer in the history of international competition ever was forced to take worse punishment than Hagen took at Deal. But he carried on to the end and played every dreadful shot until the last putt had been holed.

And after he had passed through the ordeal and knew that he had finished in something like fiftieth position in the field, behind a number of amateurs as well as a great number of unknown professionals, he walked to the official scoreboard, which was surrounded by strangers, and there he saw to it that the record of his failure to score well was set down for all the world to read.

But the wires and the cables did not record that when to have picked up his ball and quit would have been merciful relief and the easiest way out, when it was mental torture to keep going, Hagen stuck to it and continued to try—first to regain his stride, to find the touch which had carried him to the top in America, and when he could not do this, to keep trying just as hard and to play the game to the finish.

As Hagen walked away from the scoreboard he was dragging his bag of clubs, having discharged his caddie. Three American newspapermen joined him. Walter smiled and made some humorous remark; then becoming serious he said: "I couldn't get going. I didn't have the touch. I am discouraged now, but I am coming back to England. I hope some day to play well over here."

Then he went to France and won the French Open from a fine field of many of the stars who had been at Deal, including George Duncan, the Deal winner. And last year Hagen went back to England and tied for sixth in the British Open at St. Andrews.

And then he won at Sandwich.

But to those who love an athlete who is game and can take a beating as well as win a championship, Hagen never appeared to better advantage than he did holing that last miserable putt on the home green at Deal in 1920; not even when he won at Sandwich.

After finishing his final round at Sandwich, England, this year, Walter Hagen used a pair of field glasses to watch the rest of the field in their unsuccessful efforts to match his score.

Hit the Ball BY EDDIE LOOS

A Valuable Lesson of What Concentration
Really Means

A GOOD MANY YEARS AGO I HAD A PUPIL WHO worried me. He could swing perfectly without a ball. In practice, he would hit fifty per cent of his shots with a surety that made your heart rejoice. But in actual play, he was the most erratic performer that ever topped his approach, missed his putt, sliced his drive, or dubbed an iron shot.

The more lessons I gave him, the worse his performance got. And the worst of it was, I liked him personally, so my feelings as well as my pride as an instructor were at stake.

He laughed—I guess he liked me too—I was an earnest if not a fully competent boy—and he told me something like this: "It isn't your fault, Eddie. I've been to some of the best instructors in the country before I came to you and while you haven't helped me, my game isn't any worse than it was before you took hold."

This was scant consolation for a young fellow who really wanted to help his pupils and who laid awake nights trying to figure out how —if you can imagine such a thing in golf.

I talked to some of the older pros. Outside of the fact that they were not much interested —in my problems, at least—the best I got was: "It's mental—"

I studied and I pondered and I questioned, but the more I questioned them on this "mental" thing, the closer I came to the conclusion that they had read it somewhere—didn't know what it meant.

My pupil himself gave me the clue—unwittingly. He came out one day, to take another lesson, and with the courage born of desperation, I told him the truth. "It isn't any use taking any more lessons. I just simply can't teach you anything and I don't want to take pay without giving something in return." And I needed the money, too.

He laughed and told me not to worry about that side of it, then he asked me a question.

"Eddie, what do you think of when you hit a golf ball?"

I had never considered the question before, so I stopped and thought carefully and when I answered, I told him truthfully. "I just think of hitting the ball."

My answer, incidentally, with a slight addition would be the same today. And then, on the spur of the moment, I impulsively asked him the same question. "What do you think of when *you* hit a golf ball?"

He looked at me, and then he replied, "Well, I think of my grip and my stance and keeping my head still and swinging back slowly and maintaining the correct arc and rolling my forearms as I come into the ball and not swaying—and following through—"

I stopped him—I was astounded. "Do you mean to say you think of all those things when you hit at a ball?"

"I try to"—he said slowly.

And then it dawned on me that I couldn't hit a ball myself, if I tried to keep my mind on anything besides actually hitting it, let alone a dozen things—the swing is too fast to permit of consecutive thinking, although I didn't argue it out that way then.

He took a practice swing as I stood thinking. It looked fine—the arc was true—his wrists worked properly—everything co-ordinated perfectly.

I had an idea, and made a beginning. "I'm going to give you a lesson after all," I said, and teed up a ball, "but—" I added—"I'm going to learn more than you do and you've got to do just what I say."

He laughed and agreed.

"Now," I said slowly, trying to get my idea clear, "I want you to step up to that ball and look at it. Then I want you to make a swing without an idea in your head except to hit the ball—hit through it."

He did—and since this isn't a fairy story, I'll have to admit that he tightened—and the ball was badly topped.

I scratched my head. "What did you think of?" I asked.

"Hitting the ball," he answered.

"Anything else?" I asked.

"Well"—he grinned a little—"I guess I thought of hitting it—*hard*."

"Let's try it again," I said, and teed up another ball.

"I want you to hit this ball a hundred yards—only a hundred yards—do it by swinging easily not by trying to shorten your swing," I told him.

"Hit it a hundred yards," he repeated and then stepped up to the ball.

Out it sailed—two hundred and ten yards—the longest ball he had ever hit in his life. He reached for another ball without a word, started his club back and stopped.

"Getting ready to slug it," he explained. "Guess I'd better try again."

He did and the next ball went around two hundred.

I pulled the driver from his hands and gave him a mashie. We were both learning something.

At the end of that lesson, he had hit more perfect balls than ever before in his life at one sitting—or standing.

And from that time on I gave that man lessons by simply reminding him to hit the ball. His swing was all right except when he spoiled it by thinking about it or by tightening up to try and slug the ball.

When he realized that clean hitting brought distance, the tightening disappeared—and when he got the knack of thinking about hitting the ball, his handicap inside of one season went from 25 to 14—no miracle, but a splendid improvement.

And that was the beginning of my realization of something which has been of immense value to me in my teaching ever since. In my own mind, I make a distinct differential between teaching the swing and hitting the ball. In spite of the fact that practice swings mean nothing, a man with patience can better learn to play golf without a ball than he can with one—simply because every time he dubs or slices, or hooks or tops, he begins to make a change in his swing and thereby defeats any possibility of really developing skill in the swing.

There are two sides to golf—the mechanical and the mental. And it's mighty simple and a sure recipe for improvement if you'll let it sink into your system.

The mechanical side is the swing—when you have learned the correct swing that part of your game should be behind you. It is a tool you have acquired and its use is in hitting the ball.

And the mental side of golf is not intense, wrinkle-browed concentration—it's simply stepping up to the ball with the determination

Walter Hagen recently lost a special match to Gene Sarazen at Oakmont, near Pittsburgh, possibly because he was finding it difficult to keep his mind off the gallery.

Jess W. Sweetser, of New York, recently supplanted Jesse Guilford as National Amateur Champion. A student at Yale, Sweetser is also a capable performer on the cinderpath, where he specializes in the half-mile.

to hit it where you want to go, or "hit through it," whichever expression you prefer—with no other thought in your mind—none whatever.

When I step up to the ball, no matter where it lies, I look at it—I determine the path it is going to take and suddenly I find my club has snapped it into space right in the direction pre-determined. When I try to think of anything else, my shot is spoiled.

No thought of turning wrists or top of swing or anything else—just hit the ball where you want it to go. Even people with ugly swings who have this knack can secure surprising re-sults.

We all know men whose swings look like nothing this side of the nether regions, yet they shoot good golf. Their minds are on hitting the ball where they want it to go.

It's far better fun to play golf with a good swing than with a bad one, but the man with his mind on hitting the ball, no matter what his form is, is going to play better golf than the fellow with splendid form who is trying in a fraction of a second the golf swing takes to think of sixteen different parts of his anatomy.

I have talked with hundreds of professionals. They all tell me the same thing—when they're frank—their thoughts are on hitting the ball.

Their analysis of the swing for teaching purposes is the result of observation. Their swings are not consciously executed. Their instructions to you are the things they have noticed in their own swings when they studied them for tuition purposes. This plus the mouth to mouth methods of transmitting golf lore that have always been prevalent in professional ranks.

Golf is no more difficult than driving a nail or swinging an axe. True, the planes in golf are a little confusing to the beginner, but the most difficult part of golf is the part that we inject into it by making a mental thing of something that should be mechanical.

Try this experiment.

Go out and make a few practice swings without a ball—make sure your clubhead grazes the ground and comes through on a straight line for a few inches before and after the spot where the ball ought to be.

When this comes easily and naturally, lay down a ball. Fix the direction you want to go and step up to the ball in the same mental state that you would start to swing an axe. Think of the objective, not the physical motions necessary to attain it. Step up to hit that ball straight and true—never mind distance —just as you would drive a nail or chop a tree.

You may surprise yourself.

Now, of course, a good many people will feel that by taking this attitude, I am discounting the value of professional instruction, but this could hardly be true, considering the fact that I earn my living in that particular manner.

Professional instruction develops the ideal swing—the "good form" with which every ambitious man wants to play golf. And for that reason alone, professional coaching will always be in demand.

But the man who is going to play a good game of golf, with or without professional coaching, must make up his mind to divorce the mechanical and the mental sides of golf.

He will learn to swing so that his control over his club is exercised without any more thought than he uses a hammer or an axe or reaches for a glass of water.

And then, when he plays, he will forget his swing—put the mechanical part of it behind him. His mind will be on hitting the ball the distance he wants to go. His attention will be concentrated on that little flight path that starts a few inches before the ball and ends several inches past it pointing in the desired direction.

And with his mind and his attention concentrated right at the bottom of the swing where it belongs, he will find that handicaps go down and balls fly straight and true.

I firmly believe that a clear understanding of this principle will do wonders for any golfer.

And just as a last word—a confession. I have observed that when a shot fails to come off to my satisfaction, that my mind was elsewhere than on hitting the ball.

The danger of the amateur lies in filling his mind with so many things that he can't center on hitting the ball.

The danger of the professional is that his certainty is so great and his swing so true that he may let his mind wander entirely off the golf course.

And the fact that even when he does this, he brings off a good shot most times, shows that a good swing—a formed habit—is well worth cultivating.

The Style of Walter Hagen BY O. B. KEELER

A Close Inspection of America's

Leading Professional

WALTER HAGEN, RATED THE PREMIER PROFESsional match-play golfer of the world, has been about all the kinds of champion a professional golfer can be in America—National Open, Western Open, Metropolitan Open, P. G. A. Champion, North and South Open, Florida West Coast Open, and a good many more. But his winning of the British Open in 1922 probably was the crest of his championship career to date, being the more noteworthy by reason of a startling contrast. In his first venture in that classic three years previously, he finished a sorry fifty-fifth in the great field, so his bound into first place caused even our staid British cousins to raise their eyebrows a bit.

Hagen is a thoroughly interesting type to study, on the course and off it; and before the end of this little sketch is reached I hope to let you in on a factor of his amazing success as a golfer that, to my way of thinking, has at least as much to do with that success as his fine, sound style and his powerful play. Perhaps more; you can't tell about such things. No man can be a golf champion these days without a sound style and plenty of power. But there are many who possess both these requisites and are not champions, and have not been cham-

pions, and very possibly never will be champions.

The first impression you get of Hagen's golfing style is that it is free, slashing, and of enormous power. I was interested in the views of Damon Runyon, the well-known sport writer, who saw his first golf at the National Open Championship at Skokie in 1922. It was getting the view of an intelligent chap and a good writer utterly unsophisticated in that particular line. He called Walter Hagen "The Big Fellow" in his articles.

And it was easy to see where Mr. Runyon got the idea. Hagen is not a "big fellow," in the sense that Dempsey and Firpo and Ted Ray are "big fellows." Hagen is a well-proportioned man of about five feet ten, weighing, I should guess, around 175; not a "big fellow" at all.

But watching him tear into a golf ball for a full shot, with the tremendous drive of his right side carrying all his weight far forward onto his left foot, it is impossible to escape an impression of bulk; the vast power of the man seems to dilate him; the action is expansive, in a way. I do not wonder that Runyon called him "The Big Fellow."

And this dynamic style is most interesting to

analyze; easy, too, if you go about it the right way, taking the swing by sections and not allowing yourself to be dazed by the smashing effect of the stroke as a whole.

Walter shoots from a firm foundation. He employs an exceptionally wide stance; I know of no golfer of his height whose feet are more spread for the full stroke. The stance is fairly open; it has to be, to permit the astounding use of his right side that is one of his leading characteristics.

As he takes his stance and addresses the ball, you may note another Hagen characteristic. Since you took up golf you have been told to keep your eye on the ball; but have you ever paused to wonder which eye? There is a master-eye in golf, the same as in rifle shooting; and in most golfers, as in most riflemen, it is the right eye. With Walter Hagen it is the left eye, as with Bobby Jones. Offhand, they are the two leading exponents, so far as my observation goes, of the left-eye style of address—and it is the style that favors the right-hand golfing swing, because with the left eye lined on the ball the head naturally is turned slightly in the direction the body must turn in the pivot that brings the club back; hence, there is less strain in keeping the head in one place as the backswing progresses.

Hagen and Bobby Jones, when concentrating on a stroke to the limit, give the impression of "cocking" the head, so immobile is the cranial pose as the club starts back. You may see this in any photograph of these players at the moment of address.

Hagen's swing is neither upright nor flat, but is nearer the former. He takes the club back smoothly to a position just dipping past the horizontal; a full swing, it would be called these days, though far short of the "St. Andrews' swing" of a generation ago. The left arm all through the stroke, until the ball has gone, is rigidly straight; but that is a characteristic of all first-class players, practically; only Harry Vardon, the Old Master, eases the backswing at the top by a slight bend of the left elbow, and he brings it out straight again early in the downswing.

At the top of the swing, Hagen's right leg is rigidly braced and his weight seems to have moved back on to it, but the left foot is gripping the ground firmly; the foundation is solid all through the stroke. But once the downswing is under way, Hagen does not hesitate to shoot the left hip into a leading position, and at impact his right heel is well off the ground—his weight is coming through with a rush as his right side goes driving on. But his head remains still until the ball has gone; the rush of his right side fairly yanks it from its position. I never have seen Walter play in a hat or cap, but I firmly believe that that terrific snap would flip his head from under its covering. He finishes the stroke with his right shoulder the nearest portion of his anatomy to the objective, and his weight so far forward that a photograph of his finish looks as if he were running after the ball.

This is his big shot, and it is a grand effort, and an impressive one. He is one of the greatest wood-club players of our generation; perhaps of golfing history. But there is another stroke of which he is master, a wee one, that I fancy even more as a bacon-bringer.

This is the chip-shot, that inestimable economist of golf; the greatest shot-saver of all the game, when it is working for you. And Walter is peculiarly adept with it.

A casual inspection of Walter's game around the green might incline you to the notion that his chipping game is complex: he uses this club one time; that club another; a third—even a fourth—for a tiny shot up to the pin.

But Walter has his very good reasons for the change of clubs, and as he explains it himself, the use of three or four different tools actually tends to simplify the business.

It all depends on the proportion of chip and roll he desires. If his ball is, say, twenty yards from the edge of the green, and the cup is pretty close to that side, Walter will take a mashie-niblick so as to get more chip than roll, lifting the ball over the intervening fairway, or rough, or trap, and dropping it on the smooth green with the brakes on it, so the roll is curtailed.

If the proportion is fifty-fifty, he will take a deep-faced mashie; and if he is close to the edge of the green and the cup is well back, he will use a mashie-iron or even a mid-iron, giving the shot less chip and more roll.

But in every shot of this nature, and with every club, Walter hits the ball the same way; a smart, crisp blow, the club just snipping the turf and taking the ball fairly in the back. That is the secret of simplicity in his chip shot. In place of varying the stroke to get more pitch and less roll, or vice versa, he varies the club to suit the situation—and hits the ball the same way every time.

To keep the body absolutely immovable—as essential in the chip shot as in putting—he keeps most of his weight on the left foot, well advanced. I do not recall any stance for any shot where his feet are not well separated; his putting stance is about the same as for the chip shot, with the weight well forward.

And permit me to say just here that when

This action shot shows Walter Hagen lacing out a 250-yard drive down the long, winding third fairway at Pelham, New York, during the final of this year's P.G.A. Championship. This hole is 530 yards in length. Hagen got his par-five, but it wasn't good enough, as Sarazen, after driving 270 yards, played a 260-yard brassie shot to the center of the green. No small part of the crowd was banked in back of the tee, out of range of the camera—and on beyond the green.

The vigorous finish of Walter Hagen after tearing into a wood shot.

Walter Hagen prepares for a chip shot from any location close to the green, he is not trying merely to get the ball close to the cup; he is trying to hole out. And it is astonishing how many times he succeeds. And if the ball doesn't drop he usually has an easy putt for his next shot. Jerry Travers some ten or fifteen years ago, and Alex Smith, the one with a jigger, the other with a plain mashie, were Walter's nearest rivals I can recall at this important detail of play.

Hagen is, of course, a fine iron player, though I never have regarded his intermediate game as up to the long and short ends of it.

So much for the interesting mechanics of the first American home-bred to win the Blue Ribbon of British golf. Briefly I would set out in conclusion a factor that has nothing to do with style, yet has supplied the main impetus, I feel sure, for the brilliant career of the remarkable young man who started the season of 1923 by winning four of the first seven tournaments in which he played and at Belleair Heights, Florida, set a new record for a medal round in competition with a score of 62.

This factor is the competitive instinct, which I believe to be more highly developed in Walter Hagen than in any other modern golfer.

) Walter Hagen never steps on a golf course except to win whatever match or competition he may be engaged in. As Ty Cobb will fight just as hard in an exhibition game against a college team as in a championship struggle in the American League, so Hagen "puts out" every time he takes his club in hand. He plays to win, and to win as decisively, as crushingly, as overwhelmingly as he can. A friendly match with Walter is a friendly match, all right—but he will beat you if he can, and as much as he can. He never eases up. In his famous match with Abe Mitchell, the Englishman who, it was said, had not lost a money-match in three seasons, Hagen was four down at the turn of the last round; but he won the match, with an outburst of birdies that swept the Englishman fairly off his feet.

He plays that way in any game. On tour with his partner, Joe Kirkwood, and their manager, Bob Harlow, the three often played pool in the "tank towns," waiting for late trains. And I have it from Harlow that at the end of a four-hour session at pool, for no stakes at all, Hagen would be found playing the last rack with all the care, all the keenness, all the intent to win, that he displayed at the start.

"I believe," said Bob, "that if Walter got in a game of tiddledy-winks with a couple of kids on the nursery floor, he would try as hard to beat them as he did to win the British Open."

That, if you please, is the competitive instinct. Hagen cannot play any other way; he does not know what it is to ease up, winning or losing.

The finest example of that spirit I know of was shown in one of Walter's most disastrous performances: the British Open at Deal, in which he was hopelessly off his stride and finished fifty-fifth. Yet he played the closing holes of the last round with as much care and as much pains and as much determination as if he were aiming at first place. After the tournament he was asked why he didn't take it more easily. Walter grinned.

"Why," he confessed, "I found I had a chance to beat out the chap I was playing with for some place or other—fifty-fifth, it turned out—so I just kept on plugging."

The difference between fifty-fifth and fifty-sixth places was enough to make Walter Hagen put out all he had. It was the competitive instinct. Nothing else would have kept him "plugging."

And this is the factor of success I promised to tell you about. Walter Hagen is proverbially a fine sportsman; a courteous opponent; a good loser, when he loses. He never kicks about his luck; he takes the breaks as they come. Bob Jones once said to me:

"I love to play with Walter. He goes along, chin up, smiling away; never grousing about his luck, playing the ball as he finds it. He can come nearer beating luck itself than anybody I know."

And always and everlastingly, he plays to win. That is one reason he usually does.

St. Andrews BY BERNARD DARWIN

Observations on Play at the Shrine of Golf

I HAVE JUST FINISHED A ROUND AT ST. ANDREWS with a feeling of profound thankfulness for not having committed infanticide. From the last tee my ball leaped lightly over the left ear of a small and quite unconscious boy who was walking along the road that crosses the links and leads to the shore. All day long there is a procession along it of motor cars, perambulators, children and old ladies, and the golfer, learning perforce to be callous, drives over, round, or through them from the first and from the last tees. Mr. Horton, the starter, in his box periodically shouts "Fore" at the people in a voice of thunder or, rather, he makes some horrific sound with no distinguishable consonants in it, but nobody pays any attention and, which is more surprising, nobody is killed.

St. Andrews in August is distinctly different from St. Andrews in September. September is the month of the public Vase and the Medal when "everybody as is anybody" feels bound to come here and one meets all the golfers one ever knew in the clubroom. In August there are plenty of members here, but it is pre-eminently the season of the golfing tripper from Edinburgh, from Glasgow, from all over the place. Most of them play golf and all of them putt. Excluding the ladies' club putting course, which is select and genteel, where you must be accompanied by a member and must

play with a putter of wood on the sacred turf; excluding also the children's links on the far side of the road by the seventeenth green; there are three public putting courses.

You pay twopence or a penny. You hire a putter, if you need one, and a ball from which the vestiges of paint have long since vanished, and you putt. These greens are just outside the white railing between the shore on one side and the fairway to the first hole on the other. One of them is in considerable peril from the sliced drives from the first tee and I apprehend that on this one you only pay a penny, because of the enhanced risk to your life. The greens are not very good (how could they be with the constant tramping?), but they are very amusing and there is something extraordinarily friendly and jolly about the whole performance. You feel that putting is not the solemn and agonizing business that you have so often imagined it, but a popular pastime with vast scope for rollicking humor, like going on a switch-back railway at Coney Island.

Of course, there is plenty of solemn golf too. At this present moment there is a big open tournament on the Eden course with so many entries that the qualifying rounds take two days. In it are playing such well-known golfers as Mr. de Montmorency and Mr. John Caven, both of whom have played for Britain against

America, and a host of those artisan golfers with whom Scotland abounds—golfers who from lack of time and means seldom go far from their home courses but who have all the dash and style of the professional and want only something of his steadiness and experience. There are big crowds watching the plays, for the Scots never tire of watching golf, but this does not seem to diminish by a single man, woman or child the crowd that is playing on the Old Course and on the New. They were hard at it when I looked out of my bedroom window at eight o'clock this morning and they will still be hard at it when in a few minutes I strike across the edge of the last green to dress for my dinner at eight o'clock in the evening. And nearly every match is a four-ball match because it takes three hours to get round, and to play a single is to become a martyr to impatience on every tee.

There is one curious thing about playing here which always strikes me. One never seems to notice the players in front of one and at the end of the round scarcely remembers who they were. The reason is, I fancy, that it does not in the least matter who they are. They might be three old ladies playing by mistake left-handed. It would make no difference. They would go the same pace, which is the pace of the green, which is three hours a round. And yet, I suppose I am not quite accurate. There must be some players so portentously slow that they take three hours and a quarter. I suppose so because there is now an official of the links called the "Ranger." He wears a red band as a badge of office and stands up on a little hillock among the whins, by the tee to the Heathery Hole, overlooking the links. If he sees any players who are not keeping their places, he goes and prods them on with a metaphorical bayonet.

Nothing demonstrates so well the unique fascination of St. Andrews as the fact that golfers who might go anywhere else come here year after year and gladly suffer all the slowness and all the inconveniences in order to play on the Old Course. That is the magnet. The New Course is a very fine one. If it were anywhere else in the world, except under the shadow of the Old, it would be very famous. It is even argued that judged by orthodox standards of architecture it is as good as the Old. Yet everybody wants to get a place in the ballot for starting times on the Old and nobody but regards the New as a last resort. The Calcutta Cup foursome tournament is played on the New Course. Yet I remember that two years ago, not one single player took the trouble to go for a preliminary round of exploration on the New. They just played it "blind" because they would not spare one precious moment from the delights of the Old. There is nothing like it anywhere else, though I am sure I cannot explain why. The best reason I know is George Duncan's "You can play a damned good shot there and find the ball in a damned bad place!"

The eighteenth green on the Old Course at St. Andrews during the finish of a round in the 1921 Open Championship. In the background, to the left, is the clubhouse of the Royal and Ancient.

The Three Types
of Pupil BY ALEXANDER "SANDY" HERD

Which One Are You?

PEOPLE WHO COME TO ME FOR GOLF LESSONS may be divided into three classes—learners, unlearners, and improvers.

Suppose you come to me as a learner who has never yet played a round. I take you to a quiet part of the course, out of everybody's way. There is no need for balls. My first concern is to teach you the golf swing.

If you will give me patient attention, I shall put you on the right road—only a short way to begin with, but a yard on the right road is worth a mile on the wrong road. At least fifty per cent of golfers still play golf hopelessly after years of practice. If you are wise, you will be warned in time.

The pleasures of golf are increased a thousandfold when it is played correctly. Those who merely knock the ball about, trusting to luck more than to good guidance, miss all the charms and pleasure of the game.

It is easy to play golf well very soon. I could tell of a well-known Yorkshire player who came to me at the age of forty-five as a learner.

"I want to advance by slow but sure stages, Sandy," he said.

"You're my man," said I.

After a series of lessons I saw no more of him for three months. Then one day he wrote, asking me to play him a round and give him half a stroke a hole. We played and halved the match.

I asked him where he had been and what he had been doing to make such wonderful progress, for he played beautiful golf, without the semblance of pressing in his tee shots. I half feared he might say that he had been taking lessons elsewhere.

"I have been practicing hard since I last saw you," he said. "I made a careful note of all you told me, and have practiced for two hours a day since."

That is the sort of pupil to do credit to a teacher. He now does credit to a handicap of plus 2 in a South of England club.

As a learner you must not attempt a full swing for some time. The golf swing consists of five sections—the quarter swing, the half swing, the three-quarter swing, the full swing when the club lies horizontally over the shoulders, with the toe of the head pointing to the ground, and downward swing, when the club descends on the line by which it ascended.

These sections must be distinctly understood by the pupil, as he proceeds to graft them smoothly into each other. There is no need to be alarmed. It is all easy with careful practice.

And, this above all, do not imagine that golf cannot be played without the full swing. Everything depends on the build of a player, as to the length of swing he should stick to. The part of the swing that determines the flight of the ball consists of about three feet before it is struck and one foot afterwards, however far momentum may carry the club-head round.

It is perfect timing that works all the wonders. When this is attained, the pupil looks up and smiles at the ease with which an astonishingly fine shot is made. Golfers can recall shots of this description, and many pray for their return. Their prayers would be answered at any time, if they had an intelligent idea of how the shot happened.

This is why I want the learner to begin with the scales, so to speak, and not to want to play classical music in a month.

So now take up your driver. I place a brown leaf on the grass or direct your eye to a daisy. Why not a ball? Because the result of your first efforts would tend to dishearten you.

The first section of the swing consists of taking the club back with a straight left arm, till the need for bending the elbows is felt.

The left heel is slightly off the ground, and the left knee is just beginning to bend. These things happen naturally. There is hardly any need to think of them. They come of themselves.

The reason for straightening out the arms at the start of the backswing is to get the hands well out for the final blow. The golf swing is not made like a cartwheel. It is almost an oval —the hands must go well out to come swiftly through.

I shall ask you to make this half swing many times till you seem to have got the hang of it.

Of course the half swing is too short for long driving. But tag the next section on to it, and the advance is most encouraging.

Now the elbows come into operation. El-

bows and wrists play a great part in golf. Having thrown the left arm well out, you bend the elbows in going on with the upward swing, till the clubhead lies over the right shoulder, considerably short of the horizontal.

Swings cannot be adapted to inches. The best of us vary the length of our swings, and it is certainly true that the trend today is towards shorter swinging for accuracy.

In making this three-quarter swing, the eye, of course, rests on the ball, or the place where the ball should be. The head remains comfortably still, neither lifting nor swaying.

From this position you can make a rhythmic swing that will give you a sense of speed and power. There must not be a vestige of jerking or stabbing, just a nice smooth, swift sweep through, after the wrists have come into position at the top.

Whatever you do, don't hurry. Don't fall asleep at the top, either, but perform the shot in the way that commands power and keeps direction. The long straight ball must come. There is no road to it but correct golf. It is the character of his shots, not the length of them, that marks the golfer.

Now we go on to the full swing. The club must not be "lifted" or "pitched" or "dragged" back. It must be "swung" back. When the horizontal is reached, a barely imperceptible pause may be made, by way of making sure that the left wrist has come almost under the club shaft.

What I mean is, that you must not begin the downward swing as if you were anxious to get it over. Haste spells disaster and disaster is disheartening. I am always on the look-out against a pupil becoming downhearted.

That is why I am constantly saying:

"Wait for the wrists! Wait for the wrists to come into position!"

We all go wrong at times through neglecting this fundamental guiding principle.

Haste throws the hands in front. All the vim then goes out of the shot. Try hitting a nail with a hammer. The right sort of blow is made when the hammer head "falls" on the nail.

"Let the clubhead do the work" is an excellent rule to follow in golf. Do this, and you will immediately see the force of it.

The full swing is the ideal swing, but it must not be too full. A three-quarter swing is better than a swing that causes the player to lose control of the club. You should work up by degrees to the full swing, going smoothly all the time.

Suppose now you have reached that stage when the full swing seems to suit you. Don't trouble about the "open" face and the "shut" face. Such things are not for you yet—in fact, they are of no very great importance to anybody.

No golfer took fewer liberties with the natural swing than Harry Vardon, whose golf in his prime was the best the world ever saw. His style was always capable of being imitated. Hundreds of good golfers owe their success to the study of Vardon's natural methods.

At the top of the full swing, the club should lie horizontal with no dip of the clubhead. By dipping or dropping the clubhead after the swing is completed, you lose control and balance, thus throwing the swing out of gear. The left arm forms a half circle at the top of the swing.

Your club in coming to the horizontal across the right shoulder, a few inches out from the nape of the neck, arrived there by the line it must take in the downswing. There is no going up one way and coming down another.

Be careful not to pull the hands in towards the body in coming down. Throw the clubhead out from you at the start of the descent. The effect of this is to bring the club well behind the ball—and not down on it—for the blow. There must be an element of sweep in the hit, or an element of hit in the sweep.

But unless the club comes at the ball almost on a plane for two or three feet, the result will be a high, short shot at the best. The reason for this is easily seen. Without it there can be no follow-through.

One great golfer, we know, decries the "follow-through," and says he gets his long drives without it. I have watched him, and found that he follows through quite as much as any

of us, but does not finish over his left shoulder. That is all the difference. His backswing is full. He comes down at such terrific speed that he has no choice but to follow through.

A last word to the learner.

Be sure you know what you are doing. Don't be always playing matches with men of your class. Go out alone and practice, as I have been telling you. Proceed by degrees. Don't doom yourself to be a comparative duffer for years when patient study will put you on the sure road to success.

I know young men, strong as lions and supple as panthers, who have golfed, after a fashion, for years and can still be beaten easily by men old enough to be their fathers, who have studied the game and know what they are doing.

The young man in the twenties or early thirties who, after playing for years, is yet not good enough for a low single-figure handicap —well, there is no excuse for him and his only hope is to join the great body of unlearners.

By unlearners I mean golfers who have gone so far along the wrong lines that they need a thorough overhauling. They are a constant source of disappointment to themselves and their partners, one day playing fairly well and the next as badly as they played at the beginning, ten or a dozen years ago.

In their case I generally find that the removal of one or two radical errors should put them right—the occasional good golf they play proves that it is in them.

Do you belong to this class? If so, let me see what I can do for you. It must be true of erratic golf that the rhythm has gone out of your game. All golf shots, with any club, have this one feature in common—rhythm. Only this way comes what is called a "sweet" shot, when the ball is propelled with a click.

"Timing" is the result of rhythm. Jerking and "bashing" are the opposite causes of all your troubles.

Men are not all built alike, but to be good golfers they must all play alike in this respect, whatever be their styles. Ted Ray and the caddie boy who swings a stick cut from the woods observe the law of rhythm—unconsciously, it may be, but none the less certainly.

All golfers who begin as boys play properly. You began as a man, when the muscles were set. Therefore, you must think it out for yourself and overcome this natural handicap.

Amazing results may be achieved if you make up your mind to give the science of golf a real chance with you. Shed all your bad habits on the spot. They have thrust themselves in your way long enough. There is greater joy in playing nice golf than in winning a match merely because your opponent played still worse than you.

It would be easy to set your head in a whirl with directions. I shall not do that. Just play with easy confidence and, above all, play *smoothly;* and don't stiffen the wrists when hitting the ball.

In quest of more length come through quicker, but still smoothly. With wood clubs, or irons, throw the clubhead after the ball *smoothly*. This applies to the mashie as well. There is no need for trick shots.

In putting, follow through with the clubhead, like a pendulum, feeling the wrists working nicely. The good habits will rout the bad ones in due time. If you value your peace of mind, obey these directions.

The improver may be a golfer with a low handicap who wants to come down to scratch but gets no lower than, say, three or four. He has been standing still for a year or more.

If I had him before me, I would see at once what was the matter. Not unlikely he is making the mistake of substituting eagerness for concentration on the principles of golf. He worries himself out of the realization of his ambition. Most probably his hazards are mental.

But, aside from these things, the shot that does most to make a genuine scratch golfer is the mashie shot up to the pin—not merely up to the green. Anybody can do that. So to approach as to leave the ball practically dead at four holes in a round might make all the difference. It is the mashie that makes putting easy—or difficult, according to its manipulation. Nineteen mashie shots out of every twenty are short with average golfers. Two-putts, or three, may be required.

There is no road to scratch this way. The mashie must be mastered. I saw a scratch man playing a two man the other day. It all turned on the scratch man's ability to play mashie shots up to the pin.

Though born and bred at St. Andrews, where they play the run-up shot, I advocate pitching and stopping with the mashie. The Americans, among whom I recently spent three months, practice this shot in all their spare time, before or after matches. They know its value.

The way to stop a mashie shot is to give what we call in Scotland a "dunsh." This is done by bringing the head of the club under the ball, with the back of the left hand facing the flag. Underspin is thus imparted, without the ball being deflected. It drags forward a short way as the underspin pulls it up.

I do not believe in cutting a shot by drawing the clubhead across the ball. There is no certainty of direction in this method. The "dunsh" shot is surer and simpler. You can pitch at the pin with it. I do not know any shot more calculated to help the improver to take strokes off his handicap.

But to all classes alike one counsel outweighs every other in every department of the game. Bring the club down by the line you take it back and up—smoothly and rhythmically. Your return ticket, so to speak, is not available by another line. That is the only royal road to golf, or, if you like, the common-sense of golf.

The End of the Hike BY GRANTLAND RICE

Details of Bobby Jones' First
Championship Victory

THERE ARE TIMES WHEN VAGUE AND DIM IMPRES-
sions, off the line of strict accuracy, suddenly
become more luminous than actual facts.

There seems, in this connection, to have
been a general understanding far and near
that Robert Tyre Jones, Jr., of Atlanta, has
always been something of golf's stormy petrel,
moving along at an erratic, zig-zag pace, the
victim of fate, circumstance and other imped-
ing details out the road.

So far as the National Open is concerned,
this impression has been entirely incorrect.
Bobby Jones' procession to the top throne of
the game has been almost as orderly and im-
mutable as the orbit of the stars. He started
the long championship journey at Inverness in
1920 at the age of eighteen. Here has been
his upward line of march—

Inverness, 1920—tied for eighth place.
Columbia, 1921—tied for fifth place.
Skokie, 1922—tied for second place.
Inwood, 1923—tied for first place.
Inwood, 1923—Open Champion (play off).

Here was a drive for an objective where a
definite advance was made in each charge, as
definite as any advance charted by some Chief
of Staff. There was no slip, no falling back, no

break in ranks. Merely a steady, even, unbroken march to the main goal.

Through May and June, Jones in practice
rounds had been having trouble with his approach shots from intermediate distances. His
full shots, full mashie or full iron, were well
under control, but the shorter pitches and the
half-irons had not been working any too well.
It was only the night before the championship
started that he finally admitted he was hitting
the ball in much better fashion than at Skokie,
where, as he said, "My putter kept me in the
chase."

When the qualifying test was over, practically every favorite had slipped safely
through. There were good men left out, fine
golfers in fact, but none picked to win. When
the crack field finally got under way for the
first day's thirty-six-hole test, the qualifiers
were facing ideal weather over the hardest test
that had ever known a championship in the
United States, perhaps in the world.

Certainly no other links or course had been
as heavily and as closely trapped, calling more
persistently for both length and direction, with
a terrific stroke-and-distance penalty for eight
or nine out-of-bounds. There was no resting

A study in young Bobby Jones' graceful swing. This was
snapped at Brookline last year when he lost in the final.

After receiving the Open Championship trophy from
U.S.G.A. officials Thomas B. Paine, Charles O. Pfeil and
James Francis Burke, Bobby Jones spoke in glowing terms
of his opponent, Bobby Cruickshank, in the play-off.

Jones holing out after playing a mid-iron six feet from the hole on the eighteenth during play-off.

place along the entire journey. The drive had to be hit far and true and then the problem of the second shot arose with all its baffling details. There was no easy drive, no easy approach upon any hole of the eighteen. And one mistake could lead to almost instant disaster at any moment.

The eight favorites to win included Hagen, Sarazen, Hutchison, Kirkwood, Barnes, Jones, Mac Smith and Farrell. Bobby Cruickshank was given a good chance, on the outer edge of the group favored by such dope as golf permits. And when the first day's play at thirty-six holes had been completed, Jock Hutchison seemed to be a certain winner. Jock was leading with two great rounds of 70-72. Jones was next at 71-73. Cruickshank was third at 73-72.

The big shock came in the crash of so many favorites. Here within one day Gene Sarazen, defending champion, and Jim Barnes, 1921 titleholder, were completely out with two high rounds, more than fifteen strokes above the leader with the gap too wide to be ever closed.

Mac Smith and Kirkwood, field leaders in the qualifying pace, were almost gone, barely on the rim of a forlorn hope. Walter Hagen, always a powerful figure, was ten strokes away at 152 through two rounds where he had taken a world of punishment to keep in sight. His first 77 for anyone but Hagen might have been an 85.

While Forrester, Gallet, Watrous and others had done well, extremely well with a fine display of golf, it became evident by Friday's gathering dusk that Hutchison, Jones or Cruickshank would be the new Open Champion of the United States. Such leading amateurs as Ouimet, Evans and Sweetser had failed to show winning form and were all struggling far out of even a fighting chance.

Now, Jock Hutchison, one of the most brilliant golfers that ever lived in any clime or any age, is a performer of moods. On certain days he is unbeatable. He had been unbeatable Friday and he confidently expected to lead the field by ten strokes. In that frame of mind the Glen View Scot is nearly always a tiger, no matter what the occasion is.

But golf has its sudden and unexplainable turns. Still confident as he took his early morning practice on Saturday, Hutchison discovered at his first few practice shots that he had lost all touch with his irons. There was no accounting for the change but the entire feel from the day before had left. With this knowledge his confidence slipped away. He still hung on until he took a 6 at the eleventh hole and followed this slip by pitching into the water guarding the green at the 110-yard twelfth, a mashie-niblick shot that usually left him putting for a 2. By losing four strokes on these two holes, Hutchison finally finished with an 82, dashed from the heights with only an outside chance.

The third round is generally figured to be the vital round of an Open Championship. It is usually the round that makes or breaks. Jones finished his third round with a steady 76—41-35—for a 54 hole total of 220. In place of trailing Hutchison by two strokes, he was now four strokes beyond the harassed Jock, who, as it turned out, could have won the championship with a 77-76.

The next two men to be considered were Bobby Cruickshank, the wee Scot from Schackamaxon, and Walter Hagen. At the fifth hole of the third round the news swept over the bunkered battlefield that Cruickshank had cracked beyond all repair and that Hagen was coming like the wind. The sound of Hagen's footsteps whirling up from behind is always an ominous echo for any leader.

This report was soon verified. Hagen was under par and Cruickshank had started 4-6-6-5-7. Hagen had caught him within five holes, starting with a seven-stroke deficit. Here was Cruickshank only two under even 6's for five holes, almost hopelessly wrecked. But from that point on the lion-hearted little Scot, who had served in the big war with the Seaforth Highlanders, showed his fighting soul.

In place of quitting he got a new grip upon his nerves and settled down to one of the greatest uphill fights ever seen. Hagen continued his mad march until he pitched over the green at the ninth out of bounds. But for this slip he would have been out in 36. As it was he was out in 38 with Cruickshank at 42. On the homeward route Hagen had another bad dip at the 172-yard fifteenth, where his tee shot dropped in heavy grass under the matted branches of a small tree. This break cost him a 5. Despite these two ripples he was around in 73 where he might have had a 69.

And Cruickshank marched steadily along to a homeward 36 for a 78.

The tide had turned to Jones. Only the terrors and difficulties of the long Inwood test made the result uncertain. There were too many places where two and three strokes could be picked up on a single hole. Jones got out safely in 39. This was just two strokes over par, not so bad under the conditions.

Then began the most memorable inward march we know of. Through six holes Jones held himself in front by either fine putting or miraculous recovery from trouble. He started home 3-4-3-4-4-3 by sinking two good putts and by smashing niblicks from the sand dead to the cup at the fourteenth and fifteenth.

After this sensational whirl it seemed as if nothing could hold him down. He needed three 4's for a 33 to finish, a 72 for the round and a 292 for the entire journey.

But on the last three holes he continued to hook his iron shots and the recovery gift suddenly went away. At the 430-yard sixteenth, after hooking his approach out of bounds for a penalty of stroke and distance, the shot that saved his scalp was the next attempt, a full iron to within seven feet of the pin for a five, where a six looked certain and a seven probable. With still a 4 left to cinch the championship at the eighteenth green, Jones hooked his iron approach, missed his short pitch, found a trap and took a 6, leaving him at that moment the most wretched individual between two oceans. There were deep circles under his eyes, a weary sag to his body and the look of one who had been mortally hurt.

Hutchison, by this time, needed a 32 home to tie, so he was through. When Hagen took a 7 on one of the early holes he gave up completely, playing the rest of the distance in a haphazard fashion that finally netted an 86, the highest mark he ever took in any championship round.

So only Cruickshank was left. The wee Scot at first was struggling. But after reaching the sixth tee he played the next seven holes in these amazing figures: 2-3-3-4-3-4-3, only one over even 3's. He had now caught Jones and seemed to have the championship as surely tucked away as Jones had had it forty minutes before. For he still had that 5-5-6 finish of Jones to shoot against.

But Cruickshank slipped a trifle at the next three holes, playing them in 5-5-4 where Jones had only needed 4-4-3. This left Cruickshank with three 4's to win on three of the hardest finishing holes ever tackled.

His big crash came at the first test, the sixteenth, where after a fine drive he cut his iron approach to the rough up near the green, came out too gently and then took three putts for a heart-breaking 6. But Cruickshank's heart is not easily broken. He still had a 4-3 or a 3-4 left for a tie. When he had a wild hook at the seventeenth any final hope looked as dead as the mummy of Rameses. Not an earthly chance seemed to be left. But after reaching the seventeenth on his approach he almost holed a sixty-foot putt over two ridges, got his 4 and then played one of the greatest and most important shots on record by slashing a mid-iron to within six feet of the home green for his tying 3.

Golf, with all its spectacular turns, had known nothing quite like this miracle effort in any past championship. It was a golf shot that only a great golfer with a stout heart could ever make. It lifted the name of Cruickshank high in the roll call of the ancient game. It made him famous among millions.

So now Jones and Cruickshank were left alone to fight it out. The next man, Hutchison, was six strokes away at 302. Most of the big headliners were far back in the mists, completely outdistanced. And the big Sunday gallery that romped and raced after the two survivors saw a golf match they will never forget.

In place of breaking, the two game young

scrappers began to rip the hide off par. At the fifth hole together they had beaten par by four strokes. Four birdies in five holes—three for Cruickshank and one for Jones. This pace seemed to be faster than Jones could stand and when he missed a two-foot putt for his 3 at the sixth and was two strokes down, the pressure on him at the nerve-breaking, hope-wrecking, baffling narrow seventh with its double flanking out of bounds was terrific— more so than usual when Cruickshank was just short, fixed for a sure 4 and a probable 3. But Jones responded with a valiant effort, reached the green, got his 3 and picked up a stroke when Cruickshank missed a six-foot putt.

One of the big turning points of the match came at the eighth hole where Jones was short of the green on his second and Cruickshank, after a magnificent iron, was only five feet away from the cup. But when Jones had chipped up and got his putt, Cruickshank again missed and then proceeded to miss fairly short putts at the ninth and tenth in the wake of this other lapse.

Jones almost holed his tee shot at the 110-yard twelfth and so picked up another stroke with a 2. Cruickshank got these back at the fourteenth and fifteenth, where, at the former, he played one of the greatest iron shots of the year—a mighty wallop through a narrow entrance 230 yards away.

The ding-dong, nip-and-tuck battle continued when Jones took the lead at the sixteenth and lost it at the seventeenth where Bobby the Scot came out of a trap and holed a seven-foot putt.

So after eighty-nine holes they were just where they had started—still all square. They had each taken just 368 strokes to reach this point since the championship proper began. And this was the hole that on the day before had made Cruickshank and had wrecked Jones. All the psychology of the occasion was on Cruickshank's side. But a hurried backswing gave him a low, half-topped hook to the left of the course while Jones' long tee shot found the rough at the right.

Cruickshank was forced to play for safety— his effort leaving him a mashie pitch for the green in 3, and a sure 5 if he needed it. Jones was called upon for a deadly choice—to play safe for his 5, or go for the green and either take a 4 or a 6. For if he failed, waiting water meant elimination and another year to wait. The ball was one hundred and ninety yards from the green, resting in loose dirt amid the rough. He took the gamble of a champion at heart, slashed into the ball with a mid-iron and as it soared upward against the dark gray sky, heavy with the threat of an approaching storm, he saw his dream coming true upon the trajectory of a ball that was headed straight for the fluttering flag. The ball struck ten feet short and stopped just seven feet beyond the cup. Jones had not only won an Open Championship with this shot but through it he had also proved that he had a firm and certain grip upon the last strand of nerve in his body. To prove that the right man was in the right place, the records showed that in the last four Open Championships Jones is fourteen strokes ahead of Walter Hagen, in second place, for a total count.

The long hike was over at last. The weary, slogging march was ended. His 1263rd stroke through four championships and a play-off had turned the trick at twenty-one, with greater years still ahead.

The hardest shot is a mashie at ninety yards from the green, where the ball has to be played against an oak tree, bounces back into a sandtrap, hits a stone, bounces on the green and then rolls into the cup. That shot is so difficult I have made it only once.

ZEPPO MARX

Pola Negri is shown playing a round with
Charlie Chaplin. Both are enthusiastic members
of the golfing set in Hollywood.

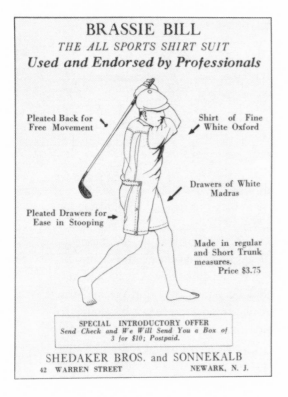

Physical conditioning has an important place in
the golfing scheme of Congressman Samuel Wins-
low of Massachusetts. Hence, the trainer who
accompanies him around the course.

There is nothing comical about the golfing style
of humorist P. G. Wodehouse.

Although he had a busy program during his recent
visit to the United States, Prime Minister
David Lloyd George found time for a round
of golf, now and then.

At the Close of the Round BY FRANCIS OUIMET

Casual Observations on Some of the
Many Phases of Golf

NO MATTER WHAT THE SPORT MAY BE, WHETHER it is tennis, baseball or golf, there is a certain element among the spectators who persist in engaging the player in conversation at a time when he is doing his best to keep his mind solely on the task ahead. When the golfer is walking to his ball after playing a shot, one of these chaps is almost bound to pop up and place himself in the player's way long enough to say something that invariably requires an answer and which serves to take the player's attention away from his next shot, sometimes a mighty fatal thing to do.

My experience with this sort of person first occurred the day I managed to tie Harry Vardon and Ted Ray at Brookline in 1913 for the United States Open Championship. Things were not breaking any too well for me at the time, and as I was playing the fifteenth hole, one fellow, who had played in the championship and who had done very well, took me by the arm as I left the tee and proceeded to tell me of the wonderful chance he had of winning. Bad luck overtook him on the last few holes and I had to listen to that hard-luck story while I was also trying to figure out my next shot.

I have a vivid recollection of trying to let his conversation go in one ear and out of the other, but somehow I couldn't do so because he had a tight hold upon my arm and only released it when it came time for me to play my second stroke.

That second shot was a terrible failure and sliced off into the rough, but as I started in the direction of my ball my erstwhile friend caught up with me and proceeded to finish his sad tale. I did not wish to cut him short, but his conversation bothered me so much it was all I could do to be nice to him. After he went off I settled down and was able to concentrate entirely on my own game.

Another great trick of well-meaning friends in a gallery following your match is that of telling you how you should play your shots. Without trying to pass bouquets at myself, in almost every instance I could start some of these friends several holes up in an eighteen-hole match, yet they will dare to tell you how to play a mid-iron shot!

That is the worst pest of all because they offer advice, unsolicited as it may be, in such a way that it greatly irritates you, and it is several holes before you can control yourself, during which time your opponent may have moved out in front with a nice lead.

I am of the type who enjoys a word or two with a friend while walking from the tee to my ball, but I want the chatter to be short and sweet, so that when I come to think over my shot I have not got a dozen other things to think of. I think a few pleasant words with people whom you know greatly reduces any strain you may be under and the slight opportunity to relax must be a fine thing for the mind.

At Inwood one fellow came up to Bobby Jones as he was walking toward his ball the day he played off with Bobby Cruickshank and asked him if he would not come and spend a week at his summer home. Bob Jones had never seen this chap before and politely told him to come around after the match was over. Not satisfied with this answer, the thoughtless fellow insisted upon an answer then and there. But Bobby wisely slipped off and was not bothered thereafter.

Again going to another hole, a fellow greeted him like a long-lost brother at a most critical stage of the round and on being told to keep away until the round was finished, got indignant. He did not realize the importance of allowing Bobby all the chance in the world to concentrate on the shot before him, but if allowed would have carried on a five-minute conversation over nothing, you might say, considering what was at stake.

The great golfers have troubles of their own, even as the most ordinary players, and there has never been a golfer who could go year after year without having some sort of bother. Harry Vardon had his trials on the putting greens. So did Chick Evans. Jerome Travers in the midst of his brilliant career lost the knack of using his wood clubs and it was several years before he got it back. J. H. Taylor, the master of the mashie, found his skill in this respect had deserted him and for three years playing a mashie shot was a lost art.

Among the American professionals there are four men who stand out among themselves from the rest of the field—Hagen, Barnes, Hutchison and Sarazen—and I doubt if there is a more finished quartet of golfers than these men. They all hit a golf ball in a different manner, yet each one is a very great player. With all their skill, however, they have known of instances where some little thing has gone wrong and try as they would they could not correct the fault.

Jock Hutchison, always a model to follow in iron play, was telling me at Inwood that this year he was playing his iron shots worse than he had ever played them. This seemed almost unbelievable, since Jock is a wonder with an iron club.

On the other hand his driving, he said, had never been better. My own experience has been that if my driving was good the rest of my game invariably went along all right because I seldom got into difficulties from the tee. Therefore if Jock was driving well it was difficult to understand why he did not break a record each time he started out, unless, of course, it was, as he said, poor iron play.

He was more or less worried at Inwood before the championship and spent much time practicing with his midiron and mashie. At last he got to the stage where his old confidence had returned and he could shoot the ball in any direction he wished, and he was pitching them close to the hole every time. Just as he thought he was back in his true form his driving left him and he had something else to worry over, which is, as he said, the game of golf over and over again. You no sooner get one thing than you lose another.

The stars of the game sometimes give one the impression that they do considerable worrying over poor shots, but such is not the case. Hagen, for instance, is of the type who believes if a tee shot finds the rough the recovery will more than make up for the bad tee shot. He is willing to believe all shots cannot be played perfectly, and though he does play most of them faultlessly, a ragged stretch of golf will not dampen his ardor, for he thinks in the end all things are evened up.

A short missed putt on one hole will be evened up by a long one on another. Or a poor pitch shot that misses the green can be overcome by a deadly chip.

The great players all seem to have periods where nothing goes right. Sarazen, for example, on his final round in the Open played as well from the tee to the green as any man living could do, his driving being flawless and his second shots superb.

However, Gene's only chance to finish well up with the leaders was to try and hole long putts. He putted boldly for the hole and sometimes slipped so far past that he missed coming back, but to those who realized what he was after, it was the thing for him to do and in no way did his game show any deterioration.

In his unsuccessful match against Max Marston at Flossmoor during the recent National Amateur Championship, Francis Ouimet got slightly damp while battling for a half on the seventh hole. Marston defeated Jess Sweetser, one up on the thirty-eighth hole, in a thrilling final.

What Makes a Golf Course Great? BY GRANTLAND RICE

One of America's Leading Architects Speaks His Mind

IT IS NO DIFFICULT ASSIGNMENT TO LAY OUT A golf course that will be a championship test. It is no crushing burden to lay out a golf course that will give the average golfer his chance. But there is a big job in between.

This job is to build golf courses that will be championship tests and at the same time give the average player his chance to live, breathe and spend a few minutes each round outside of a trap or a bunker.

Charles Blair Macdonald, who designed the National Golf Links at Southampton, Lido at Long Beach, The Links on Long Island and the Mid-Ocean in Bermuda, among others, has distinct and artistic ideas along these lines. Mr. Macdonald believes in obtaining all the beauty that is possible from any given tract, in giving the average player his chance to live and, at the same time, punishing pride and lack of control as he makes the star work for his par.

"The object of a bunker or trap," says Mr. Macdonald, "is not only to punish a physical mistake, to punish lack of control, but also to punish pride and egotism. I believe in leaving a way open for the player who can only drive one hundred yards, if he can keep that drive

straight. But the one I am after is the golfer who thinks he can carry one hundred and eighty yards when one hundred and sixty yards is his limit. So I believe one of the best systems of trapping or arranging bunkers is to let the player make his own choice, from either the shorter or the longer route, and go for that.

"This helps to make a man know and study his limitations, and, if he is inclined to conceit, he will find his niblick has drawn a hard day's work. I can see no reason at running a trap across the course one hundred and forty or one hundred and fifty yards away when a large number of golfers can't possibly carry that far. For that same reason I rarely believe in putting traps across the front of the green where the second stroke is more than a pitch.

"A bunker or a trap," continued Mr. Macdonald, "is supposed to be a place that calls for a stroke penalty, not a shallow dip where the golfer can walk in with iron or spoon to get one hundred and seventy yards, or where anyone can use a putter. If I had my way there would be a troop of cavalry horses run through every trap and bunker on the course before a tournament started, where only the niblick could get the ball out and then out only by a few yards. I have seen a number of traps and bunkers that afforded better lies and easier strokes than the fairways. This, of course, is ridiculous.

"There should be a reward for the golfer who can hit a long, straight ball or else there is no premium upon skill and control. This doesn't mean that the shorter player is to be hopelessly handicapped. He must be provided a shorter route. The diagonal effect will nearly always take care of this, but the one who can make the longer carry should have the easier shot to the green.

"In building a golf course there should be beauty, interest and variety as well as a first class test for first class golf, a fair test for all who play. There must be variety and general interest. For this reason I am against an endless succession of greens with rolls, bumps and dips. I believe each course or each links should have at least four or five greens, well distributed, that are practically flat after the nature of the ground, with less artificial building up. One gets extremely tired of putting on nothing but mounded greens with sudden dips and rises to work out. A few of these, when not overdone, are well enough, but there should be variety.

"There should be, also, variety of distances. Some of the best holes at the National are under three hundred and twenty yards. And they are testing holes, too, calling for as much real golf as those over four hundred. Nothing could be more monotonous than a stretch of long holes from four hundred to five hundred yards in length. Three of the first four holes at the National Links are under three hundred yards. There are six holes on the links under three hundred yards, yet I have heard of few who looked upon the National as an easy spot for low scoring.

"Fine short holes and fine drive-and-pitch holes are nearly always the most interesting to play, for skill is a greater factor here than mere physical power. I am also against the two hundred and ten or two hundred and twenty or two hundred and thirty-yard type of short hole, except under rare conditions. This type is rarely interesting. For short holes I like the range of distances from one hundred and thirty to one hundred and eighty yards, calling for mashie, iron or spoon—depending on the wind—and not the full blow with driver or brassie.

"I don't believe in pampering any class of golfers, nor yet in forcing average players to attempt impossible strokes with no other outlet. For example, the National is hard to score on consistently in low figures, yet it is extremely fair and an extremely popular spot for golfers who play between 90 and 105 or 110. For here each player can name his own medicine and take only as much risk or attempt only as long a carry as he thinks he can handle.

"There must be variety, and variety without too great length. How many golfers care about tramping around a 6700-yard stretch? And what is the need of this when testing courses can be built from 6100 to 6300 yards?

"This brings me up to an important point—the number and the placement of tees. I believe in at least three sets of tees for every hole, where the idea is practicable. In the first place the direction and the force of the wind can change the entire character of the hole, if there is but one tee to play from. In the second place, with a variety of tees it is possible to have a variety of tests for all classes, to run the distance from 6000 to 6400 yards. You can have then a simple course or a hard one, or a moderately hard one as you may elect. This is quite an important point, a point that doesn't receive near the attention and consideration that it deserves."

These are all valuable suggestions from one of the greatest of all architects for those planning changes or those planning new courses. Here you find the answer to the old question as to whether the average golfer prefers a hard course or an easy one. He prefers a fair course that gives him his chance, yet a course that calls for golf. He doesn't want a croquet lawn to play over nor yet to be called on for impossible carries where there are no open ways to play for.

Getting Distance on the Drive BY TED RAY

The Essentials of Long Hitting

from the Tee

LONG DRIVING IS OF PRIME IMPORTANCE IN GOLF. It need not be long enough to make the world gasp. But it must be long enough to give the golfer some chance against par, and to put him on good terms with himself.

I think this can be done almost in every case as soon as the underlying principles of long driving are correctly understood. The intelligence must play a part in this branch of the game as in every other branch. There may come a day when habits have been so permanently established that good golf is played mechanically. I suppose, like other leading professionals, I may be said to have passed the thinking stage.

Of the great bulk of amateurs, however, this cannot be said. They are still thinking—and very hard; wondering, in fact, what every shot is going to be like, and too often wondering why things do not happen as they should.

When amateurs talk over their games it will generally be found that the length of their drives—or the lack of length—forms the chief topic. When a man is able to say that he has carried a bunker at some prodigious length, he is very well pleased with himself. So when golfers talk of others, who are noted for the length of their drives, they do so with a mixture of admiration and envy. Professionals who go playing before the public all over the country would attract very small gatherings if their tee shots belonged to the commonplace, no matter how scientifically executed the iron or mashie shots might be.

There is a spectacular charm about long driving alike for those who look on and those who play the shots. To see one's ball soaring into the air and gathering what looks like a new lease on life on its journey is indeed a rare pleasure, even to those of us who are more or less addicted to drives of this description.

We have all seen amateurs, not necessarily of scratch quality, make magnificent drives once or twice in a round. It must be particularly tantalizing to these gentlemen when drives of this description are followed by very indifferent specimens. It is here that the need for knowledge comes in and brings with it good reason for hope. It has always seemed to me that the greatest of all drawbacks to long driving is the tendency to lean forward on the left foot while taking the club back, and then to fall back on the right foot in bringing the club through again. The ball is not driven in this way, but might be said to be scooped into the air.

So again one often sees another common error in operation. I refer to the over-tightening of the right leg at the top of the swing, bracing oneself, so to speak. It can never be possible to drive a ball a very long distance in this fashion. Everything becomes too taut. There is no play in the knees, wrists or shoulders; at least, not the necessary amount of play which goes to the making of a long tee shot. In dealing the blow with the clubhead—and I am an advocate of hitting—both knees should be slightly bent, so as to permit of the right shoulder coming well through after the ball, just as the left shoulder has been swung under the chin in taking the club back.

Everything in the nature of tightness must be eliminated from the swing of the driver. I do not mean that slackness cannot be overdone. I rather mean there is much greater danger of tightness being overdone. I suppose I am one of the most powerful golfers in the professional ranks today, and one of the longest drivers. That, at any rate, is how they speak of me, and I cannot see any reason for differing from the popular belief.

I am supposed to hit with all my might. So I do. What better use can "might" be put to? What is the use of having driving force if you allow yourself to be theorized out of employing it? But don't let it be imagined that mere brute force could be relied upon without the careful direction of it.

Sometimes it is said of me that I belong to that class of golfers who rely on swaying—and the timing of it—for length. I do not sway so much as may be thought. In fact, I should say that the camera would support my contention that all the swaying I do is after the ball has been dispatched. Then I often feel myself, not only throwing the right shoulder through and the head with it, but actually getting off my right foot and walking after the ball. That may be called swaying, but it is the kind of swaying that a boxer uses in delivering a blow.

It is necessary to get the weight of the body slightly on to the right leg at the top of the swing; for only then can one be in position to heave the body at the ball. The whole weight

then comes into play. Of course, perfectly exact timing is required here, and the art of perfect timing is not acquired in a day. There is nothing in all golf that is so much deserving of study as timing.

Another danger to be guarded against as one of the reasons for short driving, is that of over-pivoting on the left toe. The grip of the ground has then practically gone and the player is almost reduced to the physical handicap of standing on one leg.

I have always been known as the unorthodox golfer. But I am not so unorthodox as some people think. My method of playing golf is one which might with advantage be adopted by the generality of golfers. The underlying principle of my style, if it may be called style, is that of attacking the ball without taking too much account of grace. I am not advocating anything in the nature of clumsiness, and I am not pleading guilty to that offense.

What I am trying to get at is that the clubhead must be, so to speak, flung at the ball without any conscious restraint. I should say that a very large percentage of players, who find their handicaps rather stationary, would at once discover an element of progress coming into their game if they would let out more at those shots, whether from the tee or the fairways, which call for length.

I have seen golfers make a tee shot in a way that suggested that they were posing for the camera, instead of playing for results. I have seen them bring the club over their left shoulder at the finish of a swing by the deliberate act of lifting it there. That is no use at all. Wherever the clubhead finishes, it must get there entirely by its own momentum. In fact, the finish is of no consequence, except in as far as it indicates the completeness of the follow-through.

A humorist once described my method of teaching golf in these words:

"Keep your head down and hit as if you meant to knock the cover off the ball." In principle he was not far wrong. But there is hitting and hitting. The kind of hitting I am speaking about is no mere punch and done with it. It is rather a blow and on with it. The right arm and right shoulder cannot follow too far after the ball, but they can easily fail to follow far enough. I cannot tell you, and nobody has been able to tell me, whether the ball and the clubhead part company the instant they meet, or whether they stay together for some inappreciable period of time. And I don't care whether they do the one thing or the other. All I care for is, as I have been saying, that the clubhead shall go after the ball as swiftly and as far as possible.

While discussing this very question one day with a scientific gentleman, I remember it was raining and the face of the clubhead had become very damp; so to a certain extent had the ball. After I hit a long drive, I examined the face of the club and showed it to him. There was a mark as round as a shilling and perhaps a little larger, dotted like the cover, which proved that the ball had flattened a bit in consequence of the vigor of the blow. I thought that this afforded evidence of the clubhead and ball remaining together for the fraction of a second. My scientific friend was inclined to agree with me.

Well, now, how is this hitting of a golf ball accomplished? What position must be taken up by the player when he wishes to drive the longest ball of which he is physically capable? Suppose him to be a strongly built man, or a lankily built man, which involves strength as the term is applied to golf.

First of all, he must get into the right relation to the ball at the top of the swing, whether it be a full or a medium swing. Speaking for myself, I always know one thing; that if I get my body in the right position when commencing the downward swing a good drive becomes a practical certainty. Above every-thing, it is necessary to be on one's guard against letting the weight of the body fall forward onto the left leg at the top of the back-swing. In my view, it is absurd to expect a good drive from such an attitude.

Let the right shoulder go back an inch or two while the head is kept fairly still; let the right leg share with the left leg the weight of the body in about the proportion of three-fifths to two-fifths; it will then be felt that you can hit the ball with all your might, and in doing so bring the right shoulder smoothly through after the ball has been struck. The speed of the clubhead must be considerably faster by taking up this position than if more of the weight were thrown on the left leg than on the right.

Objection is sometimes taken to this theory —though I don't like the word theory where facts are concerned—on the ground that by throwing the weight on to the left leg the body is more easily pulled through. The body must not be "pulled through." It must swing through, giving the player the feeling that he has been released from a spring and needs to make no effort in the nature of pulling his right shoulder.

Try to do as I am telling you, and do not entertain any fear of hitting the ground; for the faster the clubhead flies through, the more likely is the ball to be cleanly hit. It is the lazy, unnecessarily leisurely downward swing that is most apt to come in contact with the ground before the ball is reached, or at the moment of impact.

It must not be supposed that driving on this model would make a toil of the game. On the contrary, it makes a real pleasure of it by giving the player the rare satisfaction of hitting good tee shots.

I am still undecided as to which of these two is the hardest shot in golf for me—any unconceded putt, or the explosion shot off the first tee. Both have caused me more strokes than I care to write about.

RING LARDNER

The Eight-Inch Golf Course BY EDDIE LOOS

Establishing the Proper Mental Patterns

EVERY GAME OF GOLF THAT HAS EVER BEEN played—whether the medal was 68 or 168—has taken place on a golf course that measured eight inches more or less. I arrived at the dimensions of this golf course by taking a ruler and measuring my own head from back to front. Of course, every game of golf is played—every shot is played—in your mind before the ball actually starts on its way.

You've heard before about golf being a mental game. So have I. But my objections to most articles on the mental side of golf have been that the nut or kernel of the message seems to be that the mental side is vital, but then what?

If a woman wants to cut a dress—if a foundry wants to make a casting—if an architect starts to design a building—the basis of the finished product is a plan or pattern. The finished product, properly erected, is an exact reflection of the original plan or pattern.

If you wanted to learn a verse—wanted to learn to speak it effectively—you would commit it to memory, with every inflection and emphasis necessary to make a good delivery. This would be your "pattern."

And—when you wanted to deliver the verse—mentally you'd fish out your pattern and go ahead—practically the same every time, gaining skill, ease and certainty with repetition.

It is exactly the same thing with the game of golf—every shot, successful or otherwise, is the result of a mental pattern.

Of course, in speaking the verse, your voice is the vehicle through which the pattern is reproduced.

And your voice is more or less easily controlled.

On the other hand, the mental patterns used in the golf shot express themselves through many, many muscles.

So, the patterns—the *right* patterns—must be slowly and painstakingly built up. Their part is so impressed upon your "muscular memory" that their execution requires no conscious thought.

The mental patterns of the professional are so set that when he steps up to his ball, his only conscious thought should be where he wants it to go, and then the decision to send it there.

Ask any professional you know if he carries any thought besides these after he has decided upon the playing of his shot.

The stance must be built upon a mental pattern. When that pattern is developed, you are able to step up to your ball and—without conscious thought—know where the ball is going as the result of the position you assume in relation to it.

The "grip" of the club is the subject of another mental pattern.

When you have the right mental pattern of your grip, you know that the face of the club is not going to turn over or turn up when it comes to the ball; it's fair, square and true.

The arc of your swing, the timing, the feel of the clubhead—all of these things are basic mental patterns which find execution through your muscular memory.

In the putt—short or long—direction is simpler to visualize than distance. Thus, the better the mental pattern of the proper force of the blow, the closer the ball comes to the cup.

I know this *sounds* complicated. I don't believe that, once understood, it will be so, however. On the contrary, I firmly believe that it is the greatest step possible toward simplification of golf instruction.

The oldest golf instruction extant in the early days of the paid professional coach was to take the beginner and make him swing a club without a ball for days before he actually hit one. Then, to make him hit shots with the various clubs various distances without actually playing a game—this for a month or so. This system, a wonderful one, was based—although I never heard it so explained—upon the building in the beginner's mind of proper mental patterns, free from the obstructing strain of actual play.

I learned to play golf with the flat swing of Willie Andersen, my idol. I created my mental patterns upon this method of play. When I changed to the "upright swing" and the "game through the air," I was forced to completely change my train of mental patterns, those relating to the arc of the swing, the stance and the timing. Of course, my grip and my "club feel" patterns remained the same. My game went back. But once the new mental patterns were correctly established, by experiment and practice, my game became better than ever before.

Here is the way mental patterns evince themselves.

I stand up with an iron. My usual shot would be a high, long ball to drop dead upon the green. But a strong wind is blowing against me. So I call to mind my mental pattern of a push shot, get my direction and execute it.

You must realize that these mental patterns are not—decidedly not—a set of directions memorized on "how to play the shot." They are muscular memories—the physical repetition of the way previous successful shots of this character have been played.

John M. Sellers of Chicago, a great golfer and a keen student of the game, has—I understand—made an observation that is very interesting.

He says in effect that the fancy, full, free swing of the professional in casual play or practice is a decidedly different thing from the "money shot" that he settles down to where there's a stake up.

Of course, he's right. I like the term "money shot." And, with Mr. Sellers' permission, I am going to take the liberty of commenting on this shot.

While the professional is playing a casual round, he feels that he can take a chance—experiment perhaps. So his mental patterns are of the kind of swing he thinks his fellow players like to see—the slashing, bold, take-a-chance set of patterns.

On the other hand, when there's a cup or a prize at stake, the average professional calls up, or tries to call up, that set of patterns that minimize the chance of error—the mental patterns where every bit of unnecessary flourish, of useless motion, is eliminated. In short, the "money shot."

I firmly believe that one of the things that holds back hundreds of professionals from far better scoring is the possession of these two sets of mental patterns. Men like Walter Hagen have only one set of mental patterns——the money shot. The shot that minimizes chance results is the one that their muscular memory reproduces.

I do not mean that they do not take chances, but I do mean that their chance-taking lies in the daring of the shot, not in its execution.

Concentration in golf, to my mind, is simply a matter of eliminating all outside matters from the successful reproduction of the mental pattern of the shot about to be played.

"Looking up" is an interruption of the duplication of the mental pattern. Permitting noise, movement, fear of water or hazards to spoil shots can all be traced back to the interruption of the execution of the duplication through muscular memory of the proper mental pattern for the shot.

Build your patterns—increase your skill in executing them; distance, direction and a handicap that takes the winter thermometer drop will be your reward.

That eight-inch golf course in your head will do wonders if you'll take the time to plant the seed of proper mental patterns. And the longer you own them, the better they are.

Author-actor Frank Craven, between puffs on his dainty dudeen, assures movie star Tommy Meighan that the first million slices are the most aggravating.

Gene Sarazen gives Master Jackie Coogan a few tips during a visit to Hollywood.

Combating the Wind BY TED RAY

Chances Are You Are Going About It All Wrong

A GOLFER'S EDUCATION IS FAR FROM COMPLETE unless he is able either to defy or to make use of wind. First of all, take the wind that's with you. Players whose handicaps range from, say, eight to eighteen, feel comfortable in driving down wind, but it is astonishing how comparatively little advantage they derive from this favorable circumstance. Many make the mistake of building high tees then, evidently under the impression that that is the right thing to do in order to bang the ball up into the air so that the wind may carry it well away. The danger of a high tee always is that of hitting under it.

When the wind is with you, try a low tee. You will then find that a greater command is obtained over the ball. It will also rise high enough to add the additional length which might be expected with the wind's assistance. The reasonableness of this should appear at a glance. A high tee generally results in underspin being imparted to the ball, which is just what is not wanted in a following wind. By teeing low the underspin will not be so pronounced. The wind will then carry the ball in the air much farther than if it had, as billiard players say, "bottom" on it.

What then about the wind in your face? Here again, the same sort of error is commonly made. The wind inspires a measure of fear.

The player feels that his drive is going to be seriously shortened. With this lack of confidence he adopts the lowest possible tee, hardly, in fact, any tee at all. His idea is to bore through the wind, or play under it, as we say. So far, so good. The intention is all right, but the method is all wrong. At any rate, I can show you a better method, which may seem a little difficult at first but the advantages of it will appear soon enough to warrant your approval of it.

Tee high when playing into the wind, with the wind in your teeth. The harder it blows in this direction, the greater the need for teeing well off the ground. I do not mean that your tee should be two inches high, but an inch might not be too high. You will take up your stance with the ball slightly nearer the right foot. The thing to do then is to hit as if you meant to impel the ball along a plane. In a sense, you actually try to knock it down. You must hit hard, and the effect will be that the wind will lift the ball instead of letting it drop to the ground.

This is one of the most beautiful shots in golf, when the ball, after traveling like a telegraph wire for 120 or 150 yards, then begins to rise and still go forward to a respectable distance. You have "used" the wind like a golfer who knows what he is doing, and knows how to do it. The shot needs practice. But every shot in golf needs practice, and it is for lack of practicing useful shots like this in the way they should be played that many men describe themselves as fair-weather golfers. They cannot live within strokes of their handicaps on a windy day. And yet, without wind, golf would become a very much less interesting game than it is.

That is two winds we have disposed of. Take now the wind that blows from left to right. I do not believe in playing any tricks with the wind. I very much more prefer to form a correct idea of its strength. I do not ask

Macdonald Smith is shown facing squarely to the hole at the finish of a drive during this year's British Open, at Prestwick, Scotland.

British star Ted Ray always punctuates his philosophical remarks with puffs on his brierroot.

it to do very much for me, but I set myself to the task of ascertaining what may be expected of it. Let a good stiff breeze be blowing from left to right as indicated. There is no need to try to impart slice to the ball. The thing to do is to hit the ball truly, taking an aim some distance to the left, according to the wind's strength. The ball will go on in the air for perhaps 150 or more yards without being appreciably affected in its course.

But as it tires, the wind will begin to exercise power over it. This is exactly what the intelligent golfer should anticipate. As the momentum expires, what happens is this: the wind carries the ball over to the right into the middle of the fairway, or on to the green. I am, of course, assuming that the drive has been correctly made. Any attempt to cut the ball in the act of hitting it, when the wind is blowing in this direction, can only have the effect of shortening the drive and exaggerating the "bend" of the shot as it finishes.

I am writing for the generality of golfers with the view of putting them in the way of progress and pleasure. There are numberless trick shots in golf but it is well to postpone fantastic juggling until the time comes when such things can be done with some certainty of advantage. We cannot all be Sandy Herds or Joe Kirkwoods. Herd learned his golf at St. Andrews, where the wind is never still. He had to master it and play tricks with it instead of letting it play tricks with him. But Herd cannot be imitated, and there is no great need to imitate him when simpler methods can be made to achieve sufficiently good results.

When the wind blows from right to left, you may attempt the pull shot as a means of gaining length, but here again I contend that it is only necessary to hit the ball clean and truly, taking the proper line to reap all the advantages the wind can give.

A tee shot in these conditions should be made as if the flag were on the right-hand edge of the green instead of being somewhere near the center of it. Take no further thought of the wind than the strength of it. You must judge for yourself what the wind is likely to do

to the ball as it nears the end of its flight and begins to slow down. While it is traveling at its fastest, the power of the wind is reduced to a negligible quantity. It cannot catch the ball, always providing, of course, that it has not been made to travel with any sort of side-spin.

It is amusing to watch what happens when the wind begins to gain the upper hand. The ball has been well swung away to the right, without any "bend" on it, and the most the wind has been able to do so far is to slightly retard its flight. Watch what happens as the ball begins to hang in the air. The wind takes possession and blows it over—all things being equal—into the middle of the course, or somewhere agreeably near the green.

You have often heard the remark made after a shot with any club, but particularly with the driver, that the wind had no effect on the flight of the ball. This happens when the shot has been made without any kind of "side." The ball has revolved vertically; I cannot believe that it traveled without revolving at all, as some argue might happen. But it has been truly hit and the wind has been defied. A shot of this description is really only made difficult by the player himself fearing what disastrous effects the wind may have when he has dispatched the ball into its power.

It may amuse some of my friends when I tell them that I bring autosuggestion into my golf. I could name professionals who ought to have won an Open Championship years ago, if they had cultivated the mental side of the game. It is of great importance in playing a golf shot, whether with wood or iron, to believe that you can play it as required.

Many years ago that great master of the brainy aspect of golf, J. H. Taylor, impressed upon us all that it was a good thing to foresee the character of a shot, not merely in respect of length, before the shot is made, but to see it as an accomplished fact. I entirely agree with Taylor on this point. Nothing does more to steady the mind regarding a shot that might reasonably inspire some doubt, than concentration and confidence established this way.

Left-Handed Golf Courses BY RUBE GOLDBERG

Our Greatest Need

I HAVE BEEN TRYING TO PLAY GOLF FOR THE LAST seven years and have been reading about the game for twice as long. I get no comfort out of the continuous flow of golf reform literature that bellows and splashes against the shores of duffer island. Those who are suggesting new improvements are tackling the game from the wrong end.

When I read that the new rules prohibit the use of corrugated club ends it has as much effect on me as if I had just heard that the Gaekwar of Baroda had issued a decree calling for purple tassels on all elephant saddles on Mondays and Fridays. The only good my backspin mashie ever did me was to use it as an onion grater when we were fortunate enough to have caviar sandwiches on picnics.

Some people think the new metal shafts are a great improvement over the old wooden ones. I have tried both and I would do just as well with rhubarb or asparagus. Every time they bring out a new ball called "The Purple Flash" or "The Comet's Tail" or "The Galloping Dandruff" I laugh so loud I wake up my caddie. I made the best drive of my whole golfing career with a meat ball I had picked up by mistake from a passing lunch wagon.

Another thing that seems to take up a lot of time and energy among those who are sincerely but unwisely seeking new antidotes for

the duffer's poisonous mistakes is wearing apparel. I have actually gone out on the links carrying eighteen sweaters—one for every hole. Each one of the sweaters, according to the ad, was built to give the player a particular advantage in playing certain shots. Some were fashioned to keep the neck rigid, others were made to keep the elbows dry when playing chip shots out of the ocean, and still others were designed with special cartridge belts for carrying spare pencils with which to write down extra large scores. The sweaters were all different, but my shots all remained the same.

I even went and purchased a pair of those terrible-looking English knickers that are baggy enough to hold a radio set, and stop somewhere between the knee and the ankle. They don't look like short pants and they don't look like long pants. They are a first cousin to balloon tires but don't give you near the mileage. I played one round in the pair that I bought and my caddie said to me just before he left, "Gee, your old man must be a pretty big guy, if you can wear his pants cut down and they're still too big for you." I gave the pants to my wife's sister who was having a garden party at her place in the country. She used them for Chinese lanterns.

As I said before, the reformers are trying to reform the game from the wrong end. The thing that needs changing is not the golf ball or the golf club or the golf trousers. It is the golf course. I am surprised that nobody has ever thought of suggesting the left-handed golf course. The left-handed golf course is bound to come if the game is to survive. It is an absolute necessity—for me at least.

I forgot to mention that I am left-handed—and there must be thousands of other unfortunates in this country like myself. I have been advised to switch to right-handed. But why should I? I have been eating soup for forty years with my left hand and I am not boasting when I say that my shirt front is as clean as the average man's. In the ordinary course of things it is no handicap to be left-handed. No woman ever refused to bow to me when I tipped my hat with my left hand—that is, no woman who knew me. I never made a waiter sore by handing him a tip with my left hand.

When I take a practice swing at home people look in through the window and say, "Good morning, Mister Sarazen." But when I go out on the golf course and take the same identical swing, the ball doesn't seem to go anywhere. So I know it must be the fault of the course. Logic is logic.

Here are a few of the handicaps I suffer when I play on the regulation course:

When the average player shoots he stands facing the other people on the tee. Being left-handed I must stand with my back to the crowd. Besides wondering whether or not they are giving me the raspberry, I must try to be a gentleman and say each time I step up to the ball, "Excuse my back." And you know that any talk during a shot throws a man off his stance—even if it be his own voice.

In standard golf courses most of the out-of-bounds limits are on the left side of the fairway. A sliced shot always puts me out-of-bounds. So I naturally stand well around to the right on every tee to play safe, so my drive will slice back into the fairway. Then for some reason or other I don't slice at all. My shot goes straight and I hit the president of the club, who is playing three fairways to the right. This puts me in continual bad standing, be-

sides giving all the club members the extra trouble of finding a new president.

Another thing. When I make a beautiful shot right on the green next to the pin I invariably find that I have played for the wrong green. My left-handed vision has given me a cock-eyed idea of the course.

My greatest handicap is in the traps, where I must admit I spend a good part of my weekends. It takes an experienced miner to go down into a hole with nothing but the blue sky as his only area of vision and still keep his sense of direction. After the seventh shot, my left-handed leanings force me around in an angle of ninety degrees without realizing that I have turned at all. Then elated with the wonderful "out" I have finally negotiated, I rise to the surface only to find that I have shot right back through the foursome behind me and lost about sixty yards. I once had a series of these mishaps and spent an hour and a half on one hole continually losing ground. There was an insane asylum across the road from the course and it took my friends quite a while to convince an attendant who happened to see me that I was not an escaped inmate.

There are many other disadvantages that we left-handers must suffer, including the fact that they're building suburban homes closer and closer to the golf courses. The left-hander, when he dubs a shot, always lands in somebody's back yard and this isn't very pleasant when they're cooking cod fish.

I think I have made my case clear. What golf really needs is a course where left-handers can be segregated like smallpox patients. It would be simple to lay out one of these courses. A golf architect can take a plan of any well-known course and build it backwards. He may run into a few snags in the locker room. It will be quite a feat of engineering to get the attendant to mix cocktails standing on his head, and the water to run uphill in the shower baths. But trifling difficulties have never stopped the march of progress. Did snags and prejudices stop Lysander J. Lentil when he started to construct the first portable sink, now socially known as the finger-bowl?

Refugees from a fire which destroyed the Breakers Hotel in Palm Beach, lugging belongings.

Bobby Jones harvests a laugh while giving some pointers to some visiting opera stars at the Druid Hills Club in Atlanta. Madame Lucrezia Bori is driving.

The Role of the Left Hand BY EDDIE LOOS

A Clear and Comprehensive Analysis

of Its Function

THE LEFT HAND IN THE SWING IS ONE OF THE three fundamental actions that make the ball snap away from the club, clean and true on its mark, whether it's leaving wood or iron. If you will get out that mid-iron, we'll try to get a clear picture of not only "left hand action," but the way it fits into the swing as a whole.

First of all, let's get one thought in our mind as a foundation to build upon. *The golf swing is a back-handed stroke.* Therefore it is a left-handed stroke—just like a low "backhand" with a tennis racquet.

That is advanced merely to get a general picture of the action in your mind. Put it in the back of your head—it is to be a subconscious thought rather than a conscious action.

That brings us to the nub of the whole situation. *Properly executed, the swing requires no conscious thought.* It is easier to execute it right than wrong. It is harder—much more difficult for a professional or good amateur to hit a ball improperly than properly. The above is not idle conversation, it is a cold, hard fact. The effort—the exertion, the strain—comes in only when execution is faulty. And what is more, the incorrect swings we see men using everywhere are much more difficult to execute

than correct movements.

Now let's take that club—wasn't it a mid-iron we found?—and stand up. Take the club in the left hand only—just the one hand. Stand up and address an imaginary ball. Now, with the left hand alone—without thought of wrist or twist or pivot or feet—keep your eye on the ball and swing easily back and through. If you had a mirror to watch yourself in, it would be helpful. At night in a lighted room, a window serves the same purpose.

Do this several times—slowly—keeping the club under control. And except for two things, you have made a perfect golf swing. We'll come to these two things later.

Your club has described the perfect arc—naturally—without effort. The face has turned square to the ball at impact and slid smoothly through. What is more important than anything else, the club has come to the ball on a line from the inside and passed through on the outside—the perfect line through the ball, the one all professionals use.

The two things in which it differed from the regular swing were, first, you had only one hand on the club; second, the head lacked speed at the bottom of the arc.

Now, let's take the right hand by itself and do the same thing—make a one-handed swing. What happens? In the first place, the clubhead travels faster. The hand back of the club handle makes speed automatic. But the arc is wrong. The right-handed swing is erratic. The clubhead comes in from outside the line.

Now, let us combine the two. The left hand swinging the club throughout will give us easily and automatically a true, fine swing. If we use the right hand for anything in the world but to add speed at the bottom of the swing and through the ball, we are complicating and probably ruining the work the left hand, permitted to do as it will, performs.

So then, the swing is a completely left-handed swing, with the right entering only at the bottom to give the speed and power the left or back-hand stroke lacks.

How are we to get this speed; to put the right hand in? By the "wrist flick" or the "turn-over" or the "hit?" There is a simple way to do it. Keep your wrists flexible—don't tighten them.

About the time you feel the clubhead progressing at an easy, uniform speed near your right hip, without quickening, without tightening, push your right hand evenly and smoothly right toward the hole. Don't quit until the swing is completely finished.

Your right hand has not entered into the swing at all until the club enters the speed section. The thought is not one of effort, but to support the weaker left hand and keep the clubhead from lagging behind. The pushing right hand prevents it, and speed comes without effort. You'll be surprised at the speed the clubhead will gather and the crispness and surety of the ball's flight.

Now let's pick up the mid-iron again. I'm going to give you a tedious exercise, but it is the key to the use of the left hand.

Right at the start of the swing is where the most mistakes are made. That strong right hand closes in tight and overpowers the true swinging left. And that's the end of accuracy and trueness. Leaving the ball on the backswing, once it is accomplished, is sixty per cent of the battle to use the left hand.

How should you leave the ball? Clubhead low to the ground—left hand in control—smoothly and without effort.

Here's the way to do it. Imagine a point about two feet back of the ball—a little stick, say, two inches high. With your left hand alone—the right a passenger—the right arm *limp—push* the club back so that it slowly and smoothly passes over or knocks down your imaginary little stick.

From then on, the rest is easy—the right is simply a humble, unassertive assistant to the true swinging left, until the club is nearing the right hip. Then—without effort—it pushes smoothly through right to the end of the swing.

Take your right hand, with the arm extended, about six inches short of the right hip. Go through the motion of throwing a ball underhanded—not fast, but like a slow motion picture—and you'll understand what the right does and *all* it does.

The body? It followed throughout when you swung with the left alone, didn't it? Well, let the left hand take care of the body action for you.

At the beginning of a match do not worry yourself with the idea that the result is likely to be against you. By reflecting thus upon the possibilities of defeat, one often becomes too anxious and loses one's freedom of style.

HARRY VARDON

What You Will Encounter
in Nassau BY RING LARDNER

Mr. Lardner Studies Folk Lore and Hears a Golf Story

LAST TIME WE WAS TALKING ABOUT NASSAU IN the Bahamas and this time we will very the monotony by disgusting the same subject once more. I will leave it to others to describe the clear waters of this section of the Atlantic where you can see the flamingoes, lizards and fish wading on the bottom of the ocean at a depth of 40 ft. and will also refrain from references to other liquids that frequents these premises and which I did not taste same on acct. of it not being no fun to drink where they's no law against it, but will confine myself to a few wds. in regards to such attractions as Honest John Kelly and Jock Hutchison and similar incidence of our all too brief sojourn on fair New Providence isle.

Mr. Kelly denies that he is called Honest John so as to distinguish him from all other Kellys. He is the prop. of a palatial club house on the ocean front where you can eat and drink and also be merry provided the right numbers comes up, but you can eat and drink anyway because Honest John has a heart and won't charge you nothing for beverages or for food neither if he feels sorry enough for you.

He felt sorry for the undersigned and no wonder as my favorite numbers, the numbers which had made me a rich man in Cuba and Monte Carlo, acted on Mr. Kelly's wheels like they was quarantined. It was on the occasion of my 5th. visit to Honest John that I give up the idear of retiring from the field of classical literature and supporting the wife and kiddies from a comfortable seat on the clients' side of a roulette table.

However I don't know no worthier charity who I would rather contribute to than Mr. Kelly as he treats you fine win or loose and even sent flowers and good wishes to the ladies the day we sailed away so that instead of being mad at him we was all very sorry when he left the end of a finger in a taxicab door.

Jock Hutchison is the genial pro at the Nassau golf course where hooked drives on the 1st. two holes costs a dollar apiece unless your caddy is a fish. I had not met Jock since 7 or 8 yrs. ago back in old Chi and he didn't remember me on acct. of not having no mustache at the time or now neither as far as that is concerned, but any way he says he was glad to meet me and that reminded him of the story about the Scotchman and Cohen. It seems they was a Scotchman and a man named Cohen and they didn't neither of them have anybody to play golf with so they decided to play together and then Cohen asked the Scotchman what he genally went around in, but if you ain't heard the story you must of been dead at lease 6 mos. and if so they ain't no use repeating it to you. Well I laughed as hard as I could and done pretty good for a man that hadn't heard it more than 124 times since last summer.

While playing on Mr. Hutchison's course a couple days before we come away, I beckoned to a friend of mine from N. Y. named Mr. Levy to go through us as I was playing with Mrs. G. Rice an exasperatingly slow golfer. Well Mr. Levy thanked us and in part payment for our kindness he says he would tell me a golf story, so I says go ahead and he told me the story about the Scotchman and the man named Cohen.

It seems they was a Scotchman and a man named Cohen and they didn't neither of them have anybody to play golf with so they decided to play with each other and then Cohen asked the Scotchman what he generally went around in. They being a lady present and Mr. Levy being a brother Friar I resisted the temptation to end it all with a niblick.

It leaked out some way another that I was a wonderful musician and interested in folk songs and etc. so we was adviced to take a carriage ride to a little settlement of natives called Grantstown where they said we would hear some weird Bahamian melodies sang to the guitar by moonlight so we took the trip and sure enough the streets was filled with native citizens chanting Blues of Tennessee and What'll I Do by that talented West Indian composer Irving Berlin. We finely did run into a hack driver that knowed the Nassau songs and was charmed by one number which was a kind of a lyrical history of the burning of the old hotel. Here is a few of the verses:

Do Aunt Nanny, do Aunt Nanny,
Do Aunt Nanny, how do you do?
Hay, Hay, do Aunt Nanny do.

One Friday morning bright and soon,
The hotel burned down smack and smooth,
Hay, Hay, do Aunt Nanny do.

The hotel burned down smack and smooth.
The white man run and left his shoes.
Hay, hay, do Aunt Nanny do.

It seems that the white man also left a lot of liquor in the hotel and Aunt Nanny rescued it and had a wild night and her experiences is all related in the course of the song and I only wished I could remember the rest of it.

Which reminds me as Jock would say that they have got a Friday closing law in Nassau which don't refer to the saloons but all other kinds of stores and they must close up by noon and stay closed till Saturday, but if they disobey this law nothing happens unless a customer goes in the store and then the customer is fined 5 pounds while the store keeper gets off with a good scolding. The reason for this may be that the customer might possibly have 5 pounds whereas they ain't no chance for one of the store keepers being that dirty with money.

I am kind of afraid I ain't give you a very vivid picture of the Bahamas and regret that I was too busy down there to take notes like I should of, but all and all will state that I ain't never been to a more pleasanter place to spend the winter and Nassau has got a climate of which they can boast and certainly do, and also plenty of amusements and industrys of which the most important is the sponge fisherys which the biggest sponge merchant down there told me that the sponge was really the lowest form of animal life and not U. S. senators as claimed by Percy Hammond.

I am stumped when it comes to saying which is the
hardest shot in golf for me, but I know the easiest one—
the first shot at the Nineteenth Hole.

W. C. FIELDS

Hagen—Match-Play Master BY O. B. KEELER

Some Observations on His Seventy-Two-Hole Match with Bobby Jones

IN THE MOST RECENT BOUT BETWEEN A GREAT match-golfer and a great medalist, the match-golfer came out convincingly on top. Walter Hagen, professional golfing champion of the United States, and rated the leading match player of the game, defeated Bobby Jones, National Amateur Champion, regarded as the leading medalist of golf, by the impressive margin of 12-and-11 in a 72-hole match played February twenty-eighth and March seventh at Sarasota and Pasadena, Florida. The result, aside from inspiring one rather impetuous section of the critics to announce that Sir Walter had thus proved himself the master golfer, has revived the old question of match golf and medal golf, and a discussion of the curious difference existing between the problems and tactics of a golfer confronting a single human opponent and a golfer competing against the grim specter of the card and pencil.

Incidentally, it is unfair to both Sir Walter and Bobby to intimate that either is lacking in proficiency at either style of golf. Walter has won the United States Open Championship twice, and the British Open Championship twice; these are medal competitions. Bobby has won the United States Amateur Championship twice in succession—a match-play

tournament. Yet Hagen persistently is regarded as a match-player and Jones as a medalist; and that rating, based on the records which include them both, may be assumed as reasonable. In the last six United States Open Championships, in which both have competed, Jones has led Hagen five times at medal play, and trailed him once. In the aggregate score for twenty-four rounds, Jones leads his professional rival nineteen strokes. He has won the title once, finished in a tie for first place and lost the play-off once, and been second twice. In the last four years he has been either first or second—the top record for consistency in the Blue Ribbon event. Hagen in the last six years has been as high as second once.

The inference, then, is reasonable that Jones is the better player against the field—that is, against the card and pencil. And Hagen's impressive record of losing only four set matches in the last five years, topped by his second consecutive win of the United States Professional Golfers' Championship, at match play, and his sound drubbing of Bobby Jones in their one formal match, surely should establish him as our greatest match-play performer.

The Florida encounter of these two champions affords a curious study in the psychological differences of match and medal play; and as a witness of the match I saw quite too much of that odd factor to be blinded by the conclusion that any one match, even of seventy-two holes, could establish definitely a rating between any two first-rank golfers. There is much in golf besides mechanics; even besides the patient courage and the implacable morale needed to play under the shadow of the card and pencil, generally regarded as the highest type of golfing competition.

Walter Hagen unquestionably has something in his game beyond the ability to stroke a golf ball correctly. Indeed, up to the vicinity of the green, a dozen players may be adduced who are his equal or superior. But around the green, within chipping and putting range, Hagen surely is as good as the best; and many experienced observers rank him as best of all. Hagen also is celebrated for his recovery shots, which reputation collaterally implies an inclination to wildness. The implication is accurate. Walter is one of the wildest of the first-rank golfers; I might even say he is the wildest of all the first-rank golfers of America; and this disposition to wallop the ball off the visible confines of the course, not to mention the fairways, has cost him more than one medal-play championship.

But where a stroke gone in medal play is a stroke irrevocably lost, in match play one hole may cost a competitor a dozen strokes and still be only one hole gone, which a pretty 3 may recover on the very next green—that is the vast difference between match and medal play.

Hagen is a hard man to beat in match competition for two principal reasons, and one, oddly enough, is the very tendency to wildness just considered. The other is his superb showmanship; his histrionic talent; his gift for "acting," and for making of some special shot a ceremony on which the gallery hangs with an hypnotic attention—and which his hapless opponent regards with a distinctly disadvantageous concern, not to say exasperation.

In addition to which, please never forget that Sir Walter can chip and putt with the very best of them.

With the Florida triumph over Bobby Jones in mind, let us examine these factors a bit.

After that match Bobby said to me:

"I would far rather play a man who is straight down the fairway with his drive, on the green with his second, and down in two putts for his par. I can play a man like that at his own game, which is par golf. If one of us can get close to the pin with his approach, or hole a good putt—all right. He has earned something that I can understand. But when a man misses his drive, and then misses his second shot, and then wins the hole with a birdie —it gets my goat!"

Of course Mr. Jones is not to be understood as stating that this is Sir Walter's habitual manner of playing golf; not at all. But I knew perfectly well the hole to which Bobby referred; and in my opinion it was the turning-point of the match, which had started off with Bobby playing raggedly and then beginning to settle down in the second round, as Sir Walter, also starting raggedly, seemed beginning to loosen up.

It was the sixth hole of the afternoon round at the Whitfield course in Sarasota. Bobby had just won the fifth hole with a great iron second against a terrible miss by Walter—who had the better drive—and had cut Hagen's lead to three up. On the sixth tee Bobby had a fine drive down the alley and Walter, who had missed every drive but one in that round, shoved his tee-shot out to the edge of the rough, where a tall pine tree stood inconveniently near the line of his pitch to the well-trapped green.

Hagen had to play the odd and he hit as wretched a shot as can be imagined—he topped the ball so that it fairly rolled along the turf, straight to a wide sand trap guarding the front of the green.

See now how the complexion of a hole and a match can change and change again in a few seconds. As Hagen missed that shot any sane spectator would have concluded that Jones had won a hole, and that he was only two down, and staging a rally. But the topped ball ran on through the trap and wriggled up on the green and stopped a dozen feet from the cup. Jones' perfect drive and good pitch left him a couple of feet farther away, and his putt rimmed the cup and stayed out, right on the edge and an almost complete stymie for Hagen. Now it appeared that Walter had a lucky half—instead of which, putting with incredible daring and accuracy, he trickled the ball delicately past Bobby's up to the left-hand edge of the cup, where it hung an instant and then toppled in for a birdie 3. And Bobby was four down instead of two down.

A great putt—certainly. But Walter had made one good shot and two very bad ones, and Bobby had played the hole in par.

That was the turning point of the match, I shall always believe. And on the hole just preceding, when Bobby had played his iron second beautifully to ten feet from the pin, and Hagen, with a shorter and easier shot, had messed it up almost past belief and was far over the green and to the left, as Bobby told me afterward, he stood there and looked at Sir Walter in a sort of bewilderment.

"I watched that shot," said Bobby, "and I said to myself, 'I'm four down to a man who can miss one like that!'"

You see how deadly it is to take such an attitude with Sir Walter, and to permit yourself to consider his shots instead of sticking tight to the card and to Old Man Par, who never makes a birdie and never commits a buzzard. One never can count Sir Walter out, even with trees in the way. At the thirty-sixth hole at Whitfield, and at the fourteenth at Pasadena, Sir Walter hit a tree with his drive, the ball bounded out into the fairway, and each time he won the hole with a birdie against a perfectly played par. These shocking upsets do not affect the card and the pencil, in a medal competition; but they do work havoc with the equilibrium of a single human opponent—which is one of the reasons Sir Walter is accounted so formidable at match play. Willie Park said a long generation ago that the man who can putt is a match for anyone, and Hagen can putt. In his match with Jones, he used twenty-seven putts in the first round and twenty-six in the second. Bobby, a fine putter himself, and in this match behaving like a human being about the greens, took thirty-one putts in the first round and thirty in the second. He used eight putts more than Walter, and he was eight holes down at the thirty-sixth. Bobby needed eleven putts more than Walter in the match, and was beaten by a margin of twelve holes, though it should be explained that Walter also was playing his irons better than Jones; and in justice to them both it should be stated that in Bobby's last rally, at Pasadena, he shot the concluding twenty-five holes of the match in par and went four down to Walter's amazing golf.

So Walter *can* play golf, undoubtedly. Now

"What a whale of a difference just a few cents make!"

—all the difference
between just an ordinary cigarette and—FATIMA, the most skillful blend in cigarette history.

CUTHBERT S BUTCHART
THE MASTER CLUB MAKER
WESTCHESTER BILTMORE COUNTRY CLUB
RYE NY

The New Butchart Bamboo Clubs!

What a motor is to an automobile a shaft is to a golf club. Fine upholstery doesn't make a powerful racing car any more than ornate gold lettered heads and a pretty grip makes a powerful driver. Hickory has been universally used for shafts though only a few hickory shafts out of a hundred have the tough lasting rigidity needed for a powerful club. That is why good golf clubs are higher priced than the ones made from soft second rate shafts. The problem has been to turn out tough, resilient powerful clubs, light yet strong and have every one of them perfect. This problem has now been solved for the first time in the long history of golf by the

Butchart 12 Ply Bamboo Shafts

These shafts are made entirely of the tough outer wall of specially selected Asiatic Bamboo. There are hundreds of varieties of bamboo but only a few are suitable. Twelve separate strips from different bamboo poles are

laminated together so closely as to be almost invisible, making a beautiful slender steel-like shaft. A good golfer instantly recognizes the indescribable "feel" of these clubs. There is no heavy "woodiness" but delicate suppleness and strength. Every club is standard so if one is lost it can be duplicated *exactly*.

The Butchart Bamboo Clubs have been tested the past two months by tournament use in the hands of the finest professionals and amateurs in the United States. Their verdict is that they are the finest and most powerful Clubs ever built.

Bamboo is impervious to moisture, so your prized clubs are not ruined by the heaviest rain storms.

Try these remarkable

Butchart Bamboo Clubs

yourself or ask the good golfer or the professional who uses one.

Order Butchart Clubs through your Club Professional or your local sporting goods dealer or write to us direct.

C.S. BUTCHART COMPANY INC.

GOLF CLUBS

41 EAST FORTY SECOND STREET
TELEPHONE · MURRAY HILL · 9911
NEW YORK

for that other factor—showmanship. Years ago, Patterson McNutt, a great admirer of Bobby Jones and himself an actor and a playwright, told me that what Bobby lacked in golf was nothing but the histrionic instinct.

"If he loved to 'show off,'" said Pat, "if he liked to act—to strut his stuff—they'd never beat him. But he's just a bashful kid and a great golfer. He's no showman."

The gallery has no effect whatever on Bobby Jones so long as it keeps out of his way. It doesn't bother him, and it doesn't inspire him. He doesn't care if its component members hang with bated breath on his next shot, or if they read a newspaper, so long as they don't walk about or talk out loud when he is making a shot.

Not so Sir Walter. If Hagen were not a great golfer, I fancy he would be a great actor. He loves to do his stuff, for the gallery—and for an opponent, when it is match play.

I remember once when Sir Walter was playing a quiet practice round before a certain tournament, and on the last hole his second shot went into a shallow, simple sand trap by the green. Without an instant's consideration he picked a mashie-niblick from his bag, went down into the trap, chipped the ball from a clean lie to a couple of feet from the pin, and holed the putt for a par 4. The next day he was in the tournament. He had a big gallery with him. At the home green, his second shot behaved precisely as it did the day before, in the practice round—it hopped into the shallow trap, to a clean lie on the sand, about the same place as before. But this time there was a gallery.

And Sir Walter did his stuff.

Walking slowly into the trap, Hagen studied the position of the ball carefully, and considered its relation to the position of the pin on the green. Then he chose a mashie-niblick and returned to the ball, which he inspected again with the utmost care. Then he went back to the bank of the trap and exchanged the mashie-niblick for a niblick, returned to the ball and resumed his study. The gallery by this time was on the verge of hysterics and on the

outskirts frantic units were semaphoring distant friends to hurry thither and see the sights.

After another painstaking examination, Sir Walter regretfully shook his polished head and went back to his caddie for the third time, changing the niblick for the mashie-niblick he had picked out at first. Armed with this implement he returned again to the ball, once more studied the situation, took his stance, addressed the ball—and played exactly the same shot that he had executed in three seconds in practice the day before; a neat chip, two feet from the cup, for his par 4. And the gallery, convinced that it had witnessed a golfing miracle, split the welkin up the back like a patriarchal locust.

In the match with Jones, on the way to the ninth green at Whitfield, Hagen's ball after the drive was in the short rough of a sort of valley below the green, resting against a twig the size of a pencil. From where I stood I could see that the twig could not be moved without moving the ball and incurring a penalty. But Walter, with the gallery close about him, and Bobby standing none too well at ease after an indifferent second shot, consumed all of a minute that seemed an hour, studying that twig. At last he got up from his knees and played the shot, and a very good shot it was, and won the hole. And it may or may not have been a coincidence that Bobby Jones slipped over par on the tenth, and again on the eleventh, and got only a half on each with Walter, who also was stuttering at that juncture.

A great golfer—a great match golfer—and a great showman, is Walter Hagen. His cold, confident, deliberate personality impinges on a single human opponent with such effect that we have so good and game a player as Leo Diegel, last year in the P. G. A. championship, when Hagen picked up a deficit of five holes and won on the fortieth green—we have Leo Diegel saying to Bill Mehlhorn along toward the finish:

"Bill, I never want to play him again; he's killing me!"

Possibly you never considered the possibilities of psychological browbeating in golf; or perhaps in your sphere it is known simply as the gentle art of goat-getting.

One golfer at least has been able to resist the Hagen psychology successfully in match golf—Gene Sarazen, who has defeated Walter in two out of three formal matches, one of them for the P. G. A. championship of 1922 at Pelham. It was in the final round, and Hagen tried all his golf, and all his showmanship, and all his psychology, on Gene. Gene was playing as good golf as Hagen, and he didn't bother about the showmanship, being something of a showman himself. And as for the psychology, it went right over Gene's unimaginative little black bean. So along about the sixth hole of the morning round Hagen tried something else. I was standing by the green and heard all of it, and so far as I know it never has been in print before.

The second shot for the sixth hole at Pelham is a pitch over a sort of precipitous mountain. Hagen's ball reached the green, short of the hole and to the right, about a dozen yards from the pin. Sarazen's ball was on a narrow strip of turf at the left edge of the green, where a sort of walk-way had been left between two pot-bunkers, across which golfers traveled from the green toward the next tee. The grass had thus been somewhat worn away. A leaf lay over Sarazen's ball. He asked the referee if he might move it.

"Certainly," said the referee.

Gene carefully removed the leaf. Then the official suddenly spoke up.

"That ball's in a path," said he, "and a path is a hazard."

Gene looked at him rather helplessly. Hagen began walking over toward the colloquy.

"But I picked up a leaf," said Sarazen. "What shall I do about it?"

The referee plainly was puzzled, having told Gene he could move the leaf. Hagen spoke up, loud enough for the adjacent gallery to hear.

"You ought to know the rules, Gene," he said.

Sarazen again looked helplessly at the referee.

"Well, what about it?" he inquired.

Hagen spoke again, with elaborate condescension.

"Oh, go ahead and play it," he said wearily, and walked back to his own ball.

Sarazen chipped—and his chip was three yards from the cup. Hagen won the hole, and Sarazen failed to hit the fairway with his next three drives.

There is a good deal more in match golf than ever gets into the public prints.

In this particular instance, however, there was a flareback. Sarazen was playing well enough to hold his own up to the intermission, and at lunch time—I recall it well—he said to me:

"Walter had no business to show me up in front of the gallery. I'll give him a licking for that!"

And that is what he did, though Sir Walter, game to the core, picked up a three-hole deficit in the last nine with a tremendous rally, squared the match, halved the first extra hole with a birdie 4 after the most powerful iron shot I ever saw, and then lost at the thirty-eighth green to Sarazen's miraculous recovery from the rough for a birdie 3.

But except for little Gene Sarazen, Sir Walter's golf, plus showmanship, plus psychology, has pretty well flattened out the opposition these last five years, so far as match golf is concerned. Bobby Jones' own pet system went to smash against the Hagen psychology in Florida. After Max Marston beat him at Flossmoor, in the National Amateur, Bobby discovered that by playing the card in match competition as well as in medal, he could win matches—and he won nine of them in succession, and two consecutive Amateur Championships. But in Florida Bobby made the vital mistake of going back to his original plan and playing Walter Hagen instead of playing the card, and Walter is a calamitous opponent, when you try to match shots with him. He makes such odd shots from the tee—and he takes so few shots about the green! He can be so shockingly wild and so distressingly precise, all playing the same hole! He's the great match golfer, is Sir Walter!

Mr. Eustace Storey, the dapper English player who took part in this year's National Amateur Championship at Baltusrol, in New Jersey, displays his rather unusual putting stance.

The striking finish of British star Cecil Leitch, made during a recent match at West Hill, England.

Mr. Cyril Tolley, the British amateur star, has been thrilling the English and Scottish galleries with his whistling long shots this season.

Swing the Clubhead 1927 BY ERNEST JONES

A *Plea for Simplicity in Analyzing the Golf Swing*

BEFORE STARTING ANY DISCUSSION OF THE golf swing, I should like first to say that my own impression is that most golfers go quite the wrong way about learning the game. This refers to being always on the alert to find out what is wrong instead of getting to know what is right.

I know the old saying that to know what is wrong is one way of knowing what is right. Personally, I don't think that idea is good. It doesn't seem to me to be constructive. It seems to lead to nothing but counter actions of things that are wrong. I certainly consider that it is much simpler to find out what is right, and try to keep to that standard, or as near as possible, so the thing to try to get at first is "What is right?"

Every good golfer concedes that you must have "control," that you must have good "balance," and that you must have "timing." But when one asks what is "control," or what is "timing," or what is "balance," the answers usually received are, to say the least, vague and indefinite. For instance, anyone can say that Bobby Jones has "control," but just what is meant by "control"? What does one control? And how does one contrive to control?

Briefly just what are we trying to do? There is no end of things that sound simple, in fact silly, until they are thoroughly understood.

This is one of them. Obviously what we are trying to do is to hit the ball with the head of the club. It is so entirely obvious that most golfers forget it completely in trying to think of the thousand and one tips to help them do that very simple thing. Then we can say that what we are trying to do is to hit the ball with the head of the club. Once more, obviously, to do this we must have control of the head of the club to hit the ball with it.

The next question that confronts us is "What is the action of the club in hitting the ball?" To be able to get the maximum distance with the ball, the clubhead must be traveling at the maximum pace when it reaches the ball. We must then devise a method that will enable us to cause the clubhead to reach its maximum speed as it comes to the ball.

Now let me call your attention to the action of a pendulum. At first thought the action of a pendulum does not in the least suggest pace. But a moment's consideration will convince one that there is nothing can travel faster, for if a pendulum should continue its course in one direction, the result would be a complete revolution, and unlimited speed may be developed in revolutionary motion. So then, consider the action of the club as the action of a pendulum. It doesn't matter how long or short the stroke is. This is merely a question of the degree of the angle through which the pendulum swings. Hence, when we say we are trying to acquire control, we mean we are trying to make the club move through a true pendulum motion.

Then comes the question "How do we get the control to swing the club?" Obviously once more it is possible to feel what we are doing with the clubhead only through the points of contact between ourselves and the club; that is, the hands and fingers. If we have control, it means we can feel what we are doing with it. Mostly control is intuitive. For instance, in writing, we feel control of the point of the pen on paper, or in tossing a ball we feel control to throw with the thumb and fingers. Thus we have to feel that we have the sense of moving the club in a pendulum motion, through or by means of the hands and fingers.

We now come to the question of what balance is. This too has developed into a terribly complicated problem, in that nowadays we are supposed to have to consider it in the sense of transfer of weight, in thinking of the golf swing. Maintaining balance in the golf swing involves the transfer of weight, all right; that much is agreed. But so does the simple action of walking. Here is possibly the simplest demonstration of the transfer of balance, yet we never so much as think of it at all when we walk.

Now this latter is true of the making of a golf swing with a good golfer. He never worries about the transfer of weight any more than he does of shifting the weight forward from one foot onto the other in walking. Now then I should like to explain balance in this manner. Balance without motion is even distribution of weight; that is, poise. Where there is motion involved, balance is responsive motion. For instance, in the case of a top spinning, it is the speed of the motion that maintains the balance. In the actions of a swinger of Indian clubs, balance is the responsive motion to the swinging of the clubs. It must be plainly and distinctly understood that balance is not something that has to be pulled into action. It is never an initiative action, but merely the response to an initiative one.

Now, then, in hitting a golf ball it is possible to hit only with the clubhead, and not from balance or the responsive motion of the body. The greatest trouble in golf is that the player will try to hit or force too much from what should be balanced motion. On the other hand it is equally fatal to try to keep still. If we are to put any power or force into the stroke, the body must move, and balance in motion must be maintained.

It is all very simple if one can only get the idea. The golfer's main thought must be on the clubhead, on hitting with the clubhead, and not upon other outside details. You will frequently see golfers miss a drive when the ball is teed up just as they want it—and then hit a nice shot from some bad lie. In the first case they are not concentrating on the main job of merely hitting the ball. They are thinking of arms or hands or body or pivot or something else. In the second case they are thinking of hitting the ball, regardless of unimportant details.

All this may seem to be too obvious. Yet in everything one must get back to first principles, and this is something so few golfers do. Golf is largely smoothness, ease, rhythm and subconscious effort. How can one get this? One can help by practicing swinging the clubhead through in a natural way and developing balance under control, instinctive balance just as one has in walking. You *must* have this instinctive feel of ease and balance if you ever expect to play any golf worth while and enjoy the game. You *must* have the feel of the clubhead swinging through naturally, unimpeded by any conscious movement or action.

You must understand, you must get the mental picture of hitting with the clubhead, just as you have the same mental picture of hitting a nail with the head of a hammer. That must be the start of any golf swing that will ever get you anywhere. Don't think this is too obvious to be given any thought. It is the first basis of the swing, and it is something few average golfers ever consider at all.

The hands being the points of contact with

the club must necessarily be the means of obtaining that very desirous thing in golf, "control," so that it is interesting to study the right way of using them to obtain the best results.

It is a very common error to use the hands merely to grip the club, without realizing that it is possible to get a great deal of hitting power, by the proper use of the hands or more properly fingers. This is what I describe as "dead-handed" golf.

Consider a baseball pitcher, for example. All the spin that is imparted to the ball must be done by thumb and finger action. In fact, all throwing is done by finger action.

Now, there are so many different ways of holding a golf club. Practically every first-class golfer grips the club in a manner slightly different from every other. For instance, there is the ordinary two-handed grip as used by Abe Mitchell and Sandy Herd. Then there is the overlapping grip popularized by Vardon and Taylor; also the interlocking grip so successfully used by Francis Ouimet and Sarazen. The question of which one to use must be left to the individual, but whatever grip is adopted one thing must not be lost sight of; and that is golf is a two-handed game, and one hand must help the other to get as much speed to the clubhead as possible.

It is frequently stated that the left hand does this, and the right hand does that, that one finds so many players trying to work each hand independently of one another, which is absolutely fatal to proper golf.

Again what is commonly understood as wrist action is in reality hand action. The wrists are the hinges that give in a responsive sense to the initiative actions applied by and through the hands. For instance, do you think of using your wrist when you lift your cup to take a drink? Of course you don't. Neither is a child taught to use its wrists. It is taught to hold the cup properly and use its hands.

If you stop to consider the part of your hands that are used to get a sense of touch from, it will soon be realized that the forefinger and the thumb are the principal factors. For instance, if you are examining a

piece of cloth, you feel it with your forefinger and thumb. Again if you pick up your ball you will do it with your first two fingers and thumb. If you wanted to throw it you would use the same thing.

It is the same in holding the club, in order to do something with it beside holding it. Every finger has hold of the club, but the action to move the clubhead is applied mostly through the forefinger and the thumb. I don't for one moment mean to convey that the little finger must be held loosely, but it is the natural thing for the little finger to grip tightest. A very simple experiment will soon prove what I mean. Close your fist and see which finger you can grip tightest. On first thought you would imagine the forefinger, but you will very soon see that the little finger grips much the firmest.

This is very often the case in gripping the club. The grip from the back of the hand puts the forefinger and thumb out of action, so that great care should be taken to see the club is held in such a manner that the forefinger and thumb are used to the best advantage. A good guide is to see that the tip of the thumb is in line with the second joint of the first finger.

Another point often asked is, "How tight or how loose should one hold the club?" It should be held firm enough to be able to feel what you are doing with it. I will put it this way. How tight do you hold a pen to write with? How tight do you hold the wheel to guide your car? How tight would you hold a hammer? And so on. It all depends on the amount of power being used, the hands being the means of guiding and moving whatever has to be guided and moved.

I would like to say at the start that in properly played golf strokes, there is no such thing as initiative wrist action, and that the action of the wrist in every case is that of a hinge, or responsive motion. This really is the whole thing in a nutshell, but we have all been so used to the slogan "use your wrists" that we have got to look on every motion of the wrist as a thing in itself, instead of a motion that is set in action by something else.

For instance, if you open a door you don't

try to open it with the hinge, you push the door and the hinge gives to that action. That is what I mean by responsive motion. There is not the slightest doubt that the correct wrist motion is one of the most important things in a golf swing, but it must not be looked upon as an action in itself. *The club is moved by the hands to the wrists,* and not by leverage applied by the wrists themselves.

In fact, there is no such thing as leverage in golf at all. It is speed that is required: leverage and speed don't go together. *Momentum* and speed, yes; but not leverage. In a full swing you move the clubhead with the hands as far as your wrists will allow it to go, both backward and forward, of course letting the arms, shoulders and body give, so as to get the right balance. In a shorter swing the wrists give according to how far the club is moved, so that in a short putt they would hardly give at all. For comparison take the action of a man driving a pile with a sledge hammer, and a jeweler using his hammer on a watch; it all depends on the amount of power applied.

We hear so much nowadays about the rolling action of the wrists that it is made a definite action in itself, instead of realizing that it is only action that could possibly take place, if the clubhead is moved in the correct manner. It is all a question of understanding cause and effect. When you consider that speed in the clubhead is the principal thing to aim at, you must also realize that anything to travel at its greatest speed must take the line of least resistance.

You will also realize that leverage is forcing one point against another, so that it is not possible to get the maximum speed by lever-

age, although I will grant it is the instinctive thing to do. Leverage feels as though you are using great power. So you are, but it is really all misapplied. The reason golf looks so ridiculously easy when played by a Bobby Jones or a Harry Vardon is that they can let themselves give with what they are doing with the club, instead of forcing themselves against it.

It is not right to say that the clubhead starts first in the swing; neither is it right to say that the hands start first. What should be aimed at is to start both together until you can get the sensation of momentum in the clubhead, and then try to accelerate that momentum as much as can be easily controlled.

It is equally fatal to try to swing with the hips. Of course you cannot swing the club with your hips, but they must not be held back by any means. Everything starts to give until the feeling of moving the clubhead itself is predominant.

Mention is made here of starting the clubhead first or the hands first, also of the hip action, for the simple reason that one very frequently sees these made the subject of a discussion on how to properly make the golf swing. As stated above, I think the hands and the clubhead should start together.

Also as to the hips, they play a prominent part in the swing, but get away from the idea of referring the ground work of the swing to them. They will do their part without any conscious thought on the player's part, if left alone, and trying to consciously make them take any preconceived action will simply confuse the player and detract his attention from the real task of speeding up the clubhead.

Be careful that you always stand on the proper side of the tee when your opponent is preparing to drive. At this most anxious moment for your friend, do not be practicing your own swing or move about or talk. You would be intensely annoyed with him if he did these things when you were driving. If he lost the match through a foozled drive, he would be justified in saying that you did not play the game.

HARRY VARDON

Oakmont Under the Microscope BY O. B. KEELER

Can a Golf Course Be Too Hard for a
True Championship Test?

DURING, AND AFTER, THE 1927 OPEN GOLF championship of the United States at Oakmont some of the boys were saying that Oakmont was too much golf course. Usually it was a frank admission that Oakmont was too much golf course for the boys individually, according to their confession. They couldn't quite make it, that round. Or they couldn't come close to making it. A lot of them were in that fix, at Oakmont, in June. But now and again, and with no evidence of disgruntled criticism, you would hear the opinion that Oakmont was too much golf course.

This raises an interesting question:

What *is* too much golf course on which to contest the blue ribbon event of the world?

Now, I should venture the opinion, humbly, that it is possible to array a golf course that really is too much golf course. I should say, tentatively, that Pine Valley, that beautiful and intricate, study in golfing architecture, would be rather too much golf course for a national championship. I have never got out of my head Bernard Darwin's estimate of it, delivered in 1922, I think. "Pine Valley," said the finest of all golf critics and writers, "is an examination in golf."

But does the Oakmont course as prepared

for the United States Open Championship of 1927 come under that classification?

It needs a bit of consideration. The scores were high. The winning score—I was bold enough to predict it weeks in advance—would have been an old-fashioned 300. It was 301 that wound up in a tie. Ah, I knew that course. And the changes made for this tournament, I could tell from the advance reports, made it two strokes harder than when it originally was a par of 74. Two strokes harder than in 1925, when the amateur championship was played there.

Why, it read a 75 in each round even for the man who was right. The man who lacked the thin edge—well, there was Bobby Jones, who never is far off stride. Would you have believed that Bobby Jones ever would shoot four competitive rounds on any course and never hit a 75?

Oakmont was the stiffest test of golf in the 1927 Open Championship of the United States that I ever saw anywhere. And the winning scores, or the tying scores, of 301 were an achievement that Tommy Armour and Harry Cooper may treasure to the end of the chapter as something that will assay twenty-four carats. I think the run-of-the-mine golfing fan will never understand what golf it required to shave 300 that close—and our little friend, Gene Sarazen, was one long putt from that score; and Emmett French and Bill Mehlhorn came up from relative obscurity to illustrate what the Oakmont course can do to a man who was shooting a miracle round.

Bill Mehlhorn is an interesting figure in the 1927 championship to me. He deferred his explosion to the last nine holes this time. He has been getting closer and closer. Watch for the time when he forgets to explode. He will slap some great field for a vista of furrowed bunkers. His time is coming. But the fight is harder and harder. Bobby Jones' domination slipped at Oakmont. The iron grip on American golf for the last five years loosened. He finished farther down the list, and with a worse score, than ever before. But up to the thirteenth tee of the third round he was in the best position in the field. See what four holes can do to a player like Bobby Jones—6-4-6-5, where par was 3-4-4-3—and let us resume the question as to Oakmont being too much golf course.

We will hear from Ted Ray, captain of the British Ryder Cup team, and a former champion of Great Britain and America; the last invader to win our open title, at Inverness, in 1920. "The greens were the most beautiful, and the fastest, I ever played on," said Big Ted, after taking thirty-eight putts in his third round and forty in his fourth. "It was the man with the putter at fault. The greens were wonderful. I could not play on them."

"Ted's trouble," volunteered George Duncan, never at a loss for a theory, "was this. In Britain when the greens are terribly keen, they are brown. We don't water them, there. Here, they were as keen and slippery as ever they get in Britain, but they were green and the texture was apparently substantial. I never saw more lovely greens. But fast as lightning. And Ted, for all his superb touch, could never get himself in the mood to realize he was putting over racing greens. That's the reply."

Big Ted shook his gray head—one of the wisest heads in golf. "I thought of pasting a bit of stamp-paper on my putter blade," he said. "That slows your ball up a bit. And I tried three putters—a rare thing for me. But I couldn't get the touch. Mind you, it's myself that was wrong; not the greens. But I couldn't do it."

Well, when Ted Ray, one of the finest putters in the world, especially on fast greens, needs thirty-eight and forty putts in two rounds of a national open championship, playing finely otherwise, we may judge fairly that the greens were a problem at Oakmont.

Yes, the greens were a problem. They are, I firmly believe, the finest we have in America today. Are they a trace too fine? With the rolls, I mean. They are largely undulating. Is the texture too speedy for a fair test, with the undulations?

One more point, for heaven knows the layout of Oakmont today is as near impeccable as a golf course can be. "These bunkers, now, with the ribbed sand," said Ted Ray. "I'll give you an illustration. What sort of game do you shoot?"

He was addressing me. I blushed and confessed that at best I was a feeble sort of 90-player.

"Yes," resumed Ted, "and I'm a fairish sort of professional and a big chap, to boot. And when we both get into one of these ploughed bunkers, all I can do is knock more sand out of it than you can, because I am bigger and stronger. We have to play the same shot, whether we shoot 90 or 100, or 75. There is no option. Two hundred yards from the pin, or twenty yards, you pick out the niblick and blast.

"Now, I think that is not as it should be. The recovery shot from sand—wind-blown sand; not ploughed sand—is a distant golf shot and a fine one; it calls for great skill and accurate execution. The green may be a couple of hundred yards away, and a mound at the front of the bunker in line. I don't care for the mounds, as another point. In the furrow, as on this course, you, or I, or any man, has nothing to do but explode. We are all on a level. We are reduced to the same place we would be if the area of the bunker were drawn on the grass in whitewash, and the rule was that when the ball went within the lines, it should be chucked out a few yards, and the stroke counted.

"The bunker recovery shot is a great golf shot, for the man who is skilled and bold enough to make it. Two hundrèd yards from the green, and a mound in line, he may play a boomerang spoon shot, either drawn or cut, to the right or the left, and a master-stroke will put him on or near the green. I say that is a golf shot, and one that should be offered the player—for ruin awaits him if he misses in the least detail. But here, the 100-player, the 80-player, the 75-player, has only one shot to play from the sand; and neither boldness nor skill will help him correct a position which may not have been all his fault in the first place. He has one shot—the blast. That is all."

You know, I heard Walter Fovargue say that same thing, back in 1925, when the Amateur Championship was played at Oakmont. It set me thinking. Of course, the idea of the furrowed bunkers at Oakmont is that you do not need to be in them, and in them—penalty. I should never say casually that Bill Fownes, Oakmont's chairman, is wrong, if he says a bunker shot should carry a designated penalty. Perhaps he is altogether right, and thinking ahead of many of us, in leveling the position in the bunker to a common penalty; for we all know that in the wind-blown sand one ball sits up and another snuggles in a heelprint. This is very likely advanced theory in championship golf. But it is an interesting aftermath of Oakmont, a very great tournament, grandly run, on America's finest golf course.

Broadway producer John Golden has been playing a good deal of golf at St. Augustine this winter.

While using only a three-quarter swing, Rex Beach, the novelist, is one of the longest hitters in the game, amateur or professional.

How Armour Does It BY WALTER R. MCCALLUM

The Secrets of His Superb Skill and
How He Acquired Them

It didn't come about by accident, born overnight by the golfing genius of a master of wood and iron. It came out of the fierce heat of competition, born of an overmastering desire to conquer the game he loved and literally forced on him by the varying moods of Scottish weather—this closed stance and firm grip with the iron clubs which make the game of National Open Champion Tommy Armour stand out as one of the soundest in golfdom today.

Three outstanding characteristics dominate the Armour game: the skill with all clubs that crushed Harry Cooper under the dominance of a Scottish-bred game, learned on the hills of Edinburgh and tempered in the fire of international competition; the game that found its owner tied at the end of the seventy-two-hole championship distance with the dashing English-born Californian and outclubbed him the following day over Oakmont's rugged stretches.

Supreme ability to wait for the clubhead on the tee shot, never hurrying the stroke, and never forcing the body in to gain extra distance.

A closed stance with the right foot well behind the left to give free play to the push of the body and the roll of the hips as the ball is met.

Hands well over the shaft, the ball of the left hand controlling the grip and working with the fingers of that hand to keep the club in full control at all times. This particularly with the iron clubs.

These are the outstanding characteristics of the game of the National Open Champion, this rugged, loosely-knit Scot, who won his war spurs while barely out of the University of Edinburgh, and came out of the conflict with the sight of one eye gone and pieces of German shrapnel still embedded in the left shoulder that remains so firmly on the line as the national champion hits a screaming tee shot. The same co-ordination of hand and eye that won for Thomas Dickson Armour the reputation of being the fastest man behind a machine gun in the war and gave him an official trial before the King of England, stayed with him through those trying days at Oakmont, admonishing him never to forget the fling of the clubhead, the firmness of the blow with the iron clubs and the roll of the body from the hips that characterizes many of the imported leaders in the game.

Tommy is modest about it all. He claims he got the breaks at Oakmont, and there is little question that he did. But isn't it a truism that the champion always gets the breaks, and that he creates them more often than not? The sixteenth hole of the play-off will never be forgotten by those who saw the lanky Scot deliberately play for the left edge of the bunkered green, knowing he would at least get a fair shot at the pin, while Cooper, level with his rival, chose the shorter and more dangerous route to the hole—and lost the championship.

But it is of Armour's Scottish style that more would be known. And when it is analyzed it seems somewhat unlike the style of the typical Scot. But here again there are similarities in those inner secrets that great golfers alone know. For we find Armour with an exaggerated closed stance, noticeably closed, even while Bob Jones stands square to the ball, his toes on a line to the hole, Hagen and Sarazen noticeably open, their right feet well advanced, and Cooper even more on the open stance order. Why does Armour adopt the closed stance when most of the masters of the game today advocate the moderately open stance, and surely not the unusually exaggerated stance Armour advocates, with the right foot several inches back of the left on the line to the hole?

"Simply because it permits of freer body action and gives greater play to the arms as they go into and through the ball." That's the way Tommy explains it, not at all dogmatically, but because he has thought it all out, experimented with all ways and found this way the best, at least for him. Armour, who holds down the professional berth at the Congressional Country Club near Washington, believes the moderate closed stance best fitted for the golf stroke because the arms do not have to work across and in opposition to the body as they do if the stance is open at all.

But here we have another consideration. With the closed stance, is not the right elbow apt to fly out and away from the side causing a loop in the clubhead and throwing the entire swing out of alignment? Ah, there is the secret of the closed Armour swing, the meat in the cocoanut, the germ of the whole idea.

"If you let your right arm stray away from your body, the whole thing is thrown out of gear. It must be kept in close, first for firmness, then for accuracy and last of all, for precision and smoothness." Again the Open Champion speaks—from a wealth of knowledge and years of practice. "Keep that right elbow in close to your side. Don't let it get away from you."

And what of the ability to wait for the clubhead—that characteristic which dominates the whole Armour game from tee to green and has made of him one of the admitted great masters of the iron clubs. That, the champion declares, is something that must be acquired solely from within the player. It is the exact antithesis of ducking, lunging, rushing through the stroke, or any one of the scores of evils that beset the average player and cause the loss of more strokes than there are boll weevils in Texas.

"Wait for the clubhead; and then throw in that roll of the hips and the flick of the wrists. Don't attempt a wild fling that throws the entire swing off balance. Lunging won't do it, but smoothness will. Wait for the clubhead. Imagine it on the end of a string. But wait for it. If you don't, a smothered shot will result. And if you do, Utopia will be yours."

Simple, isn't it? But it might be worth trying after all. For words of wisdom as simply spoken as these of this champion are worth a trial, at least.

Now Tommy Armour has something all the professionals—and the amateurs too—admit in overwhelming measure. That is supreme control with the irons. The ability to take an iron club from the bag and hit with it a ball that never deviates from the straight line to the pin. Such a shot was one of the vital factors in winning his championship at Oakmont on one of the few occasions he faltered. He half hit his tee shot to the fifth in the last round, and was left with a 220-yard shot to a terrifyingly trapped green. Out came a one-iron, and up went the ball to within twenty feet of the pin—almost all carry. He calls it his "forcing" shot—and "forcing" it is, for the ball travels low on a dead line and does not run. It is played far off the right foot and the hips are rolled through fast to keep it low and firm. It probably won for him the chance to beat Harry Cooper in the play-off, for a 5 looked certain on the par 4 hole and none but a champion would have tried the shot.

Armour's grip with the iron clubs is most unusual, his delicacy with the short irons and the moderate pitches from one hundred and forty yards down, mastery itself. He employs the orthodox Vardon grip—the little finger of the right hand overlapping the first finger of the left, but it is in the alignment of the hands on the grip of the club that it is unusual. Armour's two hands are well over the top of the shaft. They work in perfect rhythm, these two big hands, attached to unusually powerful wrists, and, to see them in action, flinging up a high mashie shot of one hundred and forty yards is like watching the flying hands of a Paderewski.

Armour plays a symphony with the irons— backed by this unusually high grip which puts the burden of the weight of the club well down on the palm of the left hand and permits free play and use of the fingers. It is purely a finger grip, this grasp of the club by the master of the irons. Nothing else to it. If Tommy permitted his club to slide back in the palm, all the delicacy of touch and hit would be lost, the rhythm destroyed and the efficiency lost.

So, like all the other factors in the game this title-holding Scot has developed, there is reason to it. Let the heel of the shaft press against the heel of the left hand, keep the club in the fingers and hit firmly.

So it is with Armour, an unorthodox champion in some things and a mightily orthodox man in others. No single flaw can be found in grip or stance, and reason is behind it all. That and the training of more than a score of years of the game—bred on the wind-swept Braid Hills and the lengthy reaches of Musselburgh. Firmness and closeness of swing dominate it all.

Encountered just before starting a round near Tokyo recently are H.R.H. The Prince of Wales and Crown Prince Hirohito, who lately ascended the Japanese throne.

Bobby Jones' Conquest of St. Andrews

BY BERNARD DARWIN

His Skill Captures a Championship and
His Bearing Wins the Plaudits of the Crowd

I WISH BOBBY JONES' ADMIRERS IN HIS OWN country could have witnessed the scene at St. Andrews when he rapped the putt of three inches into the hole that made him, by six strokes, again British Open Champion. They would have realized that there is one respect in which Britain declines to be beaten by America, namely, in enthusiasm for Bobby.

It really was an astonishing, almost a terrifying scene. There were, at a conservative estimate, twelve thousand people round the last green. As soon as that last putt was holed, the crowd flung away stewards as if they were straws and, caring nothing for anyone else who was going to putt on that green, stormed the slope. In a twinkling of an eye the champion had disappeared. "One moment stood he as the angels stand" and then "the next he was not." He was just swallowed up. Either he or somebody else seemed bound to be squashed to death, but after what appeared an age, but was, I suppose, only a few seconds, he reappeared, borne aloft on willing shoulders and in turn himself bearing aloft his precious putter.

His cap soon vanished, but after the crowd had surged this way and that with their load for several minutes, he and his putter were safely on dry land again—not, however, before a rescuing party had set out from the Royal and Ancient clubhouse to save him.

There was another great scene when Bobby was handed the cup, but this time he was safe inside the clubhouse railings where he made his very modest and charming little speech of thanks and announced that he was going to leave the cup in the care of the Royal and Ancient Club, of which he is a member.

These scenes of unexampled enthusiasm were, of course, evidence of a very great personal popularity, but I think they were also evidence of something else: a general conviction that Bobby was so superior that it would have been a shame and an outrage if anyone else had dared to win. For a visitor to be able to force that conviction upon the whole of an intensely patriotic Scottish crowd is an astonishing thing, altogether outside the power of any other golfer in the world.

I am not going to tell again at length the story of the four rounds which has already long since been flashed across the Atlantic. It differed from the story of most of Bobby's triumphs in that he made his own pace and led from start to finish. As a rule, he has come up from behind. This time he got in front right away with his 68, and then had to stay there. To those of us who were looking on, there never seemed any real doubt that he would stay there, but to Bobby himself, I fancy that this making of his own pace was a very exhausting business and that he would have felt the strain less if he had only begun to come away from his field towards the end of the third round.

There were really only two moments when he looked like being in the least pressed. One was on the second day—Bobby had reached the turn in 37, when we heard that Ben Hodson had added a 70 to his first round of 72. That meant that Bobby had to come home in 37 for a 74, which would make him tie with Hodson. Thirty-seven home at St. Andrews against even a slight wind is very good golf, and he was not playing convincingly. However, he took himself by the scruff of the neck, came home grandly in 35, and kept a lead of two.

The other doubtful moment was at the beginning of the last round. Fred Robson had gotten within four strokes of him and Bobby had started quite badly with five holes in 23. There was just a doubt, but a hole or two afterwards Bobby had begun to do his four 3's in a row, and that was that, once and for all. All through the tournament Bobby's driving was magnificent—magnificently long and magnificently straight. If one thing more than another won him the championship it was his wooden club play. The two long holes at St. Andrews, the fifth and the fourteenth, are both well over five hundred yards long, and apart from their length, the nature of the ground makes them particularly hard to reach in two. The ordinary rank and file were working reasonably hard to play them in 5's apiece. Bobby himself could not quite reach the four-

teenth in two, but his total for those two holes played four times each was just 33 shots. They gave him his great chance in the last round of gaining a clear stroke from lesser men and he certainly took it.

His pitching, on the other hand, was hardly up to his proper standard. Of course, he made many beautiful pitches, but he also made some downright weak ones; he was always inclined to be short with them, and once, on the last day, he fluffed one into a bunker in front of his illustrious nose.

But if he occasionally pitched weakly, he nearly always saved himself by his putting. Now and again, being mortal, he missed a putt, but he holed a great many and his approach putting was a model of free, clean hitting.

It was a long putt holed—ten yards at least —at the second hole in the first round which set him off on his 68. That hole had looked like a disaster, for it ought to be a 4, and it seemed almost certain to become a 6. He had drawn his tee shot slightly and had been trapped; he had failed to get out with his first effort, and finally, when he reached the green in four, he was a good long way from the hole. And then down went that priceless putt for a 5, which was worth more than many orthodox, featureless 4's. He never again came so near to doing a 6 as at that hole, and, in fact he went around the old course four times without a 6, a thing that has never been done before.

It is no derogation from Bobby's wonderful score of 285 to say that the conditions were ideal for scoring. The plain fact of the matter is that the weather came very near to making a fool of the classic course. Not only was there practically not a breath of wind, day after day, but the ground was unnaturally slow and grassy after much heavy rain. Those who know the course will realize that it was not its normal and interesting self in these circumstances. It was dull golf, with all the subtlety gone out of the shots, and none of that variety which an ever-shifting wind usually introduces. A big drive and then a high pitching shot, with some sort of spade mashie played right up to the pin in the sure and certain hope that it would not run over—that was the story of hole after hole.

There were just two or three holes which gave the great player his chance against the merely good player; otherwise he could only assert his superiority by a slightly greater steadiness in the playing of obvious shots. Whatever had been the conditions—if it had snowed ink—it is my firm conviction that Bobby would have won; but a stiff wind and a faster ground would have made it more interesting to watch him do it. As it was, he did marvelously, but the battlefield was hardly worthy of the victorious hero.

Francis Ouimet ready to try a carom shot off the wall across the road back of the green on the seventeenth hole at St. Andrews during this year's British Open.

One of his brilliant stretches of play will land British professional George Duncan an easy winner one of these days.

The Greatest Record in Golf

BY W. D. RICHARDSON

Hagen's Victory in the P. G. A. at Dallas Makes It Four in a Row

ONE RETURNS FROM DALLAS, THE BATTLEGROUND of the 1927 P. G. A. championship, with a conviction of having witnessed an epochal golf event. Having watched Walter Hagen snap his fingers in the face of fate and make new golf history by winning the P. G. A. title for the fourth successive time, one cannot help but feel that absolutely nothing remains to be seen. When you stop to think that here's a man who has matched his wits and skill against the wits and skill of the best golfers America can muster and won twenty consecutive matches—five each year for the last four years—the deeds of other golfers, present and past, seem small and insignificant. That's what Hagen has done. More than that he's played in six P. G. A. championships all told and lost only one match out of thirty. The only man who holds a decision over him is Gene Sarazen, who defeated him on the thirty-eighth green in the final at Pelham in 1923.

There was at least an element of luck in that defeat, for when Sarazen drove over the trees playing the second extra hole against Hagen nearly everybody in the gallery (Jim Barnes, then pro at Pelham, included) thought that Gene's ball was out of bounds. It did hit the branches of the trees, but went through and landed just short of the green. A great pitch out of the long grass by Sarazen, a head-up chip into a bunker by Hagen and the match —one of the greatest finals ever played—was over.

Had it not been for that defeat at the hands of Sarazen, Hagen would now be celebrating his fifth consecutive victory in the P. G. A. instead of his fourth. But four is enough. No other man has ever gained four major match play titles in a row in all the years that golf had been played. That ought to be honor enough.

This year we, like many others, journeyed to Dallas with a feeling that at last we were going to see Hagen knocked off his P. G. A. perch. We had seen him win at French Lick Springs in 1924, we had seen him squeeze out of at least two tight places at Olympia Fields year before last, we had seen him breeze home with the cup at Salisbury. We knew him to be a slippery fellow, but we thought that the mathematical odds, generally reliable in golf, would get him at Dallas. We were prepared to eulogize Hagen for what he had been and to acclaim his successor. Even after he showed his heels to the others in the final qualifying round we still felt that Hagen's time had come and after the draw—one of the most lopsided draws that had ever been perpetrated—we felt even more convinced of the fact that Walter was on his way toward Waterloo. Up in his half of the draw were Tommy Armour, Johnny Farrell, Tommy Harmon, Bobby Cruickshank, Olin Dutra, Al Espinosa and Harry Cooper, to mention only the top-notchers. Imagine starting out to wade through a field such as that to get into the final!

Hagen was in the upper quarter along with Armour, Farrell, Harmon and Cruickshank and luck was with him when Tony Manero upset Cruickshank and when Armour and Farrell were drawn together in the first round. The unexpected defeat of Cruickshank by Manero and Armour's four and three victory over Farrell helped, but Hagen came preciously close to elimination at the outset. Another Farrell, Jack of North Shore, playing in his first tournament of consequence, had Walter four down at the end of eighteen holes. Against anyone else that lead might have been sufficient. Two birdies, one on the seventeenth hole and another on the eighteenth, enabled Farrell to get a bigger lead than Hagen relished, but when the pair of them came into the locker-room at noon Walter was the least excited of the two. Farrell ate little if anything for lunch; Hagen had a good meal and took his time eating it. By the time they returned to the first tee to start the second round, Farrell's nervousness was such as to make it apparent to all.

If he could hold his lead only a little while longer his reputation was made. The fish he had on his line was too big for him, however, and by the turn Hagen was one up. Next came Manero, a good putter. According to Cruickshank a great putter, Tony had holed everything against Bobby; against Walter he couldn't hole anything. His was a pathetic collapse which may be charged to over-eagerness.

Then came the match with Armour. Both he and Hagen wanted to win that one badly and

the game Walter gambled on to beat Tommy with was to let Tommy beat himself. A good method if it works. It did. Armour, somewhat fatigued after his two hard matches with Johnny Farrell and Tommy Harmon, made one mistake on the fourth green. He stymied himself and permitted Hagen to win a hole that should have been halved or perhaps won.

That was the turning point of the match right there. First thing Armour knew he was three down and that was all Hagen needed. When Walter popped in two birdies on the last two holes of the morning round to be four up, the match was as good as over right there. Please note that in this match Hagen had a 71 with a 6 on the par 4 third hole and that in the first round of his match against young Jack Farrell he was in the 80's. That win from Armour brought him through his quarter of the bracket. Let's see what was happening down in the lower quarter. The first surprising thing was Cooper's defeat at the hands of Espinosa. Playing on the course on which he had broken his first 90, his first 80 and his first 70, Cooper was considerable of a favorite, but Espinosa, by playing steady if not brilliant golf from the turn on, beat him five and four.

In the semifinals were to be found Hagen and Espinosa on the top side and Joe Turnesa and Johnny Golden down below. Of the last of these two matches little need be said. Turnesa had a walk-over.

The other was anything but a walk-over. While not great from a scoring point of view it was great from every other angle. To all appearances Hagen was beaten when Espinosa won the thirty-fifth hole to be one up.

After the second shots to the home green it was as good as a certainty that Hagen had lost his crown. All that Espinosa needed was a half and it looked as if he couldn't fail to get that, for his ball was within twenty-five feet of the pin and Hagen's almost over the green. It was closer to the hole, to be sure, but his chances of getting the 3 that appeared necessary were at least one hundred to one.

As it turned out he didn't need a 3, although he almost got it. He won the hole with a 4;

Espinosa, trembling like a leaf making his approach putt, left himself a yard or more short and then missed the putt.

Espinosa did the same thing on the extra hole and Hagen won the match, just as he had won his extra hole matches against Watrous and Diegel at Olympia Fields in 1925, one on the thirty-ninth green and the other on the fortieth after being three down and four to play.

Hagen and Turnesa had a great match in the final—a match that was decided on the last nine holes. For all his 71 to Hagen's 77 in the morning Joe was only two up, but when he won the first hole in the afternoon round to be three up things began to look bad for the defending champion.

The cooling of Turnesa's putter in the afternoon round, however, left him stranded and Hagen retained his title by the narrow margin of one hole.

Both during the tournament and coming back on the train afterward we learned a great deal concerning Hagen's methods.

What is there about him that makes him such a marvel? The main reason for his success is that he plays the game of golf with his head as well as with his body and his clubs.

There's not a minute during a golf match that Hagen isn't thinking. He's just two thinks ahead of his opponent all the way.

Another reason is his wonderful self-control.

Hagen is the greatest forgetter of bad golf shots in the business. Walter starts out knowing that he can't possibly play perfect golf. He figures in advance that he is bound to play a few bad shots and he allows for them before they happen. When they do he isn't disturbed. He takes them as a matter of course and proceeds to forget all about them.

Then too he is a keen student of psychology without knowing it. Without any "goat-getting" tactics, he "works" on his opponents or at least lets them "work" on themselves, which they invariably do.

They can start out courageously enough, but the fact that it is Hagen they're playing has its inevitable effect. Sooner or later it reacts against them.

And finally he has one shot at his command that no one else has—a low mashie-niblick, a wind-cheater that lights and bites.

A great golfer, Hagen. The greatest match player the world has ever seen, and we don't mean perhaps.

Well-known professional Johnny Farrell engages in animated conversation with Aileen Riggin, the celebrated mermaid, when their paths crossed in Tampa this past winter.

Grand Slam "Gam" BY SPECTATOR

A Golfer with a Howitzer Carry

"Jim," said Leo Diegel to the godfather of the four-leaf clover, "I'll lay you $25 that boy over there can hit a golf ball farther than anyone else in this field." The field happened to consist of the group at the National Open at Olympia, so Jim Barnes wasn't particularly stinted in his choice of a candidate.

The arch enemy of plus fours was visibly impressed. "Do you mean it?" he asked.

"Absolutely," said Leo. "Pick your man."

"Let's see this boy swing," suggested Barnes cautiously and they strolled over to where Clarence Gamber of Pontiac, Michigan, was hitting some pitch shots.

"Give us a full shot with the wood, Gam," requested Diegel. Gamber picked up his driver and there was an ominous swish. Barnes' eyes widened. "Watch it as far as you can see it," suggested Diegel with a grin as the caddie turned and started on a modified marathon towards the horizon. Long Jim was silent. "Well, who do you want to bet on," demanded Diegel.

"Him," said Barnes succinctly, pointing to Gamber. "I didn't know the things could be hit that far."

At Oakmont a year ago the twelfth hole extended over 600 yards and most of the hitters used a drive, a brassie and a pitch to get home. On one round Gamber was on the green with a drive and an iron.

At Sacramento last winter a driving contest followed a tournament. Gamber, fully dressed, harkened to the pleas of Al Watrous, borrowed a club and stepped on the tee. They had about concluded the performance.

"Where is the long ball and who hit it," demanded Gamber.

Watrous pointed to a flag and added, "John Rogers." Clarence waggled the driver.

"Take off your coat and put on some spiked shoes," suggested Al.

"Don't think it's necessary," replied Gam and he smacked one fifteen yards beyond the flag. "Let 'em shoot at that," he said, simply tossing the borrowed driver back to its dumbfounded owner.

This year at Olympia, Gamber reached the fourteenth tee, where a small crowd was congregated. "They're discussing Bobby Jones' drive here," said Diegel to Gamber. "Bobby is here himself, too, so stick your tummy in one."

"I gave it all I had," said Clarence, "and Diegel estimated I was twenty-five yards beyond Jones when my ball rolled into a ditch that was supposed to catch poor second shots and I had to lift out and take a penalty stroke. Some members of the club came up afterward and told me it was the first ball ever driven in that ditch. We were back on the long tee, so I must have gotten a good one."

The Muskegon Golf Club has a hole six hundred and eleven yards long, par six. The average player stumbles exhaustedly onto the green after a drive and as many brassies as he can remember or cares to admit. Gam hit one off the tee there once, and then, to the consternation of the natives, whacked a wicked second home. This left him four putts for a par, three putts for a birdie, two putts for an eagle and one putt for a double eagle!

Citizens of Muskegon cherish this feat as a local tale of folklore and it is usually told the little children right after they've mastered the wonders of Santa Claus.

Whence comes all this power?

One of the significant factors lies in the fact Gam strips at one hundred and ninety pounds and yet does business with a thirty-two-inch waist, and if you think this is simple try it out on your own tape-measure and torso. Gam is reminiscent of Ring Lardner's first remark after glimpsing Jess Willard. "If that guy ever gets mad," said Ring, "it won't be at me."

Nearly all of Gamber's drive is in the air. Recently on the seventh hole at Bloomfield Hills, which is three hundred yards from the back tee, standing on the extreme rear of the top level Gamber's tee shot actually struck on the putting surface and yet held the green.

"I use my back, left side and shoulders to drive with," says Gamber. "When I was a kid (he's a feeble old man of twenty-six now) I was a 'hitter,' but about five years ago I switched to the 'swinger' type and I know I'm longer and straighter. Watch this," cried the strong boy. "I'm going to take my right hand off when the clubhead is three feet away from the ball on the downswing."

He teed up and cut loose. The right hand left the shaft as promised and a practice ball, agitated to the very depths of its rubber-cored soul, bored away into the distance. It was slightly off line to the right but was hooking. "The right hand would have straightened that into the fairway," he added, "but it wouldn't have gotten so very much farther. If I had taken my left hand off it would have been sev-

enty-five yards short and heaven knows in what direction.

"I'm right-handed but my left shoulder and shoulder muscles are more developed now than my right. I can lift a heavier weight with my left."

"Do you whip your wrists in?" he was asked.

"I don't make any effort to. The 'hitter' does that. I keep my left arm as straight as a gun barrel. This turns the shoulders at right angles to the line of flight or even a trifle beyond at the top of the backswing and I feel a hard pull at the left shoulder. I'm coiled like a spring."

Gamber stands slightly pigeon-toed at the address, which is contrary to the accepted theories, although Cyril Tolley does this to a perceptible degree and pictures indicate Phillips Finlay does slightly. "Turning the left toe inward slightly lets me pivot more freely," said Gamber "and this gets the shoulders further around. I concentrate on the shoulders and the left side."

If Gamber's driver were offered at public auction and sold on its merits it would bring whatever price second-hand hickory could command per cord in the open market. It hasn't one distinguishing, praiseworthy feature. "People tell me it's heavy," laughed Gam, "but I don't believe it weighed over fourteen ounces when it was new five years ago, and probably a quarter of an ounce has been battered out in the meantime. Look at this nick right in the face," he commented dolefully, and a strong man nearly burst into tears. "It's not for sale, though, at any price."

Gamber addresses the ball slightly off the heel of the club and on the backswing he cuts slightly outside the direction line, which isn't done in any of our best textbooks on "How to Drive Two Hundred and Fifty Yards." But Gam isn't interested in two-hundred-and-fifty-yard shots until someone explains how it can be accomplished with a mashie. "I didn't think that tiny push outside the line was ever noticed," said Gamber. "It shouldn't be mentioned and I never taught anyone else to do it. I think I do it because I start the swing with that left shoulder and pushing outward a wee bit seems to start the sweep of a big, wide arc and avoids constriction. I keep my elbows in, though, so my arms aren't floppy."

"What is the longest ball you ever hit?" he was asked.

"That's hard to tell, but the one I tried to hit the hardest and seemed to get good results was on the seventy-second tee in the Michigan Open this summer at Indianwood. I started 74, 73, 71 but George Von Elm was hot and I trailed him half a dozen shots. On the fourth round I was playing a few holes ahead of him and when I got on the eighteenth tee someone told me George was dropping a few strokes and as I had a par five for a 70 I figured a 3 might tie him."

The eighteenth hole at Indianwood is five hundred and thirty yards and two hundred and forty yards from the tee is an abrupt slope that runs fifty yards. Wilfrid Reid, who designed the course and is the professional there now, estimates it is two hundred and ninety yards to the top of the rise.

"I gave that tee shot all there was in me, for I wanted as short a second as possible. The ball carried over the top of the rise—it must have been in the air three hundred yards—and I got a long roll. The newspapers estimated the drive was three hundred and sixty-five yards. I don't know how long it was but I know I just had a mashie pitch left. I decided to take a four-iron and steer one right up to the flag and you know what happens to those 'steered' shots. This was just one more of the abominable breed and it skidded off and I lost the title by a stroke."

An interesting side light on the power of Gamber's game comes from his work in the bunkers. When an explosion shot is on the card it is a treat to stand by at a respectful distance and witness the spectacle.

When his niblick strikes the ground most of the bunker seems to blast its way upward in a horrible fury; the sky grows dark; and thereafter sand, pebbles, black earth, molten lava and hitherto unsuspected species of subsoils descend upon the green in a steady shower for a five-minute period. Foursomes following are diverted and forced to detour until wrecking crews can blast their way down to the top of the flag.

Gamber has spent the last few years teaching at Pine Lake. "I'm booked from morning until night," he said, "and the only golf I play myself is Saturday afternoons occasionally, Sundays and one round Monday. Next year I'm going to find a place where I can practice on my short-irons. If they'd play the Open in September, use a course where the par threes were two hundred and forty-nine yards up hill, and the other fourteen holes were four hundred and seventy-five yards or over, I'd put down about twenty dollars on Gamber to win at the prevailing odds and drive home in a Cadillac."

Always use the club that takes the least out of you. Play with a long iron instead of forcing your shot with a short iron. Never say, "Oh, I think I can reach it with such and such a club." There ought never to be any question of your reaching it, so use the next more powerful club in order that you will have a little in hand.

HARRY VARDON

A Close-Up of Bobby Jones BY GRANTLAND RICE

Explaining a Few of the Simpler
Details That Make Up His Game

THERE ARE CERTAIN DETAILS CONNECTED WITH Bobby Jones' game that are beyond explaining. These include his complete co-ordination and his almost perfect smoothness that belong to genius. They are matters not to be defined in words. They can be seen and followed, but they cannot be taken apart for any casual inspection.

But there are also simpler details of his swing which can be more accurately hung up for public view. Where one might never understand just how any mere mortal can keep hitting the ball in exactly the same way and hitting it almost perfectly round after round, one can at least understand part of the physical accompaniment.

One of the first points to notice in Bobby Jones' play is the closeness with which he holds his feet together, even on full shots. Even on the drive I don't believe his feet are more than a foot apart, certainly not more than fourteen inches. Frequently on his pitch shots there is less than six inches separating the heels. On the short chip shots his heels are closer still, while in putting they are almost touching.

This matter of bringing the feet closer together than most golfers has two distinct values. In the first place it reduces tension throughout the body. It is more natural to stand with the feet fairly close than it is to spread them out in the braced attitude so many golfers use.

In the second place there is a feeling of better and easier balance. There is less tendency to hit with the body, a fault that has driven several million golfers into the borderland of melancholy depression, year after year. If you stand, for example, with your heels touching, you will find it practically impossible to use the body in the swing. If you attempt to do so you have the feeling of falling down. The closer stance where the feet are involved is a big factor in calling more upon the use of hands and wrists and arms.

There is still another aid to be obtained from this proximity of the feet. It makes the turn of the left hip a simpler, easier matter and this also applies to the transference of weight where there is less distance to be covered. Jones gets a world of leverage from this turn of the left hip. There is a greater tendency to keep the body locked and rigid with the feet spread too far apart for any comfortable body turn.

So ease and greater freedom of swing, better

This is Mr. Jones' address for a mashie-niblick pitch. The close proximity of his feet, a Jones characteristic that enables him to execute a wonderfully balanced body turn, is evident here. His heels are not quite four inches apart.

Mr. Jones at the end of his backswing for a fifteen-foot putt. Notice how his eyes are directly over the ball.

This unusual action shot of Bobby Jones vividly shows how the champion keeps his chin tilted to the right throughout the swing and how he shifts his weight from the right to the left foot well before hitting the ball.

balance and greater use of hands and wrists are among the features that his closer foot action brings about.

It has been stated on several occasions that the straight left arm in golf is not necessary. It isn't. Vardon has a slight kink in his left elbow at the top of the swing and other fine golfers have about the same bend. But in the case of Jones he uses a left arm as straight as a rod of steel.

I watched him in practice at Brae Burn before his final match. For ten or fifteen minutes he hit almost every type of shot—drive, brassie, long-iron, full pitches and short pitches—and without exception he called on the straight left for every type of stroke. If there was the slightest kink in Jones' left elbow, it was not visible to the naked eye. It was not caught by the camera. The marvel of his swing was the way he could cock his left wrist at the top without bending the left arm. He had reduced his swing to two main hinges—the left shoulder and the left wrist. The hinge at the left elbow is eliminated. Naturally this leads to greater accuracy—the more hinges, the more chance for trouble.

Jones gives the impression of left shoulder power and left shoulder control. You can sense a feeling of strain or torsion in this left shoulder for any full swing. He also has a marvelous amount of leverage or punch in his cocked left wrist. There is firmness here, but no sign of stiffness. You get the impression that it is controlling the whip of the clubhead with the right hand coming in for the final flip or crack or blow.

There is still another feature of the Jones swing worth some study. This is the way he turns his chin slightly to the right as he addresses the ball. This was a trick that Jerry Travers always employed to make it easier and simpler to keep the head uplifted. Both seem to be looking at the ball with the left eye. When the chin is turned to the right it is more of an effort to look suddenly along the line of flight. It helps to keep the head fixed, a sort of subconscious suggestion to look away from the path of the ball where every human tendency is to see at once—often too quickly—just what has happened. This frequently takes place before anything has happened, before the clubhead has ever reached the ball.

Jones was badly bothered by his erratic putting up to 1922. I recall one round he had

at Columbia in the 1921 Open where he took three putts on nine greens and still turned in a 77. He had every opportunity to break 70, but his putter blocked the road. At that time he was experimenting with various putting styles. A trifle later he went to a putting cleek and brought his feet close together, not quite, however, as closely as they are held today.

In the United States Open of 1922 his feet were only a few inches apart, possibly two or three. Today the heels are almost touching. He has found again that this method helps him to a feeling of greater relaxation on the green and also to a slighter temptation to use the body in the putting stroke.

The Amateur Champion says he makes no direct effort to keep his body still, fearing a feeling of stiffness. But the fact is that his body seems to be completely still on all shorter putts from two to six or seven feet in length where the hands and wrists do practically all the work. So far as championship golf is concerned there has never been a surer putter from three, five, or seven feet away than Jones.

He has a light, firm touch that is as smooth as velvet. It is his idea to get the ball just about to the cup, rather than ram for the back of the tin. For in the gentler putting system there is a wider target to hit—over four inches against a trifle more than two inches. A putt just getting up to the cup with only a slight run left will usually drop in from either side. But if hit too stoutly it must find the exact center of the cup. This can be overdone by not getting the ball up to the cup, but it accounts for the fact that you almost never see one of Jones' putts from shorter ranges hit in and then hop out, one feature of golf that wrings raw agony from the most stoical of souls.

These features of Jones' play are mere segments, taken from a swing that is largely genius. One might as well attempt to describe the smoothness of the wind as to paint a clear picture of his complete swing. The co-ordination between all working muscles and between these and the eye is uncanny in a game where co-ordination, even among the elect, so often crumbles up or goes upon a zig-zag journey.

Hagen the Artist BY ROBERT E. HARLOW

Intimate Observations by His Manager

IF THERE IS ONE EXPRESSION WHICH WALTER Hagen has heard his manager use more than any other over a period of seven years of association on the road in America, Canada and Europe, it is this: "Come on, Haig; hurry up."

Hagen is the slowest-moving individual I have ever encountered. He can linger longer over playing a card at the bridge table than anyone of my acquaintance. If there is ten minutes to reach the theatre at something like the opening hour, Hagen can meet a friend, or stranger for that matter, in the lobby of his hotel and talk about nothing for thirty minutes.

Once Hagen gave me a good answer.

He was due to start in some minor open tournament and, as usual, was taking his time about getting dressed. He does the most exasperating things. When you at last think he is all ready to leave for the course, he will take a look at the hose he has selected for the day and decide that the stockings do not look as well as he had anticipated. This means another fifteen minutes while he makes a change.

On the particular occasion in question Walter was shaving and time was flying. I realized that, at the best, he would be ten minutes late at the tee. So I was being even more persistent than usual, giving him what must have been the one-hundredth lecture on not keeping his audience waiting. Of course, it did no good. This time Walter stopped, and with razor poised said, "How do you expect me to have a smooth stroke on the green today if I start by hurrying my stroke with this razor? I can't rush around now and change my pace when I start playing golf. I want to be relaxed on the course, so I must be relaxed now."

Of course, one might explain that he could have gotten up an hour earlier and thus had ample time to conduct his dressing and shaving according to the most suitable tempo for the day, but Hagen always has an answer and he would have said that getting out of bed the hour earlier would have been hurrying because he was not ready.

Hagen has the reputation of being late and he has earned it. His tardiness can be attributed to a number of causes. He is by nature very deliberate. He is likewise a leader and hews to his own path pretty much no matter what the consequences may be.

Then, Hagen is a showman, and another contributing cause and a factor of no small importance is that the public—tournament officials and others—have stood for his being late for these many years. He has never been disqualified.

Thus, over a period of years, Hagen has developed to a high degree the habit, a natural one with him, of being deliberate in all his actions. I know that no matter what the circumstances Hagen will take his time and not act until he is ready. Nothing can change his tempo, his unflinching ability to make his muscles follow his mind and at the pace that suits him best.

We have been together in a great many duck-hunting blinds in all parts of the North American continent. Hagen is usually the first man to see a flight in the distant sky and say, "Mark!" And usually the last to shoot. Nothing gives him a bigger laugh than to wait until the man in his blind fires, and, if his companion misses, for him then to drop the duck just as the bird is getting out of range. Hagen is as deliberate in a duck blind as he is on the green.

Our last shoot was near Tulie Lake in Oregon last fall. Just before dusk Hagen said "Mark!" and pointed out six large mallards coming towards our blind. Without the least show of excitement Hagen waited as they circled three or four times while the leader was making up his mind whether to decoy. These birds were very shy and seemed disinclined to come down. Finally, they got into a position which suited Hagen. He stood up and raised his automatic. There was no hurried movement. I watched as he covered the leader of the six mallards. To me it seemed a long time before he finally pulled, but he knocked the leader three feet in the air and the duck dropped, a thoroughly dead bird.

Hagen had six shells and he dropped all six ducks and there was never a hurried movement in the entire performance. It was an artistic job from start to finish. He never pulled once until he was satisfied he had the duck lined up, and then with his unfaltering eye and finished touch he fired and the unhappy bird fell from the sky. Surely there is a close relationship to Hagen in a duck blind and Hagen on the putting greens.

There is no doubt that Hagen is the greatest artist that golf has produced. I never take part in arguments that this or that golfer is better than Hagen. I never offer a protest when some of the Southern sports writers everlastingly start their copy with this line: "Bobby Jones, the world's greatest golfer," and I never complain when the journalists of London tell me that for many years Harry Vardon was never off the fairway. I give these gentlemen all the credit in the world. From a mechanical view Vardon in his day and Jones in this day both may have found a better groove in which to swing their clubs and both may have been able to everlastingly keep their clubheads in that groove.

But let a discussion commence of who is the greatest artist golf has produced and I am ready for debate. Who of the links but Hagen creates the same atmosphere one feels when Raquel Meller stands in the center of the stage in Paris and sings her songs of romance to an enraptured audience? When Raquel goes off the stage she takes something with her that leaves the efforts of the other performers almost vain. Impossible to obtain anything but standing room in the Royal Theatre in Leeds, England, on a Saturday night when she broke the house attendance record, I stood and watched Gracie Fields hold that great audience for song after song, without as much as a whisper from any part of the house. This is the greatest tribute any artist can receive, because it means complete attention.

Only the real artists get that sort of recognition from their audiences, and I noted in the crowds that followed Hagen at Muirfield, and that listened to Gracie Fields in England and Raquel Meller in Paris, the same sort of enthusiasm.

At Leeds, Gracie took call after call and finally had to tell her audience she could sing no more that night.

That was the sort of enthusiasm that Hagen got from his audience at Muirfield in the British Open this year, not alone because he was winning but because of the artistic rather than the mechanical method in which he was doing the trick. I heard one man say, "I prefer seeing this man do a 90 than any other golfer a 70."

Why did Hagen win at Muirfield? Not being at all times a mechanically perfect hitter of a golf ball Hagen needs, then, an inspiration to make him do his stuff and nowhere does he have a greater inspiration than when he stands on the sand dunes of the old country for a try at the British Open, especially when the championship comes directly following a Hagen defeat. Defeat, which he takes as graciously as any sportsman living, at the same time hurts and rouses a hidden fire within him.

Hagen went to Muirfield having been badly beaten in his singles match in the Ryder Cup at Leeds by George Duncan, an inspirational golfer who has allowed the mechanics of the game to befuddle and confound him so that half the time he is the artist that is in him, and the rest of the time he is striving to make a robot of his arms, legs, hips, wrists, ankles, knees, neck, and whatever other portions of the anatomy enter into the manufacture of the perfect swing.

Sometimes he lapses into the pure artist when everything is easy and simple and he operates not on theories but on inspiration, and then he moves majestically on in perfect figures. The only British Open Duncan ever won, at Deal the year Hagen started his career in British golf, he won in the last two rounds under the magic spell of an inspiration. On that day Duncan had no idea where his right knee was in any given position. I presume that he beat Hagen both in the Ryder Cup matches at Leeds and in the Yorkshire *Evening News* tournament at Leeds because again he was playing upon inspiration and not theory. He had a burning desire to conquer the most talked-of man in the game, and a golfer whom he believes in his heart to be inferior to himself as a striker of the ball.

Duncan is not as fortunate as Hagen at selecting the right time for the inspiration to come upon him. Hagen in his deliberate way waits patiently his hour. In the duck blind he is first to see tiny black spots against the horizon and he knows that the big flight is on, and in his deliberate, painstaking way he makes ready for the kill.

So on the links. For the past twelve months Hagen had played at golf, doing nothing serious. For the first time in five years he lost his title as American professional champion. At Chicago he made quite a bold bid for the American Open and failed, and for the rest of the summer, fall, winter and spring, life had been just a picnic for Hagen, marked by an occasional burst of speed, but with nothing to rouse him to a major effort. Tournaments for money prizes do not inspire Hagen, no matter how great the purse. If he looks at the crowd at exhibitions it is not to count them, but with the same regard as some artists in the theatre look up at the balcony to throw kisses. I have known Hagen to stay at a party until five in the morning when at nine o'clock he was due at the first tee to play the final thirty-six holes in a tournament, the winning of which would have meant ten thousand dollars to him. He was having too good a time to leave.

But the British Open, the American Open and the American Professional Championship during the years he was establishing his record run of wins in the events—then Hagen rose to the occasion and became at times in these events the most accurate striker of a golf ball in the world and by far the greatest artist of the game. That is why in his last six starts in the British Open he has had four firsts, a second and tied for third once, when if he had not attempted to hole a mashie niblick shot, he might very well have been second. That is why for four years he won the American Professional Championship, and while he has only won the American Open twice, and not for a number of years, he has often been a factor right up to the last hole.

Hagen is a most observing person. In eight years of travel with him I have been astonished by the manner in which he will take in details. He is especially interested in mechanical equipment of all sorts, and farming, and in travelling in Europe will very often point out a piece of farming machinery, and although he has never seen anything like it, he very quickly comprehends just what it is for and how it is operated. Coming from Berlin to London he quickly observed how much further crops were advanced in Germany and in The Netherlands than in England. In flying from Berlin to Vienna he pointed out that the farming communities in Germany were organized in quite a different way from those in the United States, and while flying at several hundred feet over the countryside, pointed out and described the difference.

Upon returning from the Berlin Golf Club, where he was engaged in the German Open Championship, he described to a number of people in the minutest detail, some of the ensembles worn by the women and some of the coats, shoes and other wearing apparel of the gentlemen in the gallery. On the last day of the German Championship, while he was making these observations, he scored 71-72.

And so in golf. When it is all very obvious, Hagen has no great advantage over the rest of the field, because there is no great difference in the physical gesture of striking the ball. There are many others who can perform this feat about as well as Hagen, but when it comes to ground condition and elements, there are many problems to be solved; when each stroke needs considerable thinking out, when the hole has to be visualized and analyzed, and when Hagen has a sufficient inspiration for really concentrating on the job, then Hagen becomes the greatest artist of the game.

Walter Hagen congratulates British professional Archie Compston after the latter won a 72-hole match at Moor Park, England, by the lopsided margin of eighteen-and-seventeen.

A fine study of the intentness with which Hagen approaches each shot at hand.

My Angle of Putting BY WALTER HAGEN

Some Advice from One of the Greatest
of Them All

IT IS SURPRISING HOW MANY GOLFERS SEEM TO think that putting is all a set pattern where everything is grooved and the body must be held as stiff as a post so that nothing can move but the wrists.

Sometimes I doubt if anyone ever hits two putts in succession exactly alike. I know I don't. Putting is too much a matter of feel and touch to be treated that way. And while the body must be kept out of the swing, it is a mistake to keep the body stiff and rigid.

My first thought in putting is to get comfortable in taking my stance. If you don't feel comfortable you will tighten your hands and wrists and start jabbing the ball. All I try to think about once I have taken a comfortable stance is to be sure I have a smooth swing, more of a stroking motion than a hit. Yet I often putt just the way I happen to feel that day, sometimes even cutting the ball slightly.

Putting is much more a mental proposition than it is a physical matter. Let me try to explain what I mean. At the last Amateur Championship I stood by the edge of the eighth green and watched the field come by. This green was quite keen, with some unusual slopes and grades. I saw golfer after golfer come up to his ball and apparently study the line of the putt. But you could see from the expressions of most of them that, under the strain, they were not thinking about anything but getting the putt over with. Few of them had any sharp, clear idea of what the right line was. Many of them would putt directly for the cup and then watch the ball slip well off to the right below the hole. They thought they were concentrating in the right way or actually thinking out and solving the problem of the right line, but they were not. They looked to be in a trance. At least many of them did. Or else they were still guessing as they hit the ball nervously, often lifting their heads to see whether or not they had guessed correctly, and the result was disappointing.

Then later on I saw Bobby Jones and George Voigt come by. They were different. Both lined up the approach putt and you could see from their expressions that each one was doing some clear, unmuddled thinking. They made up their minds in advance and then stroked the putt in the right way. The difference was marked.

The first thing needed for good putting is mental balance. This means mental and nerve control—coolness, lack of worry, a feeling of ease, and decision that isn't half guessing.

Make some decision on the line and the speed of the greens and then play it that way—right or wrong. You are almost sure to be wrong if you are still guessing as you hit the ball.

Have you ever noticed how often you hole a five- or six-foot putt with one hand when you are out of the hole? That means that with the strain lifted you are relaxed and you let the head of the putter have its way without checking it or hurrying it. When golfers begin to miss short putts of two, three and four feet it is usually because they are gripping too tightly, the sign of too much tension. Loosen the grip a little, try to pick out a more comfortable stance and keep the swing smooth. This will often help a lot.

I keep my weight largely on my left foot, but such fine putters as Bobby Jones and Jerry Travers keep their weight almost evenly balanced. The matter of weight and stance doesn't matter so much, so long as you feel comfortable and natural, anything to cut down tension and the feeling of stiffness and tightness. Keep your body out of all short putts or fairly short ones, but that doesn't mean to turn your body into a stone post. There can be no feel when you are that way, all tightened up. I've seen a lot of good putters use a lot of different methods, but I never saw a good putter who looked stiff and uncomfortable. They simply don't go together.

The author executing an approach putt during the National Open Championship last year.

Horton Smith of Joplin BY HAL SHARKEY

Being a Missourian Bred and Born,
He Has Shown'Em

THE NAME HORTON SMITH HAS BEEN THE THEME song of the winter sequence of professional tournaments. From an unknown outsider the Missouri boy, who won't be twenty-one years old until May twenty-second, has notched a record that is scarcely credible. It would be remarkable if it had been accomplished by some established star. As the achievement of a comparative unknown, the record is astounding.

Over a five-month span Smith has participated in nineteen open tournaments, against the stoutest opposition the profession has to offer, and he has been worse than fourth only four times. Seven times he won and four times he was runner-up, once after a play-off. In other words, he was either first or second better than fifty per cent of the time.

Playing over a great variety of courses, under widely varying conditions, this youth averaged slightly over 71½—less than even 4's—for seventy-three rounds of highly competitive golf. He did that while traveling more than 13,000 miles by rail and water.

Horton won in extreme cold weather in Oklahoma, and he was only one shot behind first place in the tropical heat of Hawaii. He was runner-up twice on rolling courses in Southern California, and he was second in the big money event on the flat prairie of Texas. He putted equally well on the sand greens of Arkansas, the cocoos bent on the Pacific Coast or the Bermuda grass in Florida. He finished first, one shot ahead of Walter Hagen, at Catalina, the shortest course played on the winter trip, and he was fourth, tied with George Von Elm, in the Los Angeles Open, over the 7000-yard Riviera layout. Most surprising, he enjoyed signal success on his first trip to Florida, where the veterans always have claimed it required experience to get the hang of playing iron shots from the sandy fairways.

In the course of his conquests Smith won from in front and he came from behind, and he scored victories by trading shots with the best in the game. He registered his first win, at Oklahoma City, on a front run, in which he triumphed by one shot from a field that included Tommy Armour, Al Espinosa and Bill Mehlhorn. At Catalina he won again by a single stroke, this time holding off Hagen. At Pensacola, where he achieved four extremely consistent rounds of 68, 68, 70 and 68, Smith won from in front against Gene Sarazen, Mehlhorn, Bobby Cruickshank and other stars. At Fort Myers, Florida, he came from behind with two 67's the final day to overhaul, among others, Sarazen, Densmore Shute, whom he later defeated in a play-off, and Clarence Hackney, former Canadian Open champion. In the Florida Open at Jacksonville, Smith matched blow for blow with Johnny Farrell and finished two shots ahead of the National Open champion.

Then came the $15,000 La Gorce Open, which brought a galaxy of stars to Miami Beach. After playing twenty-seven holes Smith appeared to be out of the race, for his first three nines were 38, 37 and 39, a pace not good enough to win. Just when he seemed likely to return a first-day total of 152 of 153, too far behind to win, Horton played the more difficult second nine in 32, four under par, and his total of 146 for the first day's play left him tied for second, three shots behind the leader. A 70 on the third round moved him up to the lead, and he stayed there by scoring a 73 on his final round for a total of 289, thus adding first prize of $5000 to his winter's earnings.

What manner of youth is this tall, slender chap whose rise to the heights has been so swift and sure? The Ryder Cup team's youngest member is also the tallest member of the squad. Smith rises six feet one-and-a-half inches off the ground and he weighs one hundred and sixty-three pounds. He has taken advantage of his height to gain leverage. He stands quite upright so that his clubhead describes a wide arc despite a shortened backswing. Horton formerly crouched over the ball, but in the course of his constant self-examination and search for improvement, he abandoned that address.

The youngster's pleasant, boyish face rarely shows any sign of displeasure. He has an easy smile and good nature looks out of his blue eyes all the time. His golf temperament is excellent. The writer has watched Horton many times and he cannot recall one word or act of temper displayed by the newest luminary of this most exasperating of all games.

If there is one trait outstanding in Smith it is foresight. His career has been carefully planned and his development shaped just as

studiously by his habit of introspection. He thinks things out for himself and he has devoted much thought to his own swing. He began figuring things out for himself when he took up the game at the age of twelve and he has kept up the analysis ever since. The result is that at twenty-one the tall Missouri lad knows exactly what he wants to do on every shot that confronts him. There is none of the hit-or-miss about his shot-making that characterizes the play of many young golfers who come by a good swing naturally without giving much thought to how or why. Instances come to mind of young competitors who were more successful as care-free hitters of the ball than they were after they started figuring out what it was all about, as the saying goes, but Horton Smith isn't one of them.

As a novice of grade school age Smith never missed an opportunity to study better players and determine whether what he noted could be applied profitably to his own game. In this way his game improved rapidly. On one occasion, after he had progressed as an amateur and was even then molding plans to take up golf as a profession, he made a trip from his home in Springfield, Missouri, to St. Louis to observe noted professionals playing in a tournament there.

"I didn't have the nerve to enter myself," Horton recalls with a smile.

A little later, when his determination to become a professional was becoming more fixed, he put himself to the test by playing as an amateur competitor in three mid-summer open tournaments in Missouri. In these trials, in 1925, the seventeen-year-old schoolboy deliberately matched his game against the recognized stars. His showing was good enough to be encouraging.

Satisfied he was not hopelessly outclassed, the amateur continued to work on his game. The following summer he turned professional, but not even then did he cease his well-planned preparation for what he had decided upon as his vocation. Realizing that a golf professional ought to know more than how to swing a club, Horton spent the summer of

1926 as a shop assistant, where he applied himself with typical zeal to learning all he could absorb about the mechanics of clubmaking. Vacation over, he returned to college, still with his plan of a golf professional's career definitely determined. The following spring, 1927, he put away his textbooks and took a club job.

Two somewhat false impressions have been circulated about Smith. One is that he is a rube type, the other that he abandoned a career as a country school teacher to become a professional golfer. Both ideas are mistaken. Horton was born and lived all his boyhood in the urban town of Springfield, a city of 40,000 which is no more rural than Broadway and Forty-second Street. Smith has a drawl and a manner that might suggest the cows and chickens, but it just happens that way. Horton's higher education was gained at a State Teachers' College in Springfield. This school, in addition to preparing school teachers, also has some general courses, one of which Smith took. Horton never considered the rôle of school-room pedagogue. From his high school days he was decided to do all his teaching in the more profitable subjects of driving, approaching and putting.

In the summer of 1926 Horton became shop assistant to Neil Crose, the Springfield Country Club professional. In the fall he won the Class B (for assistants) championship of the Midwest P. G. A. He also took time off from school to go to the Oklahoma City Open. This time he finished twenty-seventh. That was when the migratory professionals were on their way to the Pacific Coast, and when they returned the following February, Horton again did battle with them at Hot Springs, Arkansas. But they had been golfing all winter, while he was in college, and he did no better than he had in the fall. It is interesting to note that two years later, on the winter tour of 1928-29, Smith won the Oklahoma City Open and tied for first at Hot Springs.

That second disappointing showing in February, 1927, convinced Smith that to do any good in tournaments a fellow had to play a lot of golf. A month later he quit college to take a job as professional at the Sedalia Country Club. Later in the season he also contracted with the Jefferson City Country Club, sixty-five miles away, and from then on spent three days a week at each club.

That summer Horton qualified in his district for the National Open. He was riding on the train to Oakmont when he read the pairings in a newspaper. One bracket contained these names: "H. Smith, Sedalia, Mo., and George Duncan, Great Britain."

"I came near getting off the train and going right back home," Horton recalls. It's a good thing he didn't.

A calm, pleasant disposition is no small part of Horton Smith's golfing make-up.

The Passing of the Half-Shot

BY HUMPHREY L. G. FRY

Fuller Selection of Clubs Eliminates
One of the Problems of Earlier Days

"YOU SPARED IT, SIR, YOU SPARED IT," SAID THE great man, shaking his head reprovingly.

I turned to him with something like despair. "But you told me not to press—to take it easy. I wanted to play a full shot with a mashie, and you insisted on a half-shot with a mid-iron. Now look where I am," and I pointed feelingly at the ugly-looking trap to the right of the green into which my ball had ignominiously sailed.

He regarded me rather more gently, though a note of patient resignation still lingered in his tones. "Yes, sir," he went on, "I told you to take a mid-iron, and I also told you to play a half-shot. But I told you one other thing, too. I said 'take a half swing and hit it firmly.' Now what you did was to take a full swing and hit it loosely—sloppily. And I'm not exaggerating," he added, with what seemed to me unnecessary vehemence.

All this occurred in England during those halcyon pre-war days when golf was not quite such a serious business as it sometimes is today. It was before the age of super-efficiency in the manufacture of balls and clubs. You could not pay more than two dollars for a driver or five shillings for a lesson from the champion. We were, in fact, ridiculously casual about our golf, and somewhat shamefaced in admitting a desire to be too proficient. Receiving a lesson at all was much frowned upon and only undertaken as a last resort—when the outlook had become so hopeless that a man's home and family were seriously threatened.

As for putting practice between the rounds of a tournament—well, men were often blackballed for such palpable enthusiasm, though more frequently they were dragged bodily to the bar and sentenced to a round of drinks for each practice putt. It is related that some poor fellow was permitted thirty-six putts before he was made aware of the club rule by a joyous, self-appointed committee. The scratch medal in that tournament was won by a teetotaller with a handicap of thirty-six, while the victim of putting *trop de zèle* severed relations with his banker the following morning. The breach is not yet healed.

Occasionally, however, some of us were

barefaced enough to defy tradition and apply ourselves with something like zest to the improvement of our game. It was one of these occasions which led to the conversation recorded above. I had been playing my irons deplorably for about six weeks, and had long ceased to be an acceptable member of society. Drastic action alone could save me. I decided to take a course of lessons. The keen eye of the champion soon detected the root of the trouble. Underclubbing, overswinging and pressing formed the gist of his diagnosis. I had been suffering from that bane of every golfer's existence—an optimistic belief, utterly unfounded on past experience, that every stroke played will turn out to be the shot of a lifetime.

Hence, I was taking a mashie for any shot up to one hundred seventy-five yards, while a mid-iron did service from then on to the furlong mark. I was under the happy impression that I could play two hundred and fifty yards uphill and against the wind with a spoon —or was it a baffy in those days?—and my brassie was reserved for shots requiring a full carry of three hundred yards. Needless to say, these illusions were rapidly dispelled during my first lesson. Subdued and chastened, I was initiated into the mysteries of the half and three-quarter shot.

"Never underclub; always have something in reserve," was my mentor's emphatic advice. With a passing thought for my overdraft at the bank, I acquiesced. Henceforward, one hundred and fifty yards was to be the absolute limit for my efforts with a mashie, while my mid-iron was to be strictly confined to the one hundred and eighty-yard mark. Spoon and brassie shots were proportionately reduced, and with a humble spirit I passed forever from the ranks of the long hitters.

Someone may well be wondering why I did not graduate my iron shots by the use of one, two, three and four irons. Dear reader (for that is how we were wont to address you in those days), there *were* no such animals! Most of us carried a driver, brassie, spoon (or baffy) iron (later renamed mid-iron, owing to the birth of other species), mashie and

putter. A few gifted souls added a cleek—the direct ancestor of the driving or one-iron of today—while others, regarded as eccentric, experimented with fearful-looking novelties known as niblicks and jiggers. Incidentally, I believe it was Mr. R. H. de Montmorency, one of the best iron players in the amateur ranks, who first introduced the jigger. But, as I have said, the majority of us had but one iron club to do duty for all shots between the respective ranges of the mashie and the spoon. Hence the necessity for the half and three-quarter shots.

Pause for a moment, you complacent moderns, whose caddies groan under their load of sixteen clubs, who retard your fellow members while you hold your endless conferences on the merits of a three or four iron, who are equipped with a weapon for every shot in the game—pause and consider the difficulties which beset your forefathers. Imagine yourselves confronted with a one-hundred-and-sixty-five-yard approach. Today you take out your three-iron—or four if you suffer from a superiority complex—play a free, full shot and find your ball nestling snugly on the green. Were the distance increased by twenty or even sixty yards, you would play precisely the same shot, but with a different club—different, that is, in the matter of loft only. Every one of your numerous irons is made to suit the one stroke of which you are capable. To watch your swing for all iron shots beyond the short approach, one would suppose you were faced with only one kind of problem throughout the round.

But with us it was another story. Faced with that same one-hundred-and-sixty-five-yard approach, we found ourselves with no ready-made club built for the occasion. True, we could reach the pin once in a hundred times by taking a terrific crack with a mashie and trusting to a fickle providence, but unless we were afflicted with the mental disease which, as I have already recounted, sent me in despair to a professional, we had no alternative but to take out our mid-irons and play a controlled shot with a halfswing.

Anyone who has ever attempted to master

this particular shot will appreciate that it is among the sterner tasks of humanity, worthy to rank with the labors of Hercules and the crossing of the Alps by Hannibal. The first temptation is to take a full backswing, retard the downward motion, and finally make a feeble, half-hearted jab at the ball—in other words, to spare the shot in the manner described in the opening paragraph. In an endeavor to correct this, one determines not to take the club back beyond the vertical, and all probably goes well until the beginning of the downward swing. At this point some evil spirit persuades us that such a restricted swing will be insufficient to carry the ball more than a few insignificant feet. As a last resort we make a desperate lunge with body, arms and legs, with dire and lamentable consequences.

Even when we have learned to control our swing and at the same time hit the ball firmly and crisply, letting the hands and wrists do the lion's share of the work, there is yet another difficulty, perhaps the hardest of all. A mid-iron has little natural loft, so that it is impossible to play the high soaring type of shot which comes to rest almost where it pitches. On the other hand, the pitch-and-run variety may be ingloriously bunkered in front of the green. Only one solution presents itself. One must learn to impart backspin and play the kind of shot which travels with a low trajectory and yet bites the green when it lands. To be able to do this with consistent results, using only a half swing, is to be numbered among the ranks of the elect, to live in the rarefied atmosphere of those choice spirits who have really mastered their iron play.

There are such players in the world of golf today, but their ranks are thinning out. Or perhaps that is not quite a fair way to put it. There is no doubt that the majority of our great players are capable of the old half-shot, but under modern conditions they are seldom called upon to play it. In the old days a man adapted his shots to his clubs. Today the tendency is to adapt the clubs to the shot. Walk round with any well-known player in a first-class tournament and study his iron play. You will find that his swing never varies. The club manufacturer, in seeking to make the game easier for him, has standardized his play.

Some of us may regret the passing of the half-shot, for with it have departed many of the subtler phases of golfing skill. And yet, despite the clubmakers' devices, one striking fact remains. Let two players of equal skill arrange a match under these conditions: one to carry a full set of clubs and concede half a stroke a hole to his opponent, who is limited to a putter or putting cleek. The latter will win every time. If you are skeptical, try it out on your friends. It makes a splendid betting proposition.

The veteran Scottish professional Sandy Herd at the top of the swing for a half-shot with an iron.

They Can't Stop Jones—Yet BY GRANTLAND RICE

The Georgian Still Carries Too Many
Guns for the Rest of the Field

HARRY VARDON WON HIS LAST BRITISH CHAMpionship when he was in the neighborhood of forty-five years of age. Braid and Taylor won when they were over forty. Walter Hagen won his latest British Open at the age of thirty-six. John Ball was fifty when he won his ninth major title. But at the age of twenty-seven Bobby Jones has tied John Ball's record of nine national conquests and apparently he is just beginning to warm up and get started. With the swing he has and the physical development he carries along he should be good for at least another fifteen or twenty years, not good enough possibly to keep on blasting out the entire field, but good enough to remain the most dangerous single entry in each competition.

Last September, Jones retired from golf for several months. He played only six or seven rounds between September and April. But being a strong husky citizen, only twenty-seven years old, in first-class physical condition, he has the type of swing that responds quickly to a few rounds. All he needs is to oil away the rust, grind off a few kinks, and there he is again just as good as ever. In fact, the long rest brings him a keenness for play which most of the leading pros lack after months of travel and competition that were never intended to help any set of human nerves.

Jones came to Winged Foot in late spring for the National Open, feeling fit and ready, just coming on to his game. He was a bit ragged the first practice round, but after that he sent out warning that he was ready again with a series of sensational performances. In place of being worn out after his play-off with Al Espinosa he said next day that he felt as if he had just started hitting the ball and could use a lot more golf. In other championships, Jones has finished up pretty well tired out, just as the others were. But after his long winter rest he finished this championship without any touch or sign of weariness, with his nerves in better shape than they had ever been at the end of the long Open grind.

The last United States Open was not only full of astonishing events, but it came closer to proving the mysterious swirls of golf than any other ever held. What should the odds have been that Johnny Farrell, the defending champion, would not finish among the first seventy for the first thirty-six holes and would not be able to qualify for the last two rounds? What should the odds have been that Johnny Farrell, in two rounds, would not break an 83?

What should the odds have been that Walter Hagen, British Open Champion, would not finish in the first eighteen and that he would not break 309 on a fast, keen course that was all set to his style of play? What should the odds have been that Bobby Jones would lead his closest rival by six strokes with only six holes left, and, that after this, he would need a hard putt to get a tie on the final green? Here are just a few samples of the many, surprising things that bobbed up in this championship.

It has been said before that golf is full of more astonishing twists and turns, squalls and upsets, swirls and eddies, than any game ever planned or played. This championship proved it. Al Espinosa spotted Bobby Jones six strokes at the sixty-sixth hole and then caught him at the seventy-second. Yet a day later, after getting a two-stroke jump on Jones at the first hole in the play-off, Espinosa then lost twenty-five strokes on the next thirty-five holes. How could this happen? Easily enough when one is over-golfed and suddenly realizes that his timing is gone against an opponent who is hammering every shot straight for the pin.

It has been often asked, in the same way, how Bobby Jones could take two seven's on his way down the stretch, just when he seemed to have the championship won. That, also, is easy. Coming to the eighth green in the final round he had 4-4 left for a 35 going out, with a heavy wind blowing. The battle seemed to be over. Certainly here he was under no great strain.

At this hole he hit the best drive he had struck here during the championship. His high iron shot for the green seemed to be well on a line to the pin. The ball struck near the green on baked out ground and flopped to the trap on the right side. Even then he apparently had a simple five. His niblick explosion came out well, the ball hitting the narrow green well short of the flag. But with a strong following wind, it continued to roll along and finally slid down the bank on the other side under a jutting section of turf. Here he faced a tough shot to play, one that had to be blasted out and gotten up quickly, and again the ball travelled over the green into the trap he had just left.

So, there was a 7. And this 7 did more than add three strokes to his expected par 4. It broke down his confidence. From that point on he could see nothing but traps ahead, traps that might cost him another 7 or 8 and kill off his chance. He got by well enough until he came to the fifteenth hole, just four holes from home. At this point he was five strokes up on Espinosa with four holes left. He knew that Espinosa had finished with 294. He knew he had four 4's left to get his 290. "I wasn't worrying about anything at all at this point," he said later. "I knew the last three holes with the strong, following wind were fairly simple 4's. So I could take a 5 or a 6 on this hole and not have to bother about it. But I didn't want another 7. Yet you can pick up a 7 on this course quicker than you can on any other course I ever saw."

This second 7 where he figured that he had only one bad shot—his drive—came near breaking up his chance.

"I thought my shot to the green, my third, was well on," he said, "but it had struck on and slipped across behind a mound. I thought my pitch back would be close to the cup, but it was six inches too low and after hitting the top of the mound it bounded back. That 7 had exploded in my face before I knew what it was all about. I still had three 4's to win.

"At the sixteenth hole I had a twenty-foot putt for a 3. But it was downhill and it looked fast and I tried to play it safe and the ball stopped four feet short. I missed the putt and then I knew I was in for it with two 4's left for a tie. But it is easier to play good golf when you are behind or tied, than when you are ahead. For in the first two cases you go out for everything and in the last case it is hard to keep from playing safe. I took three putts when I tried to play safe, and I got down in one putt, a twelve-footer, when I had to go for it."

Jones was hitting his irons better than ever before in this championship. Outside of about four bad holes, he was playing the best golf he had ever played before. Winged Foot is one of the most testing courses the championship has known. No other course has so punished a mistake. It was in perfect condition and on the easy side after the long drought, but it still carried a bundle of fangs that were full of poison. One hole cost Farrell an 8 after one mistake. One hole, the sixth, cost Bill Mehlhorn a 10. Al Espinosa needed 8's on the four-hundred-eighty-yard twelfth hole his last round and again in the morning round against Jones. Espinosa lost six shots to par on this one hole in two rounds. And they were playing it as a par 4 over the hard, fast ground.

Jones' four best rounds, out of the six, were 69, 69, 71, 72. This is 281. His two worst rounds were 75 and 79. He still refuses to go as high as 80 in an Open Championship. He has played something like sixty-six rounds of Open Championship golf and has never taken worse than 79. He had a 79 at Scioto, when he won, in 1926 and he has had only one other 79 up to his last round at Winged Foot.

When a golfer as fine as Jones can vary ten strokes—from 69 at the start to 79 at the finish—and then to finish with a 69 again—you can see what can happen on a course bunkered and trapped against mistakes to the final inch.

The play of Hagen and Horton Smith was below expectations as both had played too much tournament and exhibition golf. Hagen was never near his best game. Horton Smith had a number of flashes, but he could not keep it up. He lacked the keenness of his early winter campaign when he was sweeping the field. Smith was hitting the ball beautifully most of the time, but there were just lapses enough to break him up.

Two of the great rounds of the championship were played by Tommy Armour and George Von Elm through the driving, pelting rain, mixed in with a whirl of heavy wind. Von Elm had a 70. Removing his outer shirt, the blond Westerner fought it out in an undershirt and trousers. His bare arms and his bare chest threw off running water, but he continued to hit the ball for the pin. He finished with a 70 through the worst part of the rain, one of the

greatest exhibitions of golf ever seen in any Open. This round gave him a tie with Armour in fourth place.

That same afternoon Armour had a 71 that might easily have been a 65. His driving and his iron play carried the ball up to within four, six, and ten feet of the cup with putts for birdies, but almost none of them dropped. Both Von Elm and Armour would have been well under 70, if either could have found the bottom of the cup with holeable putts.

Gene Sarazen again put up a stout fight, but couldn't quite get by. It remained for young Densmore Shute to be one of the bright stars of the field. He was an amateur only two years ago. In this championship, after a fine start, he had 4's on the last four holes to win. And no one knows how close he came to getting them. On the fifteenth hole of that last round his putt for a 4, a fairly short one, at least a reasonable one, just stayed out by an eyelash. At the four-hundred-and-sixty-yard sixteenth he hit the ball a mile and then played a mashie-niblick on his second. His drive had been longer than he thought for the mashie-niblick carried over the green, up a slope, and he needed another 5. At the seventeenth two fine shots left his ball twelve feet from the cup and his putt for a 3 just curled across the upper rim.

It is by such thin margins that things happen in a golf championship. At the finish Jones needed a twelve-foot putt to tie, and he needed the last half inch of roll the ball got. If that last putt had stayed out Al Espinosa would have been the big hero of the championship. As it was he had to struggle next day twenty-three strokes behind with a strong, sound game completely worn away, beyond control.

Winged Foot officials handled the biggest crowds in Open golf history as well as any golf crowds can be handled. They kept big galleries under good control, and big galleries are none too easy to handle when Bobby Jones begins hitting the ball. The Open Golf Championship of 1929 added another important chapter to the history of American golf.

Diegel the Dazzling BY W. D. RICHARDSON

Golf Knows No More Brilliant Performer
in His Inspired Moments

OF ALL THE GOLFERS IN THE WORLD, THERE IS no one, excepting possibly George Duncan, who is capable of soaring to such heights of brilliancy as Leo Diegel, thirty-year-old homebred who is again the Canadian Open Champion and the P. G. A. titleholder besides. Others, like Jones, Mitchell, Farrell, Sarazen, Hagen, Von Elm, Macdonald Smith and Mehlhorn, occasionally do prodigious scoring feats. But no one, no not even Duncan, can rise to such Olympic altitudes as can this nervous, fidgety, excitable professional whom everyone hails as "the Dieg."

As a matter of fact, no one has ever equalled his 72-hole score of 270, made in winning the San Diego Open in 1920. That represents an average of 67½ strokes, folks. Nor has anyone ever accomplished anything in a major championship like Leo accomplished when he repeated his 1928 victory in the Canadian Open at Kanawaki in July with a score of 274. Par for the Montreal course is 70 and, while a 70 isn't particularly hard to do, especially over a baked course and one greatly on the short side, since it has five par-3 holes, still four rounds averaging 68½ in the strain of a championship test is quite a feat.

No one else in the field was able to do it and the field contained almost all the big guns that were in the United States Open, with the exception of Bobby Jones. Tommy Armour came the nearest to Diegel's mark. But when the shooting was over, the man from the land o' heather and gorse was three shots behind. As a matter of ice-cold fact, those two were the only ones to break par on the four-round total.

Willie MacFarlane, who won the undying fame and glory by being the first man to beat Bobby Jones in a double-round play-off for the Open Championship, and a man not given to making rash statements, once told the writer he would be willing to wager that, given a week's time, Diegel would break the existing record of any course in the country.

Where was it? Oh, yes, it was at the Columbia Country Club in Washington, D. C., that Leo had a 29 for nine holes. He was playing a match with Guy Standifer, well-known amateur. Standifer made a bet that Diegel would not break 69. When Diegel took 39 to play the first nine holes, the wager seemed to be so deep in Standifer's pocket that he rashly offered to bet $100 to $1 that Diegel wouldn't win the bet.

"Take a dollar's worth," flashed Leo, who

proceeded to come home in 29 strokes. When he recovered from his amazement, Standifer paid off on both bets.

Another of his great feats was his 65 against Abe Mitchell in the Ryder Cup matches.

One could almost go on indefinitely recounting sensational feats performed by Diegel. We have mentioned the Canadian Open. The victory was the fourth that Diegel has won in Canada. Four out of seven is quite a record.

When it comes to the United States Open though, he's been something of a "bust," so to speak. He has now played in nine of them and been a contender in only two—once at Inverness, when he made his début, and again at Worcester, five years later.

He's very frank about his failures. Ask almost anyone else to assign a reason for a poor showing and you are liable to be drenched in a torrent of alibis. But with Diegel it is different. "I kicked away both chances," Leo says with complete candor in explaining his failures.

As to assigning reasons for his inability to do better than he has in any of the others, we are stumped. Let's try Leo:

"Here's the answer in a nutshell," says Diegel. "I've never yet come to an American Open Championship either keyed up or excited. I've got to be in a certain frame of mind to have a chance and I've not been in the proper frame of mind at any American Open."

That statement struck us as being queer, for we, along with others, have always felt that his whole trouble was traceable to nerves. We thought that if he only calmed down a bit, eased up, kept cool, he would do better.

We didn't see him at Inverness, where, as he says, he kicked the championship away by finishing something like four over 4's on the last five holes, all par-4 affairs, when a two-over-4's finish would have brought him in the winner. But we did see him at Worcester where he needed only to come home in 38 to win and yet finished with a 78, after going out in 34 and starting back 3, 4.

We recall that it was too much serious thinking about a certain tree to the left of the twelfth fairway that caused him to hit the ceiling there. The tree was no particular hazard, but Leo got it into his head that it was and, getting more and more wrought up over the possibility of pulling his drive behind it as the hole came nearer, did that very thing. His jig was up so far as that championship was concerned.

What Diegel means, we think, when he says he's never come to a championship excited, is that he's never been in the right mental pitch. His is the temperament of a great athlete. He's a bundle of nerves, keen, rarin' to go, and once off, going at break-neck speed either to win or to crash.

He has always been that way. He once told me about a time when he was told by his basketball coach to go into a game. "Do you know," he inquired, "that in the moment that elapsed between getting my orders and getting out on the floor my legs went absolutely dead on me?" That's the way he's been all his life. There used to be a time when the very thought of a competition made him ill.

We thought we detected a different Diegel at Five Farms last year, where he not only dethroned Hagen as the P. G. A. Champion—something no one had been able to do since Gene Sarazen accomplished the trick in a 38-hole final at Pelham in 1923—but gained the title for himself by beating Al Espinosa in the final and Sarazen in one of the early rounds.

We had never seen Leo quite so painstaking as he was there in Baltimore. We since learned that the reason was in his putting. You have perhaps seen his "standing-sitting" style. It is very homely, so homely that on occasions he doesn't use it for that very reason.

But he has implicit confidence in his ability to hole putts when he half sits, half stands and gets those elbows out so that they look like a wishbone.

"If it didn't look so terrible," Diegel says, "all the boys would use it. It is the most scientific method in the world. I've had any number of them try it out and tell me that.

"Sometime prior to 1924 I lost my nerve and to save my soul I couldn't putt in tournaments. It got so bad that I lost several shots each round—from six to eight. I couldn't hole the three- and four-footers which, as you know, are the winning putts. I was jerking the stroke. Finally Willie McGuire of Houston suggested that I get the left elbow out. It hit the nail absolutely on the head.

"In both the Shawnee and Canadian opens that year, both of which I won, I never missed a putt under four feet.

"A great many people think that it was my driving that cost me the British Open Championship this year. That's all bosh. What did happen was this. I never found a putter suitable for approach-putting on the Muirfield greens, which were lightning fast. I should have had a little more loft in order to hold the ball. Listen to this: My score for the first four rounds of the British event, counting the two qualifying rounds and the first two rounds of the championship proper, was 284. That's pretty good. But here's the point: I was scoring despite my putting. Although I had eleven one-putt greens, I also had eleven three-putt greens, and that's not so good.

"I was keyed up perfectly in the British event, driving beautifully, only in four bunkers in six rounds, but used the wrong kind of approach shot—a running shot instead of little pitch shots that would slow the ball up. In the last two rounds when the wind blew so hard, I got down in one putt only once and three-putted something like fourteen greens."

The much-discussed putting position of Leo Diegel.

Leo Diegel just after the start of his downswing. The left heel has already returned solidly back to the ground, the hips have moved to the left, and the shoulders are just beginning to unwind.

It Was a Great Championship BY O. B. KEELER

First Playing of the Amateur Classic
on the Pacific Coast

THE FIRST VENTURE OF THE NATIONAL AMA-
teur Golf Championship west of the Rocky
Mountains—or, indeed, west of St. Louis—
was something of a revelation to all of us
tenderfeet. We came, we saw, and a fine
young Middle Westerner conquered. And all
of us learned a lot of things. Personally, I had
never been closer to the Pebble Beach course
at Del Monte, California, than Denmark
Cross Roads, Kansas, where I was for my sins
snow-bound five days and six nights in the
winter of 1912-13.

I had heard a lot about California, as, I suppose, most people do, these days. I had heard
about a race of supermen who played football; who chucked the pilum and the javelin;
who ran hundreds of yards, and played golf.
I had heard of golf courses designed and
groomed to an excellence unknown elsewhere
in this favored land. So I went west, not
to grow up with the country, but to be
amazed by it.

I was.

That is, to an extent.

The 1929 National Amateur Golf Championship, won by Harrison R. Johnston at
Pebble Beach in a final bout with Dr. O. F.
Willing, is, and on the records must appear,
one of the most remarkable golf championships in history. The defeat of Bobby Jones
in the first round established one record. He
had played in twelve American Amateur
Championships and had lost in every round
except the first; and had won in all the rounds
—in the last round, four times.

So Bobby, the big shot—the ace of the
tournament—came out to Pebble Beach with
four records in view. He could, by winning
this championship, have set a new American
record of five amateur titles. He could make
it three in a row, which has not yet been done.
He could equal Chick Evans' record of winning the Open and the Amateur the same
year. And he could top John Ball's record,
with which he was tied, by winning his tenth
major golf championship. And the only
record he carried back with him to Atlanta
was that of losing in the first round, which
never had happened to him before, in a dozen
American Amateur Championships, and a
couple of British.

Hand it to Johnny Goodman, a smart
young golfer from Omaha. It was he who
ruined Bobby's greatest chance, and threw
a niblick into the works of the first major
championship the Pacific Coast has had.

It is perhaps a deplorable thing to recount, and certainly I do not so present it. But it must be said, as a conscientious reporter must say things at times, that while Omaha doubtless regards Johnny Goodman as a prime hero, California considers him a painful accident that came over two thousand miles to happen.

This, of course, is all wrong.

Johnny Goodman, a good, game kid, showed sufficient stuff to knock off the champion in round one, and so far from killing the show, I think that the elimination of Bobby Jones and George Von Elm in the first day's play left the tournament really and truly open for the first time in half a dozen years. The trouble with the California viewpoint was that California considered the National Amateur Golf Championship as a big act by Bobby Jones.

Now, there is no longer the slightest debate about Mr. Jones being the greatest of all golfers. Even after his sudden and startling defeat at Pebble Beach, the general feeling was that it was a type of misfortune, like breaking a leg or running into a lamp-post.

Nobody assumed that Mr. Goodman had suddenly blossomed into the greatest golfer, after taking two dozen strokes more than Mr. Jones in the National Open at Winged Foot. And Mr. Goodman himself, perhaps a bit dizzy from drubbing Mr. Jones, was knocked off in the next round by William Lawson Little, Jr., an even more callow youngster of eighteen, who went out in turn, after a mighty struggle, and before a miraculously long putt, to the distinguished veteran, Francis Ouimet.

There is no denying that the elimination of Bobby Jones tended to flatten out the tournament at the most beautiful course on which it ever has been played. He gave the fans a show, in practice, with one of his coruscant rounds, a 67; and he worked into a tie with Eugene Homans at 145 for the low medal score, shooting a neat 70, two below par, while a Southern Californian from Chicago, Gibby Dunlap, broke 70 for the only time in the official week with a 69 to lead Bobby the

first qualifying day. But, with too many exhibition matches back of him—and every time he starts is an exhibition match, away from home—Bobby went into the tournament a bit stale mentally, and he had no time to hit his stride, because of the undoubted courage and excellent game of Johnny Goodman.

If Bobby had got by the first day, as he had barely managed to do at Minikahda and Brae Burn, the answer might not have been so startling. But what of it? He was knocked off. And that is answer enough. With the third elimination of George Von Elm on the first day in three successive years, the tournament became an open one; and the veterans knocked the kids hither and yon, and worked into a semifinal round in which the ages ranged from thirty-four years to forty-six, with Harrison Johnston the youngest and Chandler Egan, champion a quarter of a century ago, the oldest. Johnston beat Francis Ouimet and Willing defeated Egan, and for the first time since—well, when was it?—the two finalists were above thirty years of age.

This was interesting, in view of the fact that the Pebble Beach course, revised for this tournament by Chandler Egan, had been heralded as one of the stiffest tests of golf in the world. While I would not go quite this far, I would say that it proved quite stiff enough, without the horrid back-breaking qualities of certain other championship tests I could mention. I would say that the Pebble Beach course amply upheld its reputation, as the forethought of the U.S.G.A. more than justified the choice of Del Monte as a battlefield.

Officially, 70 was broken one single time—by Dunlap, in the first qualifying round—and equalled once, by Jones. After the medal round, par 72 was not hit, so far as I observed. Jones went out in the first round with a card of 75; his conqueror did a 76. A curious record in the final match was that the card of each finalist in the morning round was 80; and that only one birdie was made all day, by Johnston at the long sixth hole, while Willing in his last two matches never shot a single birdie.

It's a tough course, as well as a beautiful one, at Pebble Beach. Indeed, that is the impression I carry away with me from the 1929 National Amateur Championship. In the South, we have no courses suitable to compare with those architectural visions on the Monterey Peninsula, and with those I saw at Los Angeles. And even along the Eastern seaboard, and on the famed black turf of the Middle West, there seems to me nothing so fine and beautiful. I honestly believe that the California courses I have seen, at Los Angeles and near San Francisco, and especially Cypress Point and Pebble Beach, on the Monterey Peninsula, are the finest golf courses in the world today.

Cypress Point is a dream—spectacular, perfectly designed, and set about with white sand dunes and a cobalt sea, and studded with the Monterey Cypress, so bewilderingly picturesque that it seems to have been the crystallization of the dream of an artist who has been drinking gin and sobering up on absinthe. And Pebble Beach is just as good, but no better. The putting surfaces, of cocoos bent, are the richest and finest I ever stepped on, and avoided putting on, for they are indecently fast and tricky in their breaks and slants. The courses in California are so much better than those in the rest of this country that I have no basis for comparison.

The climate, I should say, is considerably overestimated. The general landscape in Southern California especially, where the hand of man has not wielded the watering-pot, is every whit as ghastly as Arizona. Kerr Petrie, in a short and perfervid speech at a press dinner at Del Monte, expressed the opinion that there was likely to be more sun in one hour at Coney Island than in one week at Pebble Beach.

We have heard some quaint tales of California, and some of them are true, and some are as exaggerated as the premature reports of the death of Mark Twain. But as to golf courses, the half has not been told. The denizens of this state simply do not know how good their golf courses are. And as for hospitality, that was understated, too. In courtesy, and cordiality, and sportsmanship, straight through this 1929 championship, the Coast and California have set a pattern that will be as hard to match as the luminous mist that weaves a Maxfield Parrish canvas across the mountains that lead to Point Lobos, over the cobalt waters of Carmel Bay.

Amateur George Von Elm is flanked by Harold Lloyd and Douglas Fairbanks during the National Amateur.

Harrison "Jimmy" Johnston, the new Amateur Champion, playing a dramatic recovery from the water's edge to the eighteenth green in his match with Dr. O. F. Willing.

Still facing the fire twenty-five years after he won his first National Amateur, H. Chandler Egan gave one of the great exhibitions at Pebble Beach in wading through a great field to reach the semifinal.

Young W. Lawson Little, a California amateur, made his first appearance in the National Amateur while at Pebble Beach.

The Style of Harry Vardon BY BERNARD DARWIN

A Sketch of One of Golf's Greatest

AT MUIRFIELD LAST MAY WHEN THE GREAT body of onlookers went surging after the victorious Hagen, there were a few, liking art for art's sake, apart from victory, and disliking a crowd, who went elsewhere. This little band of connoisseurs, at once so modest and so select, was to be seen following Macdonald Smith and Harry Vardon. The one might well have won, but had had a bad time and was out of the hunt; the other, born in 1870, could not hope to win at this time of day. So they were to be watched purely because they were two of the most graceful and beautiful of all golfers.

Till they got to the greens there was nothing in it between them; the older man was fully holding his own in the power of his long game, in the crispness and accuracy of his iron shots. Only when it came to the putting, Vardon's old enemy beset him; he moved his body, he stabbed at the short ones, he went off "at half cock." Otherwise the years might have rolled away and here was still a great master and we might almost have been looking at the invincible player who had dominated golf at the beginning of the century.

I am not going to argue as to whether or not Vardon is the greatest golfer that ever lived. These comparisons are futile. It is

enough that he was *the* golfer of his time. He won the British Open Championship in 1896, 1898, 1899, 1903, 1911 and 1914; he won the American Championship in 1900. He was probably at his very best in 1898 and 1899, before his visit to America. In point of health and strength he was not quite the same man afterwards and he himself has said that he thinks he left a little of his game there. It was not till some little time later that his actual and very serious illness developed and he won two more championships after he was well again, but never again did he show the same utterly crushing superiority, which caused Andrew Kirkaldy to say that he would break the heart of an iron ox.

Of the "triumvirate"—Vardon, Braid and Taylor—Taylor is actually the youngest by a few months, but he was the first to make his name. He leaped into fame in 1893 when he began knocking down the big men like ninepins and in both 1894 and 1895 he was champion. Very few people had heard of Harry Vardon then, nobody perhaps save a few golfers in the north of England who had backed him in a home-to-home match against Sandy Herd and seen him badly beaten. In the winter of 1895-96 half a dozen leading professionals were asked to go out to play at Pau, France; someone of discerning judgment made Vardon one of the party and the rest of the world asked "who is this fellow Vardon?"

Then in the spring of 1896 Taylor, twice the champion, played Vardon on his home course at Ganton in Yorkshire and came away beaten by a pocketful of holes and declared that here was the man that he feared most in the coming championship. It was a sound piece of prophecy, for the two tied at Muirfield and Vardon won on playing off. In the next year the new star waned a little and then in 1898 blazed out in full glory.

For the next two years, if Vardon was in the field no one looked any further for the winner; he crushed everyone. He once beat Taylor at Newcastle in Ireland by twelve and eleven and Taylor was playing his game. In 1900 he went to America and after that he was, right up till the war, one of the two or three unquestioned best, but he was never again, as he had been, in a completely different class from all the other golfers.

I remember very well the first time I saw him play. It was in the late summer of 1896 and he had won his first championship in the spring. I went over to Ganton, where he was then professional, for a day's golf and there by good luck was the great man driving off. He hit just the sort of drive that he always did— dead straight and rather high, the ball seeming to float with a particularly lazy flight through the air. The shot was obviously a perfect one and yet I was not quite so much impressed as I had expected to be. The style was so different from what I had been taught to admire; the club seemed to be taken up in so outrageously upright a manner, with something of a lift.

No doubt I was stupid and uneducated. So at least were other people who ought to have known much better than I, and the general impression at first could be summed up in the learned words of someone, "These Vardons are not pretty players." Moreover, I think his style did change a little and become both more elegant and more sound. At any rate one of his most distinguished contemporaries has told

me so, adding that when Vardon first appeared he used to let his right elbow fly out a little at the top of his swing and he certainly never did that afterwards. However that may be, all the world soon became converted and by 1898 his swing was recognized not only as one of genius but also as one of surpassing ease and grace.

Well now, what were the characteristics both of his method and its results which made him so devastating a conqueror? Results are easier to tackle and I will take them first. Vardon was first of all a magnificent driver. He was with a guttie ball uncommonly long, especially down the wind, and he was very straight. Taylor had been regarded as inhumanly accurate and so he was. Now here came Vardon, who rivalled his accuracy and added to it a little something more of freedom and power. He had a gift of hitting long carrying shots and, because of his upright swing, the ball would sit down with but little run where it pitched. This gift was of enormous value through the green. The brassie was not atrophied then, there were lots of wooden club shots to be played up to the pin, and Vardon, who often played them with his driver, could and did put the ball nearer the hole than other men could with their mashies. It was his most overpowering stroke and, even if he had been a bad putter then (which he was not), it left him little putting to do.

Then, he was superb with all iron clubs. He could command great length, if he needed it, and had in particular at one time a driving mashie which was as a driver in his hand. He was beautifully accurate in all pitching shots. Taylor had got there first and acquired the reputation of the greatest mashie player in the world, but I think Vardon was just as good. He was a good approach putter and at any rate an adequate holer out, though without the touch and delicacy of the really outstanding putter.

He had a calm and cheerful temperament, the game seemed to take very little out of him and he could fight, if need be, without appearing to be fighting at all. All these were valuable qualities, but, if one thing is to be picked out that made him supreme, it was that unique power of hitting long, soaring wooden club shots up to the hole side. "Two-shot" holes could be worthy of their name then, and given a course that had a number of them, Vardon was invincible. Other men might be scrambling on to the verge of the green and getting a certain number of fours, but he was putting for threes.

As to his style, photographs of him are probably familiar to the reader and give at any rate some impression. One thing noticeable in those pictures is that by comparison with the modern school, Vardon certainly made no fetish of the stiff left arm. Another thing is the uniform beauty of the follow-through. Time after time he would come right through, drawn to his full height, the club right round over his left shoulder, the hands well up, the left elbow tolerably high. It was the ideal copybook follow-through and he did it every time with an almost monotonous perfection.

Neither photograph, however—the top of the swing nor the finish of it—gives any real notion of how he took the club up and his method is very unlike anybody else's. First of all, he was a conspicuous example of the doctrine of "hands leading." In his day the books used to tell us that the head of the club should go back first and the wrists begin at once to turn away. In fact, I do not believe that any of the good players did anything of that kind, but they thought and taught that they did and the human eye was not quick enough to detect the fallacy. In Vardon's case, however, it was clear that he did none of these things; one could actually see the hands leading and the clubhead going back for some distance in a straight line before he slung it to the top of the swing. Neither does any photograph convey the small but still perceptible touch of lift in the upswing nor the little touch of sway.

His was essentially an upright swing in the days when orthodox swings were flat and was the more noticeable accordingly. He took the club up very straight, "too straight" as any self-respecting caddie would have said in instructing his master. Then by way of natural compensation he flung the clubhead well out behind him and brought it down on to the ball with a big sweep. It was a beautifully free movement of one having a natural gift for opening his shoulders and hitting clean. And, of course, like the movements of all really great golfers, it was instinct with that mysterious thing called rhythm. No golfer in the world, not even Bobby himself, was ever more perfectly rhythmic than Harry Vardon.

One of the most notable features of Vardon's iron play was its beautiful cleanness. He just shaved the roots of the grass and made no gaping wound in the turf, and that was so, even in the shot singularly ill-named the "push-shot," about which industrious journalists wrote columns when Vardon was devastating the country. Down came the club hitting the ball first and going on to graze the turf, and away flew the ball starting low and then rising gradually to fall very dead from the undercut put on it. He played this shot often with a cleek and he played it with his iron; he had not a whole series of irons to play it with as his successors have today.

In re-reading what I have written I find I have said nothing about the Vardon grip. Well, Vardon certainly discovered it for himself and made it popular; but Taylor at Westward Ho! had also discovered it for himself while Vardon was doing the same in Jersey and Mr. Johnny Laidlay had discovered it long before either of them, at North Berwick, while those two were tiny boys. Still it is a convenient name and I hope the day will never come when some young golfer who has just learned it asks "Who was Vardon?"

The Late Willie Anderson BY ALEXIS J. COLMAN

He Set a Record of Four
National Opens

As superlatives were necessary in writing of Willie Anderson living, so he merits them in this chronicle. From the first he was in the front rank. He attained greater heights than any other Scottish pro who came to dwell here, for he won four National Open and four Western Open championships within nine years, at all times measuring skill with the best in the land. "Anderson was the first pro of the highest class to be developed in this country," said H. L. Fitzgerald of the New York *Sun* at the time of Willie's death nineteen years ago.

"How would Anderson at his best compare with Hagen and Bobby Jones at their best?" I asked Fred McLeod recently.

"As good as either one," he replied.

Strong medicine this may seem to the modern generation, which did not know Anderson.

"Conceding that Alex Smith was Anderson's greatest rival for more years than any other, in both national and western tourneys, what would you say of their relative playing ability?" I asked McLeod. He dodged.

"Willie was of the phlegmatic temperament, Alex of the nervous type," was his answer. But let Smith himself tell of this rivalry. Writing a dozen years ago, Alex said:

"In my struggles to land the open, Willie

Anderson seemed to be my Nemesis. The battle was sure to be among such players as Willie Anderson, James Maiden, Laurence Auchterlonie, Alex Ross, Gil Nicholls, Jack Hobens, Stewart Gardiner, Nipper Campbell, Fred McLeod, Isaac Mackie, George Low, Willie Smith, and myself. The greatest player of them all in point of winning titles was Willie Anderson. His record of four Open and four Western championships will stand for some time to come. He was the kingpin of the pros from 1901, when he won his first Open, until 1905. He got four Open events in those five years, and although he failed to win another national championship, he annexed the Western twice after this, in 1908 and 1909. His untimely death was a blow to his friends, who looked upon him as a player most likely to set a record for Open Championships that would never be beaten."

Anderson was the complete golfer. He excelled in all departments. One recalls his generous, sweeping strokes with the wooden clubs, his flawless long-iron shots on the flag. McLeod thinks his work with the mashie was especially his long suit. His putting was consistently good; he surveyed the line with just enough deliberation, and then, not with the quick, staccato tap of a Smith, but with a smooth, even stroke he sent the ball blithely on its way, "in all the way."

Sturdy, with muscular shoulders, brawny forearms and exceptionally large hands, his strokes bespoke a power and an ease akin to those of Jones. Students of rhythm and timing would have found no fault in him. His grip was an extreme interlock, the index finger of his left hand extending 'way through between the third and little fingers of the right, instead of allowing only the knuckle to show in that aperture. His was not the upright swing of a Vardon, but the flatter, fuller sweep of the typical Scot. Long shots to the green with the brassie—and he made much use of this club with the hard ball in his earlier years—were duplicates of his drives, far and straight. Not so deliberate as, say, Elben Byers, he was yet unhurried, and got the ball away with consummate ease.

Willie did not need any great variety of clubs. Someone asked leading pros in 1907 as to what clubs they used, and the order of their preference. Anderson regularly played with eight: driver, brassie, cleek, mid-iron, one he called a pitching iron, heavy-centered mashie, large mashie-niblick, and putting cleek. He named the driver as his favorite; then mashie, mid-iron, and brassie. These were the implements with which he showed his mastery of the game.

Modest, never given to boasting, he let his play speak for itself. He never wrote a book; but that he taught effectively, scores of his pupils will testify today. His example always was impressive; aspiring amateurs worshiped him. He was an artist, an exemplar. He dressed well, as befitted a champion, but he did not attempt to set the fashion on the links. I do not even recall ever having seen him in knickers.

Anderson had a heavy shock of black hair, contrasting with the thinning blond locks of Alex Smith when they posed together, which was fairly often. Pleased, Willie grinned broadly, showing a mouthful of large, even teeth. Although quiet, he was a mixer, and popular with pros and amateurs alike.

Nothing upset his even golfing temperament —"the best in the world," as McLeod observes. Although Freddie also came from North Berwick, he did not see much of Anderson there, due to the disparity in ages, Anderson being some five years older—"and that makes lots of difference when you are kids," as McLeod says. But Fred saw plenty of Willie and his skill over here, especially when both were attached to mid-western clubs. As to Anderson's style: "Not so dashing as Hagen; more on the Jones type," says McLeod. And as to his even temperament: "You couldn't tell whether he was winning or losing by looking at him," says Freddie. And, indeed, it was so; and this imperturbability saved him many strokes under trying conditions.

There were few exceptions to Anderson's unwillingness to take the limelight, except as his skill automatically placed him there. Probably the occasion on which he most astonished his confrères was on the first day of the 1901 open at Myopia. According to Jack Clark, who tells the story, an officer of the club, an Englishman imbued with the spirit of old-world procedure as to the relative places of amateurs and pros, announced that the pros were to eat their luncheon in the kitchen. Willie Anderson, standing on the velvety lawn before the clubhouse swinging an iron, became so wrought up that he lapsed into the Scottish dialect of his youth—and he was then only twenty-one. "Na, na, we're no goin' t' eat in the kitchen!" he exclaimed, and, whether intentionally or not, made a vicious swipe, cutting an enormous divot that flew high, before the astonished gaze of the transplanted Briton. There was a compromise; the pros ate in a tent.

Anderson came naturally by his golfing prowess, and he studiously developed his talents. Born in North Berwick—Harry Reddie, who went to school with him there, thinks it was in May, 1880—Willie may fairly be said to have come upon the scene with a club in his hand. From later developments, it may be inferred that this was a wooden putter. His father, Tom—afterward pro at Montclair, New Jersey—became greenkeeper at the historic course on the southern shore of the Firth of Forth, and the boy, although he never caddied, had the run of the links and was privileged to compete in the caddies' tournaments and join in their periodic entertainments. Later the family removed to Edinburgh, twenty-one miles distant, the father commuting at weekends to and from his post at the North Berwick green. The mother, two sisters, Daisy and Nan, and a younger brother, Tom, Jr., afterward pro at American clubs, comprised the rest of the household. Willie went into Aiken's shop as an apprentice, and for three years repaired and made clubs, ministered to the various wants of golfers, and played whenever he could.

Opportunities in America were developing, and Frank Legh Slazenger, the pioneer golfing outfitter who had left his brothers to run the London establishment and had opened his own place in New York, was instrumental in bringing Willie over in 1895, securing for him the position as pro at the Misquamicut Golf Club, Watch Hill, Rhode Island. With him came Horace Rawlins, whom Mr. Slazenger placed at Newport. Anderson returned to Scotland for the winter of 1896 and in the following February came again with Reddie. "I remember the year," says Reddie, "for it was the same in which Fitzsimmons defeated Corbett on St. Patrick's Day at Carson City."

Anderson's first bid for national honors was made that year, 1897, at the Chicago Golf Club, Wheaton, and it was then that I first saw this remarkable golfing youth of seventeen. He all but landed at the pinnacle on this first attempt, even though, as acknowledged by such critics as H. J. Whigham, Charles Blair Macdonald, and Tweedie at the time, the brand of golf put up by the pros was the best so far shown in America. Willie led in the morning, with 38-41-79, but a bunker at the thirty-fourth hole converted a possible 3 into a 5, and his second round, 41-43-84, gave him a total of 163. Joe Lloyd, pro at Essex County, Massachusetts, was the only man to be feared;

for, although four strokes behind at noon, he was playing much better. He had a par 4 to tie Anderson; none thought he could beat him. But he did. The hole was 466 yards, and Lloyd, after a magnificent drive, sent the hard ball with his brassie to eight feet from the flag, and holed the putt—a feat justly acclaimed as one of the high achievements in golfing performance here or abroad.

"The one stroke," said Samuel L. Parrish, treasurer of the U.S.G.A., "marks the difference between fame and oblivion." But it didn't for Anderson. In that championship he was five strokes ahead of two previous top-notchers, James Foulis, champion in 1896, and Willie Dunn, one of the two victors of so-called championships in 1894, before U.S.G.A. supervision began. No, it was Lloyd who thereafter was little heard from. Anderson played in fourteen straight National Open Championships, 1897-1910, and finished only three times outside the money. He won four, was second once, third once, fourth twice, fifth three times, eleventh twice, and fifteenth once. In 1898 he was third, in 1899 fifth, in 1900—the Vardon-Taylor year—eleventh. He won at Myopia in 1901, after a play-off with Alex Smith, and was fifth at Garden City in 1902.

For the next three years Anderson was undisputed potentate of the links, for he won all three National Open Championships—at Baltusrol in 1903 after playing off a 307 tie with "Deacon Davy" Brown; at Glen View in 1904 with 303, five ahead of Gil Nicholls; and again at Myopia in 1905 with 314, two in front of his great rival, Alex Smith.

Anderson's four national victories were achieved in what may well be termed a golden age in American golf—the first half-dozen years of the century. In that brief span Travis and Chandler Egan did their best work, and Alex Smith won his first titles. In the scoring game all pros and amateurs alike willingly conceded that Anderson, when right, was their master. He lowered Chandler Egan's record 70 to 68 at Onwentsia in 1906. Travis was leading amateur during Anderson's early preëminence and medal player par excellence among amateurs. (He was medalist in six of nine Amateur Championship qualifying rounds, 1900-08.)

Anderson's poor showing in the 1907 Open at Philadelphia was due to poor health; although under a doctor's care he insisted upon competing. A week later he was back, playing in the Western Open at Hinsdale, Illinois, and this time playing against the doctor's orders, he finished in a tie for second place with McLeod at 309, just two strokes behind Bob Simpson. It would almost appear that his golfing skill remained automatically with him, refusing to be thwarted by mere physical illness.

Anderson knew the United States and its golfers at least as well as any other player of his time, and few professionals made the friendship of so many golfers in all parts of the country.

"Willie was somewhat dour at times," says Tom Mercer, who came early from Edinburgh and was pro at Marine and Field, Sound Beach, and other clubs. "He was like a son to me, and if ever I missed anyone it was Willie. He used to visit us at Sound Beach. After he went, I got to calling my own son Willie, although Frank Arthur is his name. But I call him Willie to this day, although he is thirty-two. If anyone knew Willie Anderson intimately, it was I. He seemed to imagine at times that his popularity was waning. 'They don't know me—they don't know me,' he would say to me. Well, there was this about Willie; if he didn't like a person, he couldn't pretend that he did. He was not what you would call a gladhander. Yet he went the route with the rest, and probably his convivial habits had much to do with undermining his health and hastened his end."

Anderson seemed generally the personification of robust health, and his illnesses had little outward effect, nor was he ever an opponent otherwise than formidable, in any competition. And he spent himself up to the hilt, giving the best that was in him to the very last. Had the men who played with him in the three 36-hole matches of that last week of his life realized how the strain was to tell upon him they would have forced him to rest. But such was his gameness that they never suspected. On October 19, 1910, at Fox Hills, he played with Isaac Mackie, the home pro, against Alex Smith and George Low. Mackie had 76-71-147, Smith the same, Low 75-78-153 and Anderson 78-78-156. Journeying to Pittsburgh with Gil Nicholls, the pair lost on October 21st to Jock Hutchison of Allegheny and Peter Robertson of Oakmont.

Two days later Anderson and Nicholls played Pittsburgh's outstanding amateurs, Bill Fownes, then Amateur Champion, and Eben Byers, the 1906 titleholder, in a memorable battle over the Allegheny course. This proved Anderson's farewell to golf, but what a mighty gesture it was! Par was 72; the amateurs had 69-70-139, and the pros 71-69-140. Fownes went out in 35 and Byers came in in 34, so they stood two up at noon. The pros more than played them to a standstill after lunch, the match being all even as they drove from the final tee. Byers holed from the edge of the green for a 3 to win.

Anderson tired perceptibly on the last few holes. Sitting in the clubhouse, Willie said he didn't "intend to play another game this year." Two days later, on October 25th, 1910, he died at his Chestnut Hill home, Philadelphia. The cause assigned was arteriosclerosis. Anderson was thirty years old. His wife, an American girl whom he had married while pro at Apawamis, and an infant daughter survived. Willie's father and brother have since died, Tom, Sr., of pneumonia and Tom, Jr., in an automobile accident. Tom, Jr., was pro at the Inwood Country Club, Far Rockaway, and at other clubs. He played in various tourneys, but did not approach the skill of his famous brother. Willie is buried at Chestnut Hill.

"What a golfer!" said Jack Clark the other day, reminiscing. Jack came long ago from Montrose and has seen them all. "Day in and day out, in my opinion there has not been another pro equal to him."

A Lesson from Harry Vardon BY OWEN BROWN

An Interview with the Father
of Modern Golf

"No," said Harry Vardon. "Never 'throw' the clubhead. Swing it all the way through. Above all, do not make a 'hit' of it. The deliberate, premeditated *flick* or *throw* of the club —either from the top of the swing, waist high as some advocate, or just when coming on the ball—is wrong. It results in mediocre golf, not the finished play of the expert. This holds equally good for the iron shots as for shots with the wood. Aside from putting, there is no purely wrist shot in the whole realm of golf."

The Old Master, founder of the modern school of golf technique as opposed to the erstwhile St. Andrews' method, winner of seven open championships and fifty-eight other major tournaments, was going strong when we played at Totteridge, England. Vardon was well on his game and hitting them straight to the pin nearly all the way. A week or two before, using only a putter and one other club, and that a niblick, he had played the Totteridge course in an even 80; and, any member of the South Herts Club will tell you, 72, or even better, is still no infrequent accomplishment for him. Still clear of eye—he does not wear glasses—sure of swing and steady as a balance wheel on both upswing and downswing, he lashes into his tee shots with all the vigor of a twenty-year-old, and with the same undeviating, compact grace and control, putting direction always before mere length, that made him the recognized model of form on two continents.

"Do you begin your downswing by a 'pull down' with the hands, or do you simple transfer your weight from right back to left and speed up automatically as you come around?" I asked.

The answer came without a second's hesitation: "The downswing starts by a dropping of the elbows. What you term the 'pull down,' but even more so where the downswing follows a movement begun by a purely body action, such as by a full shifting of weight from right to left before the club gets under way, would surely be putting the cart before the horse. The club and arms must lead on the downswing, just as they should on the upswing. Not the hips and body first, which means shifting the weight as a preliminary to body turning, and then the arms and club, as so many teach. That would be good advice to follow, if you wanted to cultivate body sway; but it is body action of every sort you want to keep down to the minimum.

"There may be the slightest shifting to the left, or bracing movement, on starting down, but it should be very slight indeed. The erroneous notion of a complete weight shifting from right to left, which so many golfers are overdoing nowadays, as they start their downswings, before they have scarcely got to the tops of their upswings, is no doubt an exaggeration of the popular idea of getting the left heel back on the ground as soon as possible. The left heel, of course, must be back and firm at impact, but if you will only swing correctly, you don't have to think about your left heel, or anything else but the increasing speed of the club.

"As a matter of fact, there is no reason why the left heel need ever leave the ground but a very little, and those who cultivate a pivot upon the left instep rather than on the toe or ball of the left foot, seem to get the best results."

"That's quite interesting," I broke in here, "and I see your point very clearly; but exactly where and how do you apply your main hitting effort? That is, let us assume the left leg has become braced on the downswing, which, as you would say, was begun by a simultaneous action of the elbows, arms and club and *not* by a sidewise movement of the hips in the act of weight shifting. You are now 'hitting against the left,' as we say. At just what point in the arc do you apply the main punch—or 'throw'—of the clubhead?"

I was trying to make myself as clear as possible, so that Vardon's reply to my question would answer one of the most perplexing and debatable points in the whole gamut of present-day golf instruction. Vardon simply said, "I don't throw my clubhead; I don't think about the action of the head or any other particular part of the club, if that is what you mean; and it is my opinion that anything in the nature of a 'throw' or a 'flick,' commonly termed wrist action—a sort of swing within a swing—could have but one result. It would retard and not accelerate the speed of the club by interfering with rhythm and by communicating a certain amount of body action into a

movement that ought to be performed, as nearly as it is humanly possible to do so, by the arms and club alone. The wrists are a kind of hinge, but they should do their work automatically. If both hands are grasping the shaft as they should, and in the manner I advocate in my two books—that is, mainly, a firm thumb and forefinger grip—you don't have to think about where the power comes from. You'll get it all right, but you must get it through a proper swing of the club through the ball—not by any forcing methods associated with wrist action. What you want is freedom and looseness at the wrists, not the tenseness and stiffness that would result at once if you tried actually to make the shot with your wrists.

"I know that the motion pictures are supposed to show how the wrists 'uncock' and perform in the act of sweeping the ball away, but I still say that all this is automatic; quite beyond the conscious effort of the golfer who is swinging cleanly and smoothly. The golfer himself cannot possibly control it to any good effect. The whole downswing is over in the part of a second. There is no time to think of the wrists; such as what to do with them at a given instant. Not that you cannot, after a fashion, play what might be termed a 'wrist shot' by the throwing or flicking method, but you'd hardly expect to win big tournaments with that type of swing.

"Now, as to hitting against the left leg," he continued, "any first-rate golfer swings against an axis and that axis is the center of his pivot or balance. He isn't particularly *hitting* against anything, but just swinging the club. It is *leverage* that he wants, and must maintain, clear through the stroke. I won't attempt to say just where this center of balance is, for it shifts somewhat as the golfer does, but it certainly is not the left leg or any other definite part of his anatomy. A fine golfer may tell you that he hits or swings against his left leg, because, toward the end of the downswing, he is bracing most of his weight upon it, but he is probably a better golfer than he is an explainer as to exactly how he does it."

Although I had played but one game since

leaving the California Coast, four months previously, I was soon swinging in at least something resembling the manner indicated by the incomparable Harry. With scarcely half my usual expenditure of effort, I brought off many shots that were the result, entirely, of his brief but very explicit directions.

When I outdrove him on one of the long holes, a long straight ball and my best of the round, he seemed to take it as a matter of course. "You see—that time you outdrove me; and there's no reason why you can't do as well on all your strokes, if you'll just remember how you swung on that one.

"The golf swing must be regarded, primarily, as an action of the club. It describes certain movements in the air, and, on returning to the point of address, proper 'whip,' by *means of leverage only*, having been applied, it slashes through the ball of its own accord, without let or hindrance, except the final power which a finished player may apply by letting his weight come around behind the shot at the very instant of follow through. But not before, mind you; and none of these movements will come off correctly, if body action—and I might say wrist action—is permitted, in ever so slight a degree, to get into the downswing proper, which is largely executed by the clubs, aided and abetted by the arms and hands. The main function of the body is to furnish leverage, but not power; of the wrists, a connection only, like a 'universal joint,' between the club and the golfer. They should *not* be used for propulsion.

"Now if you could only think of yourself as a spectator—not a part of the swing itself but just looking on—and give everything over to the club (assuming that your other movements have been in accordance with recognized principles), you may be able to swing truly and cleanly, without that apparent effort I see you putting into some of your shots. That's the best advice I can give you. Just say to yourself: 'The *club* must do it; I must obey the club and what *it* wants *me* to do, not what *I* want *it* to do. If I do this swing *myself*, the club being simply a means to an end,

I'm sure to spoil the one big essential—rhythm—and get no sense of satisfaction out of the shot. But if I simply *swing*, largely with the arms and club, letting all effort be the natural result of the swing, and not the thing that produced it, taking care that the club is leading all the way through and not the body or any part of it, the ball will be struck with the finest degree of delicacy but with enough percussion at the clubhead to whisk it away two hundred and fifty yards or more.

"One other thing," he added a little later on. "From observation I am convinced that the great difficulty of most golfers is not so much in learning how to swing, strange to say, but in their lack of command or control to keep right on swinging as they know they should swing. They 'weaken' on their downswing and soon fall right back into the old way of doing it. They simply won't trust anything to the club, which would never fail them, if only they would let it lead all the way through.

"When about halfway down on a perfect swing—perfect to that point, I mean—they become suddenly obsessed with the notion that the swing is coming off too slowly and they fear the clubhead won't get through fast enough to give them a long ball; so they feel they must apply some special forcing or whipping action, upsetting both leverage and rhythm, with any one of a dozen results—all unsatisfactory. Or as it seems to me, recalling my own early golfing days, they become seized at this point in the swing with the idea that as the clubhead is still so far back from the ball, as yet travelling slowly and with the face quite 'open,' it won't catch up in time to meet the ball squarely at impact. In other words, they are afraid of their old enemy the slice, and feel, instinctively, that something must be done, in a hurry, to guarantee the desired result. They won't wait for the club to come through naturally and smoothly but most endeavor to sling it, or hurl it, or even to poke it through with a sudden clinching of the fingers of the right hand and a jamming of the right arm, tensed as a ramrod.

"As speed seems to them the thing most

lacking up to this point, and as most people feel capable of injecting more power into their swings by right-hand domination, they learn to rely on this right-hand action—a thing apart from a pure golf swing—instead of relying on the correct swing itself to produce the correct result.

"There, now, I guess you've had quite enough instruction for a while, and if you will just remember to let the club lead—and really *let* it—*all the way through,* you won't need any more instruction from me or anyone else!"

So saying he gave one look toward the eighteenth pin, brought his club up horizontally—very horizontally—over his right shoulder, and before the eye could analyze what took place after that the ball went travelling through the air on the straightest possible line to the center of the green. But with such ease and grace was the whole effect and result attained that one took only momentary notice of the ball, while marvelling, rather, at the rhythm and poise and virility of this sixty-one-year-old golfer, who, long after those memorable days when "golf *was* golf" and Vardon was Vardon—the golfing model and byword of both continents —can still reel off birdies and eagles, who, with his marvellous command of the "push shot" and every other stroke known to golf, was perhaps, in his prime, the greatest shot-maker of them all.

The old master of British golf, Harry Vardon, watches the results of a long-iron shot.

Bobby Jones Completes the Cycle BY O. B. KEELER

Highlights on His First Victory in the British Amateur

THIS IS WRITTEN THE SUNDAY MORNING AFTER the conclusion of the 1930 British Amateur Championship at St. Andrews with a brilliant sort of night journey between—these British, perking up of late, had a beautiful special train at the St. Andrews station for those in a hurry to get to London, and, with a considerable party of Americans aboard, it was not unlike a football train home, when your side has won.

And Bobby had won, at last. I think he was happier over this victory than over any since he broke through with a major triumph in the United States Open at Inwood, in 1923. I talked with him a little, immediately after he had been rescued by a squad of big Scottish policemen from some fifteen thousand admirers at the twelfth green, who apparently had determined to take the new champion apart and see what made him tick. That is, I talked with Bobby in his room at the hotel; there was no chance to talk to him or to anybody else in the trooping gallery. They had a band at the home green to play him in, but the band got involved in the crowd and I never heard a note sounded.

I asked Bobby, "Will this success increase your determination to win the British Open also?"

"On the contrary," said Bobby decisively.

"I'll do what I can, of course. But I can't start breaking my back over anything else for a while. I'm too happy and too thankful to have managed to win here."

"Then you regard this as the Big Shot this year?"

"Absolutely! Under the circumstances, this has been the Big Shot for some time. There could be nothing in golf today that I wanted so much. I can't believe it's really happened, now."

At which juncture word came that Bobby was to present himself at the Royal and Ancient clubhouse to receive the cup, on the same little veranda where he stood in 1927 for the presentation of the Open Championship trophy. Apparently convinced that he was not dreaming, Bobby brushed his tousled hair hastily and went out to face the huge gallery for the last time.

The story of the 1930 British Amateur Championship seems to me to confirm, or at any rate strongly to support, a sort of hypothesis that has been forming in the back of my head for years—that golf tournaments are matters of destiny, and that the result is all in the book before ever a shot is hit. Looking back over Bobby's eight matches, you may see crisis after crisis, in those furious encounters with Tolley, Johnston and Voigt, where the least slip in nerve or skill or plain fortune would have spelled blue ruin to Bobby's dearest ambition. Yet at every crisis he stood up to the shot with something which I can define only as inevitability and performed what was needed with all the certainty of a natural phenomenon.

"The stars are with Jones in this tournament," said Sir James Lieshman, Scottish knight and golf enthusiast, with whom I walked much of the time. "His luck is as fixed as the orbit of a planet. He cannot be beaten here."

Now, it sounds almost absurd to say this, but it is the gospel truth that at the moment Sir James made this remark Bobby was one down to George Voigt with three to play and had just blown a four-foot putt at the fifteenth green which would have squared the match.

From the next tee George's drive went into the bunker known as the Principal's Nose, and the match was square. And on the most dangerous hole in the world, the famous (or notorious) Road Hole, George played as brilliant a birdie 4 as ever was produced there, while Bobby, with an iron second not too good, was left with a putt of four long yards for a half—obviously to save the match—with George's ball stone dead.

There is no doubt in several thousands of minds that the match and ultimately the championship depended on that putt. All I could think of was that it was the same length and with much the same borrow as the famous twelve-footer he holed at Winged Foot last summer to tie for the United States Open Championship. And the stroke and the result made a fair replica of that other one: the ball rolled easily to the front of the hole as if in a groove and just fell in.

Bobby had something rather curious to say about that putt, too. "When I stood up to it," he said, "I had the feeling that something had been taking care of me through two matches that I very well might have lost, and that it was still taking care of me. I felt that however I struck that putt, it was going down."

Bobby had a seven-footer for a 3 at the home hole while George's pitch was very short

and he missed a two-yarder for a 4 and a half, so Bobby's miss didn't matter.

There was another putt, earlier, that meant an incalculable saving to Bobby.

Thursday afternoon he came to the home green with the American amateur champion, Harrison Johnston, one up on the heels of the most tremendous rally of the tournament. Bobby, going along in his accustomed mode, gradually had put the gallant Jimmy under, so that as they left the thirteenth green Bobby was four up with five to play, and the gallery was drifting off in squads in search of excitement. The three thousand who remained got the excitement.

Johnston took back the long fourteenth hole with a birdie 4 to a par 5, smacking a long pitch up a yard from the flag. Jones messed up the fifteenth, finally missing a four-foot putt for a half which would have left him dormie three. He got the half at the sixteenth and was dormie two. In the pinch, the American Amateur Champion then produced a magnificent birdie 4 at the deadly Road Hole. Jones very properly playing for a par 5, which he got, and leaving the burden on Johnston—which he shouldered gallantly.

At this stage I began thinking of Harrison Johnston in the Western Championship some years ago when Albert Seckel, I think it was, had him 5 down with 6 to play and Johnston won the next six holes. One glance at Jimmy showed him to be in this humor now. Another slip by Jones—another birdie for Jimmy—and the Open Champion would be out in the sixth round, as at Muirfield, for if Jimmy squared that match at the home green it was Lombard Street to a China orange he would win in the extra holes.

The furious strain was working on both the players and Jimmy's pitch to the big home green ran and ran, to the upper left-hand corner of the carpet, a good thirty yards from the flag. Here was a great chance for Jones, who needed only a half—but he needed it about as much as he ever had needed anything in all his life. Bobby, too, was wavering, and his pitch was almost a duplicate of Jimmy's, going to the same distant corner, and perhaps two yards nearer the pin. Now it was up to the putting.

Jimmy putted first—a good one, thirty inches from the hole; virtually a certain par 4.

Bobby's estimate of range and grade for once was at fault, or his deadly touch for once was wrong. The ball, apparently on a good line, curled up and died eight feet from the cup. And there remained a downhill, sidehill putt for a par 4 and a half, and, as Bobby later declared freely, the match. Not to extend the suspense, the putt went down with the same inflexible certainty that marked other crises in Bobby's campaign toward the title.

"It was the longest eight-foot putt I ever saw," said Bobby a few minutes later. "Jimmy's rally was wonderful. That's all that happened. I did my best. I gave him one hole—but, remember, he *took* the others. It was a whale of a fight and I'm awfully lucky to be in this tournament now."

As for the Tolley-Jones match in the fourth round, no more fitting combat ever was arranged between champions—the British Amateur king defending his crown; the American Open Champion attacking with all his skill and courage and determination. What an utterly amazing battle it was—squared six times; never an advantage of more than one single hole; with Jones plugging away on the last nine, one up, square; one up, square; one up, square, as the placid giant Tolley, roused by the occasion, fought the American to the finish with never the change of a line in his habitually casual expression or the faintest gesture to indicate the ferocity of the strain. I have had the utmost respect for Cyril Tolley for a great many years, but I never saw him to so wholly admirable an advantage as in that great match. Bobby's own impeccable demeanor, and the iron mask that hides his emotions, were so perfectly matched by Tolley's debonair manner that at times one might have guessed them not to be combatants in a desperate, living and undecided sporting event, but rather actors going through well-rehearsed rôles in some tremendous drama.

Bobby was extremely lucky to win that match, and he would be the first to tell you so. Square at the seventeenth tee, under a sweeping gale, it seemed destined that the argument between the "two most majestic figures of amateur golf" was to be adjusted at the terrible Road Hole, four hundred and sixty-seven yards around an angle to the right, with the best drive a dangerous crack over Auchterlonie's famous "drying shed."

Both players elected to stay well to the left; the pinch was too tight for any undue risk, with the match square. Tolley was five yards, or such a matter, ahead from the tee and Jones had to guess first on the desperate problem of a second shot to the long, narrow green with the horrid road along the other side.

Bobby took plenty of time while twelve thousand spectators stood and suffered. He walked halfway down to the green—it was a distance of about two hundred yards, I should say. He stood on a tall mound and considered the situation. I was standing with Dr. Mackenzie, who designed and built the Cypress Point course at Del Monte and other famous courses. We agreed that the most feasible shot was an iron pitched to the right—well to the right—of the diabolical little bunker set right in line with the pin, to swing leftward off the steep slope of the green and roll on toward the pin. So we were surprised when Bobby motioned to the stewards to move the gallery back from the rear of the green, near the eighteenth tee, which was well to the left of the bunker.

Then he went back and played. It was a bold shot, less obvious than the one Dr. Mackenzie and I had discussed. It was aimed to pitch in the hollow below the back of the green and roll on up, at the worst to be around the eighteenth tee with a fairly decent chip at the pin.

Bobby undeniably gave the shot a shade too much. I suppose that under pressure as extreme as he then was experiencing a man naturally hits harder than he intends. The shot was perfect in line but it came up to the level of the green on a big bound and not on a roll.

George Voigt, a slightly built amateur from Washington, D.C., makes a recovery from the haystack rough.

It struck among the very spectators Jones had asked to be moved back. It stopped where he had intended it to stop from a roll up the slope. A line from an old romantic novel hopped into my head: "Men call it fate!"

Anyway, and uncompromisingly, it was a break in luck. Tolley now had a vastly increased pressure on him, with Jones in a fair position to card a birdie 4, and a certain par 5. And when the big fellow's iron curled up short of the wicked bunker, I could see nothing but a win for Jones. I felt that no man living could execute so deft a pitch as would clear that bunker and stop anywhere near the hole, cut in that absurdly narrow plateau green with the road just across it. In the road likely—never, near the flag, I felt.

Now see how a golfing situation changes. Jones' simple little approach was eight feet from the cup. And Tolley, pitching with the most exquisite delicacy (he told me later it was the best shot he ever played in his life) stopped his ball within two feet of the flag, dead for a birdie 4. In one minute, Jones had the hole and inferentially the match in hand.

In another minute, Jones was putting for his life; a perilous eight-footer, with his adversary comfortably and convincingly established for a half—or a win, if Bobby missed.

This was another crisis. And down went the putt. Two drives, close to three hundred and forty yards down the evening breeze, in front of the home green. Two chips, neither so good. A half in par 4. Close play by the American Open Champion at the nineteenth; loose play by the British Amateur Champion, whose pitch was far outside and whose approach left him open for the stymie that ensued, and the great bout ended.

"I'm sorry it ended in a stymie," said Bobby. "But I fancy it's just as well for me that it did. It was as hard a match as I ever played in. Cyril was in a fighting humor. All the way I had the uneasy conviction that he was hitting the ball better than I was. His tiny pitch over the bunker at the Road Hole was the finest shot I ever saw. I'm lucky to have won the match."

Bobby added that it was conventional to say this. "But I *mean* it," he explained, solemnly.

In his first match, played against a relatively unknown named Sid Roper, Jones holed a mashie shot out of the Cottage Bunker on the fourth hole for an eagle 2. Jones began the match 3, 4, 3, 2, and yet stood only two up.

Cyril Tolley, the defending champion, went down fighting in his match with Jones. Jones finally won the match on the nineteenth green. The two were never more than one hole apart.

With these three hard-won victories under his belt, to say all too little about his remarkable match with Sid Roper in the first round in which he played—Bobby started against Roper 3-4-3-2-4 against a par of 4-4-4-4-5, was 3 up, and never was able to increase the margin, winning 3-2 over the stubborn ex-coal-miner— the final match was rather generally expected to turn out as eventually it did. Roger Wethered had worked his way to the last round with three very easy matches to start, followed by four very tough ones. The tall ex-champion was hitting his irons and pitches brilliantly, and his driving, traditionally eccentric, held up sufficiently for the first nine holes of the match.

The match was an astonishing replica of the Jones-Wethered combat in the Walker Cup event at Sandwich just played. Here, as at Sandwich, each did a pretty 35 to the first turn and they stood all square. At Sandwich, Wethered's game collapsed and he lost six of the next seven holes. At St. Andrews, Jones took five of the next seven after the turn and, losing the Road Hole to a brilliant birdie 4—Jones

blew a thirty-inch putt after a great recovery from the bunker—was four up at luncheon. A stymie cost Bobby the first hole in the afternoon, and again Roger made a good fight nearly to the turn, where his own missed putts of a yard cost him hole after hole, so that Jones ran away to win seven-and-six.

Despite Bobby's success in working through seven eighteen-hole matches at St. Andrews, beating on successive days the British Amateur Champion, the American Amateur Champion, and George Voigt, the new champion is not at his happiest over the short route. It was curious to observe with what a different attitude he attacked the longer problem. Where he had mixed superbly brilliant golf with decidedly blue splotches in the eighteen-hole engagements, he set about his thirty-six-hole encounter with Wethered in the work-manlike manner that characterizes his best medal-play performances. Missing no fewer than six putts of a yard, or no more than four feet, he went the thirty holes of the match in 118 strokes, or two below 4's for the day. His morning card was 35-36—71; he was out in 37 in the afternoon with a dead stymie costing him a stroke; and he started back 3-3-4, which is where the bout ended. Roger played gallantly, being simply unable to endure the pressure exerted by the great medalist over the long route.

Among the spectacular shots of this tournament with two hundred and seventy starters, I saw two which will be talked of many years at St. Andrews.

Harrison Johnston, starting in the very first round (of sixteen pairs only) was having a severe match with Bernard Darwin, a fine golfer, the greatest of golf writers, and a grandson of the famous naturalist. Through the thirteenth, each had won a single hole and the match was square. Johnston took the long fourteenth with a fine birdie 4 and they halved the fifteenth and sixteenth. One up and two to play, Johnston's drive at the Road Hole was exactly one foot behind Darwin's, and the writer lifted for Johnston to play the odd.

Johnston took a spoon and laid into the shot, going right for the pin, at a most ghastly risk, it seemed to everyone. The bunker was almost in line and outside the green was the deadly Road. Mr. Darwin told me later that when he saw the shot he said to himself, "I'll be square, here!" But the ball, pitching close to the plateau green, ran deftly past the right-hand edge of the bunker and curled up a yard from the flag.

"Believe it or not," Jimmy told me when I asked him, "I played for the pin. I figured that I could get a 5 out of the bunker, if necessary, and by bringing off the shot I might end a very severe match."

This put an end to a rumor that was gaining some currency to the effect that Johnston had not intended to go for the green and that he was as surprised as Mr. Darwin by the result of the shot. Anyway, it certainly ended the match.

The other shot that lingers in my memory was Bobby Jones' pitch from the "Cottage Bunker" 120 yards short of the fourth green, in the brilliant bout with Sid Roper, who played fifteen holes in 4 and one in 5 to hold his own

against one of Bobby's most spectacular outbursts. Jones holed a long putt for a 3 at the first, halved the second in par 4, canned another birdie 3 at the third, and down the wind drove into the Cottage Bunker, 300 yards away, from the fourth tee.

I was standing back of the green as he waded down into the bunker for his second shot. I was told later the ball lay perfectly clear on wind-blown sand. Up came a feather of white sand instead of a divot. The ball, obviously struck precisely as if from turf, came on in a rather steep pitch down the wind, struck in front of the big green with little evidence of backspin, rolled more and more slowly up to the hole, and dropped in softly, as if from a perfectly gauged putt. It did not strike the pin.

"Too bad he was in a bunker," murmured some fascinated fan behind me, while the others were hammering each other on the back and crowing with hysterical delight.

That Mr. Roper stood up to that blast of golf—Jones was five under par in the first five holes—and was only three down, and thereafter held his own to the finish, three-two, indicates the extreme peril of British Amateur Championship competition and the class of the player whose name is not in the stud-book. I never had heard of Mr. Roper before. I expect to hear a lot of him from now on.

Now, this seems a lot about Bobby Jones in the British Amateur, but you may take it from this correspondent, who has observed Mr. Jones in twenty-four national competitions, that the young man never before stole a show with such amazing spectacularity. Every day he played, and he played every day except Tuesday, Mr. Jones in some way managed to produce the Big Feature of the day. And eventually he won the tournament. So you must pardon me if I write a good deal about him and his doings. He was a long time winning the British Amateur Championship, but when he did win it, he worked over Olympus with the thoroughness of a modern vacuum cleaner —he extracted every sensation, every emotion, the great drama had to offer.

The Battle at Hoylake BY O. B. KEELER

Bobby Jones Adds the British Open
to His British Amateur

WITH DUE REGARD FOR MR. JONES' RATHER well-known modesty, I must give it as my own personal and unalterable opinion that Bobby won the British Open playing at very nearly his worst. This certainly would not sound very well except for the collateral clause that from one of his worst games he managed in some way to extract one of his best scores for 72 holes; and it is a fact that the race goes to the leading score without consideration of the manner in which it was compiled.

Now, Bobby won the British Amateur, but in a manner more spectacularly indicative of courage and determination and good luck than of an overpowering game. Bobby's attitude toward the British Open then became the subject of a lot of speculation, with two schools of thought to the fore. One group fancied that with the toughest golf title in the world in hand at last, Bobby would be fired by a super-determination to add the other British title to it; that he would be even more steamed up than he was in 1926, when he had just lost in the British Amateur Championship, or in 1927, when he made his worst showing in the United States Open and went to St. Andrews with the idea of retrieving himself.

The other idea was that Bobby, his dearest

ambition accomplished, would be content to let nature take its course in the British Open; that he would not risk busting a G-string, with the United States Open coming on three weeks later; and that he would just be out there playing another tournament.

Make no mistake—Bobby Jones is a competitive athlete. He plays major championship golf to win. And there is no question of his trying harder in this tournament or that. He tries as hard as he can in all of them. He tried as hard as he could at Oakmont in the 1927 National Open, where he finished eleventh, but indifferent preparation and perhaps a bit of over-confidence beat him there and beat him plenty.

Whatever was Bobby's attitude toward the British Open after St. Andrews, once he was in the British Open he was directing a lance against his natural rivals; the spur of competition roweled him deep; and he shot the works. I wish to say as seriously as possible that in my opinion he got more golf out of a worse game than he ever has managed before in an important competition. He was never right, in the common understanding of rectitude with Bobby Jones—as at Merion in 1924, or Minikahda in 1927, or at St. Andrews the same year.

He told me that he was not in any round ever sure for six collected minutes what his game would do.

"I simply don't know where the darned ball is going when I hit it," he said. "I guess I'm trying to steer it, and of course that's the worst thing in the world to do. But what can I do? This is a tight course. You can't get up there and slam away and trust to freedom of action to take care of the shot. You simply have got to exercise some control of the ball. And it's the most hopeless job I've ever tackled. I never have worked half so hard before."

After this statement, which was a perfectly candid expression, it may appear whimsical to relate that his first three rounds were negotiated in absolute par of the course—70-72-74—par being 72 and as tough a par as you can ask. But I ask you also to believe that in those first three rounds there was a lot beside the eccentricities of an uncertain game. There was in those first three rounds the concentrated experience of fourteen years of major competitive golf; the experience gained from seven lean years when Bobby Jones played in eleven national championships and never won one of them; the experience, and the stolid patience, and the tempered philosophy gained from years of defeat and seasons of disappointment, over every kind of championship golf course and against every type of field the game affords.

It is as far as possible from depreciating the great field at Hoylake, to say that Bobby Jones won with his game far from its top. He got from this game as good a score as ever he got before, the course considered; and as good a score as his best game, I think, was entitled to wring from great Hoylake. And the score is what goes on the board. And if his experience and patience and philosophy and grim determination were enough to extract that score from his game in its Hoylake condition, why, I for one will say that he never played a greater tournament; perhaps never one so great. There was never a round of the four in which some player, or players, did not tie or beat Jones, but, when the four rounds were stuck together,

he was on top by a couple of strokes.

I can tell you the stroke that saved the championship.

The sixteenth at Hoylake is called The Dun and it is the longest hole on the course, of 532 yards, and by the time he got to it Bobby knew he needed a 4 there if he could get it, so of course he went for it. And he was bunkered, short of the green, the ball lying well enough, if a ball can be said to be lying well enough in sand in a bunker. In his kit Bobby carried a twenty-five-ounce niblick with a concave face and a funny rear elevation, which Horton Smith had got for him this spring—the inventor had given Horton one, and Horton thought it was great medicine, and got one for Bobby. Bobby waded down into that bunker with this twenty-five-ounce niblick, and he smacked that ball out four inches past the pin, the ball rolling around the cup and trying to get in, but failing by the proverbial whisker.

That birdie 4 cinched the victory. For, so close was the going, Leo Diegel, at the last turn two strokes back of Bobby, picked them up with a 3 at each of the two one-shot holes coming in, and was tied with Jones as he stood on the tee of the 70th hole. Tied, after 69 holes! Deuced close, these Open Championships.

Gallant Leo Diegel—he went for that long hole with all there was in the bag, knowing he needed a 4, and another 4, and one more 4, to tie, on three extraordinarily tough holes of which the one he was playing was a 532-yard par 5. And he was bunkered from the tee, and only fairly out with his second, and then he wound up—a match for Bobby's ghastly play at the eighth, which gave Leo his chance—by missing a short putt for a 5. And with a 6 there, he needed a 3 and a 3 to tie, and they were not making 3's, on the last two holes at Hoylake, that day.

So did Macdonald Smith, as he came to the end of a magnificent round. He started six strokes back of Bobby, and of course that is an awful lot of strokes to spot Bobby in a fourth round. But Mac was picking them up, here and there. He lost one at the second and was seven strokes back. He gained one at the fourth and lost it at the fifth. He picked up three at the eighth, and another at the 190-yard eleventh, and another at the 160-yard thirteenth, and at that point, with five holes to play—par 5-4-5-4-4—Mac needed four 4's and one 3 to tie.

Well, it was too much to ask of the gallant veteran. He clipped one stroke off par, in that last spin of five holes, and he turned in the best card of the last round, a 71. But he could not close the gap.

In a way of speaking, I feel that I may speculate and even philosophize a bit, about this tournament. You know, there are in our native land some golfing critics who stick pretty close to the old, old policy of "down with everything that's up, and up with everything that's down." Since Bobby Jones has managed to get up, they have been finding fault with him a bit. For one thing, they have said he was the pet of the United States Golf Association; he was favored in the matter of starting times, and partners, in the open events; that sort of thing. One or two writers even have been guilty of the absurd reflection that he has been favored in rulings on matters of fact, in play-offs—that sort of thing.

Now, having strung along with Bobby through twenty-five national championships, and traveled with him some 90,000 miles, and watched him lose through seven years and then win through seven, I would like to ask these captious ones to say something about the cold and unalterable fact that he has won the last four British major championships in which he has competed, where they pull everything out of the hat—starting times, partners and all. I would like for those who have called Bobby the pet of the United States Golf Association to say something concerning the fact that Bobby's record in British events is materially ahead of his record in United States events, in percentage. But do you think they will say anything about that? Oh, no. They will wait until Horton Smith reaches the top, or Don Moe goes over the rest of the amateurs, and then they will say funny things about Horton, or Don.

You never can tell.

Remember what they said of Bobby Jones, after Willie Hunter beat him at St. Louis, in 1921?

"He's a great golfer—a great shot-maker," they said. "But he can't win. He hasn't the championship complex."

Connie Mack, who has won eight American League pennants and five World Series, is a very active member of the Philadelphia Seniors Golf Association. He spends a good part of his winters at Mount Plymouth, Florida.

Ty Cobb is caught at the end of a mashie shot during a recent match at Del Monte, California.

The Pressure at Interlachen BY GRANTLAND RICE

Jones Reaches the Three-Quarter

Mark in Quest for Four Titles

WHEN BOBBY JONES REPORTS FOR THE AMATEUR Championship at Merion in September, he will be face to face with an opportunity to make a record in golf that was beyond all fanciful imagination until he came along. This will be the chance to win four major championships in one summer's span, and to run up his list to thirteen major titles before he has reached his twenty-ninth year.

In many respects, the championship that Jones won at Interlachen in July was his greatest achievement. On other occasions, after the first or second day's play, there have been only two or three serious challengers. The others have been younger or little known stars hardly equipped to carry on the fight to a seventy-two-hole finish. But at Interlachen after the first day's play, and then after the second day's play, he found himself surrounded by such able and veteran campaigners as Mac Smith, Horton Smith, Tommy Armour, Walter Hagen, Harry Cooper, John Golden, and others, all capable of sticking to the final putt.

It was from this powerful cordon of skill and courage and experience that Bobby had to fight, and hack his way to the crest with a club that in other years had brought him many a golfing pang. This was the mashie-niblick. At Interlachen there were seven or eight holes that called for this club as one came to the green. If this club had failed him, he would have been doomed. It not only did not fail him —it carried him to his twelfth major title within eight years.

You can sense the situation. After the first two days of play, through the blistering heat from a flaming sun, Bobby found himself trailing. He felt that he must strike his big blow in the third round, and I have never seen him as keen to rip into par, as deeply concentrated on one big round, as he was when he marched to the first tee that forenoon for the third round.

He felt there were too many stars around him to slip in another round above 70. A few of them might slip or crack or fade, but at least one or two of them would still be left, if he faltered in any way. It was the fact that he was surrounded by such high class talent that spurred him on. He discarded any idea of safe or conservative play. And he gave evidence of his intentions quickly by starting 4-3-3-4-3-3-4-4. This left him with a 4 for a 32, just four under par. As it was, he was out in 33. And he kept on burning up the landscape. He started home—4-4-4-3 with two more birdies on the eleventh and the long twelfth. He came to the short seventeenth six under par with a 3 and a 4 left for a 66.

Here was Jones at the top of his game. You can catch the killing effect this march must have had on the rest of the field. All those who followed him and who had dreams of nailing him at last suddenly began to hear the thundering echo of cheers on out ahead. The big gallery of eight to ten thousand, the biggest that ever followed one man in American golf, was paying its noisy and excited tribute. As leading professionals still in the hunt came to the first or second or third tees they were greeted by the rolling echo of applause from over the hills. What could it be? What else could it be, except that Jones at last had gotten hot—that he was burning up the course. This was the terrific handicap all his pursuers faced.

The thunder seemed to increase as Bobby kept hacking away the hide of Old Man Par, on his way to a record round. It isn't so easy to face a four- or a five-foot putt on a sloping green and then hear another vocal cataclysm from some green on ahead indicating that the brilliant Georgian had clipped another stroke from the par of some hard hole.

Bobby knew the effect such a round must have. He never faltered. His face was set and determined, his swing was smooth and true, and there was no sign of any fluttering pulse. He was out to ram home the one deadly thrust that would make it none too easy for those determined pursuers, who on this occasion thought they had him in a net of steel. He held this terrific pace through the first sixteen holes. His tee shots were long and straight. But above all the shining blade of his mashie-niblick and his spade-mashie were operating on par as if in the hands of some skilled surgeon.

On three occasions his pitches from ninety to one hundred and ten yards away stopped less than a foot from the cup. On two occasions it looked as if he would surely hole the ball that ran up so close before stopping just short of the tin. For those sixteen holes, he set a pace that no one would follow.

And then in the wake of the cheering and the wild hurrahing, word began to come back to those camping on his trail. "Jones was out in 33"—"Jones started back with a 4-4-4—two under par"—"Jones is now five under par for the round"—"Jones is now six under par for the round"—"Jones will finish with a 66 sure" —these were the messages relayed back to such pursuers as Horton Smith, Mac Smith, Tommy Armour, Walter Hagen, Harry Cooper and others who had felt they had a great chance to cut off the Georgian at last.

Human flesh and blood can stand just so much. So can brain and nerves. There is a limit. The main wonder is that Mac and Horton Smith did so well. They were both keen to win this championship. They were both playing great golf. They both felt they had great chances. And then came the almost unbroken wandering western winds, sounding the knell of their hopes. Each one felt then that par was of no value. The strain was more than doubled, and there is strain enough in these Opens, no matter where you are in the field. The wild Georgian was on the rampage again. He was hotter than he had ever been before. He was locking the door, breaking up the show, blockading the open way that had seemed wide open when he started.

The sixteen-hole thrust of six under par won the title. It was a pace too blistering for even Bobby Jones to follow. He almost burned himself out in doing it, but it was the killing punch that sent the rest of the star field reeling. It helped to prevent any such counter attack in the third round, and while Jones slipped a little at the seventeenth and eighteenth, he faced the last round with a five-stroke lead over Harry Cooper and a seven-stroke lead over Mac Smith.

It was the final counter attack of Mac Smith, the veteran, that added further drama. Starting seven strokes back of Jones, the Lakeville Scot opened one of the greatest charges in golf history. He cut away four strokes on the first nine holes. He cut away two more later on through the second round and then Bobby put up the final barrier by sinking a forty-foot putt for a 3 on the last green. Just one slip here and the two would have tied. Mac Smith had cut away five strokes in eighteen holes from the greatest golfer in the world, and that is almost as big a job as winning a championship.

The final round of Jones proved his brain and heart above his golfing skill. Few had heard that Mac Smith was on his trail. He knew how close the same Mac Smith came to catching him at Hoylake a few weeks before, where he finished with a 71. And in the face of this test Bobby kept taking 5's on the par 3 holes. He was losing two strokes at a time on these shorter ranges, and Mac Smith was drawing closer and closer. When Jones had another 5 on the par-3 thirteenth, I think he gave one of the greatest exhibitions of golf courage the game has ever known. Here was the big chance to slip, to get discouraged, to get worried, to get disheartened or over-anxious. But in the face of these reverses, with the echo of Smith's tread just behind, he rallied to get a birdie 3 at the fourteenth. To hit the cup for a 3 at the fifteenth and then to drop another approach dead to the cup for another birdie at the sixteenth.

Here he felt that he had broken down Mac Smith's gallant assault. He had closed the gates at last. The fort was safe. And then just at this moment he tried to hook a drive to the two-hundred-and-sixty-two yard seventeenth, hit the ball in the heel and faded it out into a water hazard at the right, fifty yards off line. Once again he had thrown away his advantage. The best he could get at this hole now was a 5, once again two over par. And the battle was still on top of him. He still had the baffling home hole to face where it is easy enough to take a 5.

By this time, the excitement in the big gallery was tremendous. There was a general belief that Jones could not pull himself together again for the third time in one round after bad slips. His approach to this last green stopped forty feet from the cup. And over the curling uphill slope it was easy enough under the conditions to take three putts. But Jones has the knack of facing a tough situation with genius. He had to hole a twelve-foot putt at Winged Foot to tie Espinosa, he had to hole a twelve-foot putt at St. Andrews to stop George Voigt. He holed both. He had to hole a forty-foot putt to be sure of beating Mac Smith. He holed it. He may slip or skid or falter here and there, but when the big moment arrives, he always comes through, even though the odds against him at that one spot seem incredibly heavy.

A shirt-sleeve crowd hails Bobby Jones just after he sank the winning forty-foot putt to win the National Open in the siroccan heat at Interlachen, Minneapolis.

Jones Writes More History BY O. B. KEELER

Has Now Won a National Title
for Eight Years in Succession

I CAME AWAY FROM INTERLACHEN WITH A PRO-nounced hunch that it was Bobby Jones' last start in a National Open golf championship, but this is by no means committing Mr. Jones to anything. I know that Bobby's father would be just as pleased, if Bobby stayed out of the big show from now on, and I am even more certain his mother would be pleased, but Bobby—and very properly—declines to say anything about it.

"If I said anything I might have to change my mind," said Bobby a few minutes after it was definitely established that he had won the United States Open title for the fourth time.

This, by the way, recalls a little conversation we had some five years ago. Just after Bobby had won the National Amateur Championship at Oakmont, Bobby confessed at the time to an ambition, after extracting a promise that I would never write anything about it unless it should happen to be realized. "Which is not at all likely," said Bobby.

This was the ambition admitted by Bobby in 1925 when he had won the United States Open once and the Amateur twice. "I'd like to be national champion of the United States six years in succession," said Bobby, "Either Open or Amateur. Then I could feel that I had left a

sort of dent in the game. You might say it would be some kind of a record, but I don't suppose there is enough chance of it to lose any sleep worrying about."

I don't know if Bobby has lost any sleep worrying about the record he was compiling year by year and tournament by tournament, but I do know that when he finished at Inter-lachen he was National Champion of the United States for the eighth year in succession, which is two years more than his pet ambition called for back in 1925. He has won four Open Championships and four Amateur Champion-ships in the last eight years and never both in the same year; his remaining chance to equal somebody else's record is this year, for Chick Evans did this in 1916 at Minikahda and Merion.

Along with the eight American titles, Bobby has captured three British Opens and one Brit-ish Amateur, a round dozen major champion-ships in all, which puts him one title ahead of Walter Hagen, who has won four British Opens, two United States Opens, and five P. G. A. Championships.

Somehow I think seven National Open Championships is enough. Bobby should go pecking away at the Amateur Championships in this country and in Britain, if and when he is sent over with our Walker Cup outfit, and I think he might reasonably expect to pick up a couple more of these pretty titles before he hangs up his clubs. I do not think he needs to add anything more to his record in the Open Championships. He may live to be a very old man, but he will never live to see anyone else match his record of the last eight years in the United States Open, four first places and three second places, two of them after a tie and a play-off.

When Jones drove from the tenth tee in his final round the gallery lined both sides of the fairway from the tee to the green, three hundred and forty-five yards away. It is estimated that nine to ten thousand persons followed him in his final round, which is probably a record for a golf gallery following a single match.

Untrod Ground BY GRANTLAND RICE

How One Man Finally Took the Uncertain Feature
Out of a Seldom Certain Game

THERE ARE TWO FEATURES OF THE RECENT Amateur Golf Championship which blend together to make the final story. They show at last how Bobby Jones walked upon the untrod ground of a game always full of uncertainties.

The point is that in the midst of all these uncertainties Bobby Jones was never close to an uncertain turn. He almost gave the appearance of loafing through the championship, putting on pressure when he had to do so, but never crowding himself. Against Johnny Goodman at Pebble Beach last year he lost the first three holes where he started 5-6-4, two over par. Against Ross Somerville, a high-grade golfer, in his first start at Merion Jones went out in 33 and finished the round four under par. There was no uncertainty about this match from the start.

You can understand how extended or extensive the uncertainties of golf are when you recall that Jimmy Johnston, the defending champion who won at Pebble Beach a year ago, failed to qualify—

That Doc Willing, who reached the final round at Pebble Beach lost in his first round at Merion—

That Chandler Egan, who reached the semifinal frame at Pebble Beach, failed to qualify—

That Francis Ouimet fell in his first round against an eighteen-year-old entry from Detroit—

That Von Elm, Willing, Voigt failed to reach the thirty-six-hole test—

These are just a few cases. Apparently something of a highly harassing nature was happening to every star in the field—except Bobby Jones. When you consider all this and figure that Jones started at Sandwich last May in the Walker Cup matches, and never lost a match through the closing days of September at Merion—with two medal play victories over the finest professionals in the game in between, you can see just what is meant by the one man who at last was able to lift himself above the uncertainties and inconsistencies of a game that at one time or another takes them all by the throat and leaves them throttled on the field. It has taken Bobby Jones by the throat more than once. But through his famous five-month campaign of 1930 he was at last able to shake himself loose from the grim grip that marks the game.

Just consider these cold and unbiased facts:

Starting early last April in the Southeastern Open at Augusta, Bobby Jones led a field of crack professionals, including Horton Smith, Gene Sarazen, Johnny Farrell, Al Espinoza,

153 | *Untrod Ground*

The champion still finds it necessary to tape his hands here and there when he faces a whole week of steady golf.

Part of the detail of Marines who escorted Jones across a narrow foot bridge leading from the approach to the eleventh green, where his final match ended.

Jones putting on the eleventh green, where he stood dormie eight. He laid the ball dead for a 4. When Gene Homans missed his long putt for a 3, Jones' fourth and final major national championship of the year was all over.

Ed Dudley and many others, by thirteen strokes in seventy-two holes of medal play.

He led a fine field at Hoylake in seventy-two holes through the British Open.

He led a stronger field at Interlachen through seventy-two holes in the United States Open.

He led the amateurs through thirty-six holes of medal play at Merion.

Here you have a test of two hundred and fifty-two holes at medal play against the finest professionals and amateurs in golf on both sides of the Atlantic. Jones finished in front at every start.

What about match play?

Jones won his match at Sandwich in the Walker Cup play. He won eight matches in the British Amateur. He won five matches in the United States Amateur, making a total of thirteen matches, most of them over the shorter eighteen-hole route, where almost anything can happen.

When you consider these two records at medal and match play and recall again how quickly golfing form and the touch of the game can grow sour and stale, you begin to get a better idea of the job he handled through this season, through the almost endless strain that started at Augusta and then ran through Sandwich, St. Andrews, Hoylake, Interlachen and Merion.

In any other game, this record might not be listed as such an outstanding feat. In tennis, for example, if you can beat an opponent somewhat decisively one day, you can beat him the next day—or next month. Form and touch and timing don't vary so suddenly.

But golf is a different sort of game. It comes and goes. Even with Tommy Armour's wonderful 1930 record, he lost his touch at Interlachen after opening with a 70. Even the smooth swinging Mac Smith had one or two off days in tournament play. The records of Armour and Smith were phenomenal. In some respects they reached even more brilliant heights, at their best, than anything the season showed. But for unadorned consistency, the final test along the top plateau of the game, the all-season record of Bobby Jones goes far and away beyond anything golf ever knew before. And in his final stand, where the strain is usually the hardest, there was almost no contest. It was a week of slaughter.

The answer to this might be explained in these few words: correct fundamentals of swinging; ability to handle almost unlimited concentration; unusual determination; physical strength and stamina; experience of twenty-seven major championships.

This was the combination that turned the trick. To this, one must add a blend of genius that is always beyond diagnosis—that has no place in any clinic. The results were obtained with an ease and grace that were born in the system. Of the thousands of pictures taken of Bobby Jones, no one can recall an awkward pose, an awkward swing, a sign of effort beyond control.

The gallery explodes with enthusiasm as Gene Homans congratulates Jones on his almost incredible sweep of international golf.

Memories of Jones' Start BY CHARLES EVANS, JR.

The Victor in the 1916 Championship

Recalls a Few Personal Impressions

NOW, WITH THE WHOLE WORLD RINGING WITH Bobby Jones' victories, he seems to be a fitting subject for me to write about. For I won the first National Amateur in which he appeared.

Bobby was then fourteen years old—a stocky youth of extraordinary strength whose shots easily went as far as those of the grown men with whom he played. The scene was the Merion Cricket Club, near Philadelphia. In the first round he drew Eben Byers, a former National Amateur Champion and then a very fine player. It was a most peculiar match and strange rumors reached me which I later verified. Not being a highly "concentrated" golfer, my gaze was wandering over the course, catching this sight, speaking to this friend and that, and in course of time, falling upon Bobby and Byers engaged in a club-throwing exhibition. Everyone predicted failure for Bobby, although he was holding his own. I reasoned differently because I had suffered from a few such exhibitions, and unlike most grown-ups I had not forgotten them. I remembered a favorite club that went to the bottom of Long Island Sound, and another favorite club that went out of a taxicab window in Paris. Here, thought I, was a golfer of tender years whose heart was really broken by a poor shot.

Far be it from me to say that golfers should lose their tempers and throw clubs on a golf course, thereby endangering the lives of the gallery and the other players. More and more it seems that golfers of the present day are getting away from the practice. But I do say that the angry golfer gets a zip to his shots, and the calm one loses the crispness so definitely needed for the sailing qualities of a well-judged shot. I have no doubt that Bobby felt always strong enough to stand the strain of anger.

Bobby beat Byers at Merion. And the next day he beat Frank Dyer, at that time a fine player. My roving eye saw the chubby boy across the course with his three or four followers! I have often thought of that lately. That gallery of three or four has increased to thousands whenever he sets his foot upon a golf course.

Now, why is Bobby this outstanding success? For one thing, I think that his concentration is superior to any golfer's that I have ever known, and that is saying much. I noticed this in the final of the Amateur at Minikahda three years ago. He said only two or three words all day long. He did not dislike me; he merely was out to win. It was a queer sensation. Bing! A sharp report and then he was away, lost in that gallery. Now and then I would see him in the center of that great mass, but his very expression said, "Do not speak to me! I have a job to do."

On the eleventh tee in the afternoon, I have just lost three holes in succession. I am seven down and eight to play. Soon I have a very tiny putt to make it seven and seven. I fuss with it, wondering why he does not give it to me. He cannot lose, and it seems such a waste of time not to say "Take it!" if only to save time, but never a word from Bobby. Do not misunderstand me. I was not expecting a gift—just a little concession to expedite the game. In my surprise I fuss a little with the shot and accidentally my club touched it. Did it turn over? Bobby nodded, saying nothing. I congratulate him. What is the difference? Eight or seven, or one up? The better golfer won.

That night I wonder and think of the hundreds of putts given away. Now I know. It was concentration of the most perfect kind. No outside interest shall interfere! It is not a social matter, but a hard, stern business. The game over, and there is a different Bobby, courteous and friendly.

Another reason why Bobby is such a great golfer can be gleaned from this little story. We, the members of the Walker Cup team, are seated around a room at a Western country club. It is Bobby's room. Someone begins talking stocks. I, deep in market trouble, sit and listen. Sweetser talks confidently of the future of certain securities because the great house for which he works has some special information. Johnston has just made lots of money out of a stock he names. Von Elm has received a tip from an influential source in Detroit, and he is cleaning up. Ouimet says little except that he takes orders and lets the other fellow play it.

Bobby listens, too. The talk gets into the millions. Some are looking at the figures in the paper; my eyes are still sore from the day before at the translux. I close my eyes and think of the Stock Exchange, and the wrecks that lie along it, when I am startled by a remark from Bobby Jones. "What is the use of all that money?" he said. "Just enough to be even and kind to every one."

Bobby can never know how I envied him then. Not his golf game, but his freedom from worry. Just to be even and start over again.

This is how Bobby Jones appeared when he teed off in his first National Championship, at the Merion Cricket Club in 1916. He was then fourteen. He led the field in the first of the two qualifying rounds with a card of 74.

Mr. and Mrs. Marshall Field—she was the former Mrs. Dudley Coats—spent their recent honeymoon on a private course at Sandwich, England.

The game knows few more enthusiastic followers than Douglas Fairbanks, and the other half of the family—who is, of course, Mary Pickford—is rapidly acquiring a like interest and enthusiasm.

Governor Al Smith forgets his political problems temporarily in trying to get out of a sandtrap at Shinnecock Hills, Long Island.

Curtis W. Willock, a California golfer, declines to allow an injunction by a physician against trudging around the course to bar him from golf. He recently appeared at the Annandale Country Club at Pasadena, California, with the "Linksmobile."

Swing, Don't Hit BY MACDONALD SMITH

*Think of Swinging the Club If You
Want Smoothness and Control*

I HAVE OFTEN BEEN ASKED WHAT I CONSIDER the main reason for any control I might have over a golf club. To me the answer is simple. As I see it, the golf stroke is a swing and not a hit—and I think along these lines.

I believe most of the trouble in golf comes from the idea of hitting. When you think of the word "hit" you almost immediately tighten up. You lose most of your smoothness and rhythm. Hit means tension—tightening of the muscles. The word "swing" means just the opposite. You know when you swing that you can't tighten up.

Just watch the average golfer or the pretty good golfer take a practice swing. He looks like a champion. You see, there is no ball to hit, so he lets the swing take care of itself. But when you put a ball in front of him, he almost immediately forgets about swinging and starts in to hit. And nearly always he hits too soon.

You have to time a "hit" in golf. But the swing will almost time itself. I think that is rather easy to see. Just remember the power you feel in a practice swing, where you start the clubhead in motion and let it have its way. A large part of this must be mental. No one can think of hitting and then keep swinging. The thought of hitting, as I have said before,

kills the idea of just swinging the clubhead.

You will find also in swinging that you get much freedom from your hands, wrists, arms and body. They then have a chance to work naturally and easily, without any sudden kinks entering the stroke. I believe in letting the left shoulder come well around towards the right side, and, from the top of the stroke, I swing with both arms, especially the left, which is in charge at the start of the downward movement. I feel that I am swinging the club with my left hand, wrist and arm from the top. The right will always get there in time—usually ahead of time.

In this swinging motion, the weight moves more easily from left to right, than from right to left, just as the hands and arms and clubhead travel. I think the basis of control after the swing starts is hitting against the left leg. So I make sure that my left heel is back and that my left side is in place. If the left leg isn't ready to catch and hold the swing at the moment of impact, it is almost impossible to have any power left or to have any control. The clubhead will then fly off the right line, either cutting or smothering the ball. I just swing against the left side; this also helps to keep my head in place and to prevent my looking up.

I am quite sure, that, if all those now playing golf would only go in for the idea of swinging the club, they would make much greater progress. Let them swing from a good body turn where they can stroke from the inside of the line—inside out. But as long as most of them think only of the hit, they are going to have trouble. They are going to keep on lunging and tightening up, hitting too quickly, getting the body in too soon.

It seems to be human nature to hit rather than to swing. Most games are hitting games. Yet the golf stroke is such that it demands smoothness and one can get this smoothness only from swinging the clubhead in a free, easy way. You'll get all the distance you need.

Macdonald Smith is shown at the top of what is probably the most graceful backswing in all golf.

The Greatest of Golfers BY ROBERT T. JONES, JR.

A Tribute to the Rare Skill of
Miss Joyce Wethered

ORDINARILY I WOULD NEVER TAKE ADVANTAGE of a friendly round of golf by making the play of a person, kind enough to go around with me, the subject of an article. I realize that everyone likes to play occasionally a round of golf when reputations can be forgotten, with nothing more at stake than the outcome of the match and a little friendly bantering afterwards.

Just before the British Amateur Championship at St. Andrews, Miss Joyce Wethered allowed herself to be led away from her favorite trout stream in order to play eighteen holes of golf over the Old Course in company with her brother, Roger, Dale Bourne, then recently crowned English Champion, and myself. At the time, I fully appreciated that Miss Wethered had not had a golf club in her hand for over a fortnight, and I certainly should have made no mention of the game had she not played so superbly.

We started out by arranging a four-ball match—Roger and Dale against Miss Wethered and myself—on a best and worst ball basis. I don't know why we didn't play an ordinary four-ball match, unless we fancied that the lady would be the weakest member of the four, and that in a best-ball match her ball would not count for very much. If any of us had any such idea at the start of the match, it is now quite immaterial, for there is not the slightest chance that we should admit it.

We played the Old Course from the very back, or the championship tees, and with a slight breeze blowing off the sea. Miss Wethered holed only one putt of more than five feet, took three putts rather half-heartedly from four yards at the seventeenth after the match was over, and yet she went round St. Andrews in 75. She did not miss one shot; she did not even half miss one shot; and when we finished, I could not help saying that I had never played golf with anyone, man or woman, amateur or professional, who made me feel so utterly outclassed.

It was not so much the score she made as the way she made it. Diegel, Hagen, Smith, Von Elm and several other male experts would likely have made a better score, but one would all the while have been expecting them to miss shots. It was impossible to expect that Miss Wethered would ever miss a shot—and she never did.

To describe her manner of playing is almost impossible. She stands quite close to the ball, she places the club once behind, takes one look toward the objective, and strikes. Her swing is not long—surprisingly short, indeed, when one considers the power she develops—but it is rhythmic in the last degree. She makes ample use of her wrists, and her left arm within the hitting area is firm and active. This, I think, distinguishes her swing from that of any other woman golfer, and it is the one thing that makes her the player she is.

Men are always interested in the distance which a first-class woman player can attain. Miss Wethered, of course, is not as long with any club as the good male player. Throughout the round, I found that when I hit a good one I was out in front by about twenty yards—by not so much when I failed to connect. It was surprising, though, how often on a fine championship course fine iron play by the lady could make up the difference. I kept no actual count, but I am certain that her ball was the nearest to the hole more often than any of the other three.

I have no hesitancy in saying that, accounting for the unavoidable handicap of a woman's lesser physical strength, she is the finest golfer I have ever seen.

It has been six years since Joyce Wethered was active in formal competition, yet her game is reported to be as consistently brilliant as at any time since she first attained peak form more than a dozen years ago.

Competitive Golf BY JOYCE WETHERED

A Famous Star Discusses the Mental Side of Competitions

THE STRAIN OF COMPETITIVE GOLF CAN MEAN one thing and one thing only, a call upon tensely-strung nerves. However much a player may apparently be blessed with a calm and placid exterior, appearances are generally deceptive; the odds are that there is a tumult of emotions surging beneath the surface that onlookers rarely suspect.

The consolation is that this is an experience common to the majority of those who have to face, what is generally and erroneously termed, "the music." The music may be felt, if not expressed, when one steps off the last green. But while the ordeal is in progress, the discords are varied and numerous. Yet I am certain that no one can excel at any game without having to suffer from the sensations inseparable from "nerves."

The only resource one has to fall back on is to try to understand and develop a philosophy which will cope with them, and here experiences will naturally differ. I know perfectly well the two qualities which have helped me most: the first is honesty with oneself and the other is a sense of humor. We have to recognize our weaknesses, and unless we realize them and refuse to make allowances for them they will catch us out every time in a crisis. When, however, we have learned them all and

recognized that we are going to suffer from them always, it is worth a great deal to be able to feel amused by our own peculiar idiosyncrasies.

I know the feeling of standing on a tee with real fear in my heart, the match slipping away, the club feeling strange and useless in my hand; and yet I have fortunately been able to laugh at the ridiculous side of my feelings and the way they are apt to behave on these occasions. This reflection is, after all, perfectly sane and rational, and perhaps by this method of persuading oneself of its value it may be possible to regain a more normal balance.

As the mind governs the whole of our actions, everything will go to pieces, unless it is working on the right lines. Set a thief to catch a thief: set the mind to watch the mind. It becomes in moments of excitement full of fancies, fears or useless wandering ideas and it may be no easy task to tie it down to the matter in hand. Concentration is at the root of success, if the mind can be made to concentrate on the right idea. If it will persist in thinking of harmful ideas, the execution of the shot is bound to suffer. If the mind is full of the fear of failure—a dread of the next approach, a persistent thought of three putts although the green is still far away—then, in my experience, there is but one thing that can at all help and that is to see the humor of the situation.

If one is really amused (and I must admit one rarely is) at the absurdity of one's thoughts and anticipations, he can, and frequently does, respond by changing and coming back to a more practical and firm outlook on things. Otherwise if you cannot direct your thoughts into more suitable channels, they will grow worse and worse with the result that the horrible feeling that you are "cracking" badly becomes a certainty.

Confidence undoubtedly is a great asset, perhaps the greatest of all. But it must be genuine and based on facts. For myself I can never manufacture it; I can only keep it, if I know that I am hitting the ball correctly. If my method is working rightly, then I know that I can have confidence in producing the shot—and that is everything.

Of course, confidence depends on the avoidance of distraction. Big occasions are very apt to scatter thoughts in every direction. The only safeguard is to create your own little world and for the time being to live in it. I used to play my matches with one definite idea, to be entirely engrossed in my own shots and to be oblivious, so far as I could be, of what my opponents were doing; also to concentrate for the first part of the game entirely on figures and to let the match take care of itself until it took a definite form. I am convinced that to play a match hole by hole right away from the first tee is an unnecessarily wearing process. It will, more often than not, make you play down to your opponents if they happen to be off their game. On the other hand, if they are playing well, your best figures are all you can hope for in any case. The scramble will probably come towards the finish.

And while speaking of scrambles, it may be an unusual experience of my own, but I find the moments of greatest strain to be when I have succeeded in building up a really promising position—say, two up and five to go, or one up and three to go. If at this critical moment you have birdies shot at you, the situation is altered without any need to blame yourself. But when it is just a matter of steady figures to win, then there can come the biggest strain of all.

Playing against Miss Cecil Leitch at Troon in 1925, after a most grueling and exhausting battle, I at last became two up and three to go, with an excellent chance of winning the sixteenth to finish the match. Instead of that, I faltered and only halved it. To make things worse, I was unable to halve either of the last two holes, dropping a stroke at each. These were the most trying holes I have ever had to play. That I won at the thirty-seventh has always seemed to me a most unjust tribulation for my opponent.

It is just that final clinching of a match that can, with some people, be so difficult. Here what little philosophy one may possess is apt to desert one. The end is just appearing in sight; one is so near and yet so far from being secure. I have often wondered how Miss Glenna Collett felt during our match at St. Andrews in 1929. I wonder if at any time she felt quite as uncomfortable or unhappy as I did when I stood two up and four to play, or as utterly incompetent as when I had to run my ball up on to the narrow shelf of the Road Hole green to win!

It can be the greatest fun to look back on thrilling encounters that are past. But how fortunate also it is that we cannot know what trials and ordeals the future holds for us—on the links or off!

See that your head remains rigid from the moment when you have finally taken up your position and are ready for your swing, until you have struck the ball.
HARRY VARDON

The King of Bunker Play BY WALTER R. MCCALLUM

Freddie McLeod and His Method of Cutting
the Ball from the Sand

FREDDIE MCLEOD, WHO HOLDS DOWN THE PRO-
fessional berth at the Columbia Country Club,
near the Nation's Capital, comes closer than
any other golfer to absolute control of the ball
in a bunker. So say the professionals who have
played with him and paid to see the little
wizard of the bunkers play the cut shot.

You've watched a billiard master play intricate massé shots, where the cue ball strikes the
object ball and comes back down the table in a
long curve, as if drawn on the end of a string.
Well, that is just the way McLeod plays the
cut shot.

Ask Bobby Jones, who dabbles at billiards
and golf, and knows the wizardry of the little
Scot. He and hundreds more amateur and
professional golfers yield the palm to Freddie
McLeod in this involved business of getting
the ball from a bunker. He may not knock the
ball far from the tee, and he may not putt like
Jones or Hagen, but put him in a bunker and
watch him go. That ball comes out, spins like a
top around in a sweeping curve, and usually
leaves him with a short putt for the hole.

Just how is this shot played, and can it be
considered an addition to the usual repertoire
of bunker shots? Most golfers know only two
—the explosion shot, where the club literally

blasts the ball out on a blanket of sand; and
the chip shot, that most risky of strokes played
from a good lie in a shallow trap.

The cut shot, as played by McLeod, is
different from either of these. At the Columbia
Country Club, where the members regard his
wizardry with bunker shots as commonplace,
they say he can't miss because he is so close to
the ball. And that statement may have something in it, for Freddie stands only a shade
more than five feet four inches in height, and
weighs only one hundred and twenty-two
pounds. When he plants those brogans down
and wiggles them around in the sand to get a
firm stance, nothing short of a typhoon or an
earthquake can shake him.

Therein, says Freddie, lies the foundation of
the cut shot. You must get your feet firmly
planted in the sand, where nothing in the nature of a slip can creep in to destroy the accuracy of the clubhead. Cast aside your grooved
swing, for this cut shot demands a swing from
the outside in, where the left wrist brushes the
pants leg as the clubhead passes under the
ball. But get yourself set firmly first.

Lay the clubhead back until the back of the
head lies almost flat with the sand. The backspin is obtained by the wide open face and

the spin is imparted by the face of the niblick meeting the ball on the bottom. But there is more to it than that. A few grains of sand on the bottom of the ball or on the blade of the niblick form an abrasive surface between the ball and the clubface, acting like the ribbed face on those clubs which were barred back in 1922. That abrasive surface is what puts the bite on the ball, and how it comes back, even on a fast green, when the backspin gets to work. I've seen Freddie hit two yards past the hole and bring the ball back on the near side of the cup. I've seen him bring it back on a short hop or on a long curve.

But how he punishes a golf ball! If everyone played the shot as McLeod plays it, golf ball stocks would be due for a sudden rise. When Freddie hits the shot as he wants to hit it, he fairly tears the cover off the ball. No grindstone could have a worse effect on the cover of a golf ball than that fast clubface, coated with sand, has on the surface of the balata cover. One good cut shot and the ball is fit only for practice.

Freddie misses them, once in a while. If he meets the ball in the "belly," that pill shoots out of the bunker as if shot from a gun. He always makes a point to have the opposite side of the green cleared of spectators. In England four years ago, Freddie came within a couple of inches of ruining Bobby Jones. Had the ball been a couple of inches closer it might have cost Jones the championship he later won.

Bobby and Freddie were playing a practice match at Lytham and St. Annes, after Bob had won the qualifying round at Sunningdale and just before he went on to win the championship. Bob had seen Freddie play his cut shot so often with such uniform success that he disdained to stand aside on the opposite side of the green as the little Scot went into the shallow bunker at the seventeenth. McLeod hit the ball squarely in the "belly" and it sailed out of the bunker straight for Jones. Bob ducked and that duck was all that saved him, for the ball sailed right through the spot he had occupied and came to rest in the heather seventy-five yards away.

"I was playing with Bob at Atlanta," Freddie said, "and my caddie had seen me play the shot a few times. Each time I asked him to stand away from the pin, but he insisted on holding the flag just the same. Well, I hit one in the middle and it caught him in the stomach. He was a sick boy for a few minutes and you should have seen him shy away from the pin after that. I don't think he held the pin any more that day."

So much for the failures, and they are not so many. He probably averages something near sixty-five per cent good shots; thirty per cent perfect shots; and five per cent missses.

"I get a lot of fun out of that shot," Freddie said. "And I get a great kick when it comes off as I want it to." He disclaims credit for inventing it, claiming it is his variation of a shot that has been played on the other side for years.

"If I hit it right, the ball rises quickly, with tremendous backspin, spins on its axis for a brief space and then comes back in a right-hand curl to the cup. I don't know how many I've holed from the sand, but I must have holed a good many.

"There are several angles to the shot," McLeod says. "First you must plant your feet firmly in the sand, to make sure you won't slip. Then you must lay your clubface back until it is pointing straight to the sky. Aim to the left of the hole, keep your eye on the imaginary bottom of the ball and hit hard. The shot must be hit hard to come off. A half-hearted swing will probably leave you still in the bunker, and you know the main idea of bunker play is to get out in one stroke. First get out, and second, get as close as possible to the hole. But there is still another trick. Don't grip the club at all with the thumb and forefinger of your right hand. Let them lie loose on the grip, so the club can fit loosely in the circle formed by them. The shot is entirely a left-handed one, and, if you attempt to punch it with your right hand, you'll probably meet the ball above the bottom and go chasing over the landscape looking for it. Either that, or you'll be rushing a caddie to the hospital."

Freddie plays the shot with a little mashie-niblick weighing 15¼ ounces, a tool fine enough to shave with. He could play it with a sand iron, but he says he couldn't get up speed enough with the weight of the wedge and speed is the essential thing in the shot.

Bob Jones has played a lot of golf with Freddie and has tried the shot. But he admits he can't play it. Bob plays a modified edition of the cut shot, but it is a combination of explosion and cut shot, and not the true cut shot as Freddie plays it. The champion says he has tried it, with indifferent results, and has had to return to his own method.

Tommy Armour has tried the shot and plays it occasionally when a quick-rising ball with backspin is needed. But Tommy admits his percentage of failure is too high to establish the shot as a permanent one in his collection. McLeod stands alone as the king of the bunkers. His cut shot makes him that, but he can explode and chip also. How well he plays them is shown by the fact that not long ago, in a game at Columbia, I saw him play out of eight bunkers in eleven holes. Where most professionals would have been struggling to keep par in sight, Freddie was one under. This wasn't freakish. It was just regular stuff to the man from North Berwick. He was around in 70, just par for the course.

Freddie claims anyone can play the cut shot. "All it takes is knowledge of the fundamentals and close attention to your work," says Freddie. Sure, anyone can play it. Yeah.

For all of the enthusiasm and interest which she manifests in politics and matters of state, Lady Astor, the American-born member of British Parliament, finds time to indulge in an occasional round of golf. This picture was made on a London course at a match between artisans and well-known society women.

The Aga Khan, famous sportsman from India, tries out his game in a match at Roehampton, near London.

Some Experiments and Observations

BY O. B. KEELER

Time of Flight of a Well-Hit Golf Shot

IT WAS DURING THE SHOOTING OF THE SEVENTH episode in his series, "How I Play Golf," that Bobby Jones and I got to talking of the duration of the period of flight for a golf ball: the time it remained in the air. It was no new topic, certainly. Long before Bobby was born —at any rate, some time in the Nineties—I read an article setting out the flight-period of a golf ball in a full shot from a driver as being six seconds. Well, I won't say I read that article or reference in some book in the Nineties, but it must have been written then, because it was about the gutta-percha ball, which was superseded by the rubber-cored ball in 1902; the year in which Bobby Jones was born, by the way.

Anyway, we were talking about the flight-time, and I asked Bobby if he had tried it, and he said yes, several times.

"It's just six seconds, for a full shot with the driver," he said.

And that was interesting. Because, of course, Bobby had tried it with the lively ball, which could be hit thirty per cent, or such a matter, farther than the stubborn old guttie. And the duration of flight was the same for each, with the modern ball carrying two hundred and forty yards (we'll say) and the gutty around two hundred.

This suggested another line of thought.

"Did you ever try the time for a full shot from the other clubs?" I inquired. He had not.

So we tried that, during a lull in the picture-shooting. I had a stop-watch in my pocket, which we used for timing movie scenes. Bobby let fly half a dozen shots with the spoon, first. Shot after shot traveled out in a smooth and equable trajectory and as the ball touched the turf, an eighth of a mile away, the split-second hand of the timer was right on top of the mark for the sixth second.

"I think the ball can be made to stay up longer," said Bobby. And he hit a towering spoon shot, with a lot of spin holding up the projectile. It was up six and two-fifths seconds.

"But that's not the normal full shot with the spoon," was Mr. Jones' comment. And he reached into the bag for a big iron.

The big iron shot was as far as that from the spoon, carry and roll, but not quite as far in the air. The flight-period, however, was six seconds; precisely the same.

Bobby grinned, and picked up a mashie-niblick. "We'll try a full shot now," he said. And up it buzzed, a fairly steep pitch, with a lot of backspin, and a flight of (I should say) one hundred and forty to one hundred and fifty yards; more range than Mr. Jones ordinarily exacts of the mashie-niblick.

The ball touched the turf as the split-second hand touched the sixth second. Over and over again.

The bell rang then, and school "took in." So we did not try the intermediate irons or the niblick. But I think it was needless, anyway.

Judged by the flight-time of a full shot from the driver, the spoon, the big iron and the mashie-niblick, a golf ball struck by an expert with normal trajectory remains in the air six seconds from *any club* except the putter, which, of course, is not a club for making full shots. The extreme range of the niblick under normal conditions, and played as a niblick, will be only half as far as the carry from a properly struck driving shot. But the ball will consume six seconds in flight, just the same. And this apparently was true of the guttie, just as of the modern ball.

An action photograph of the queen of British golf, Miss Diana Fishwick. She arrived here in February to take part in the winter program in Florida.

When Miss Glenna Collett defeated Miss Virginia Van Wie in the final of the Women's Championship at the Los Angeles Country Club, she scored her fifth win in this golf classic, thus establishing a new record. It was eight years ago she first won.

Championship Stuff BY WALTER HAGEN

Some Valuable Information on How
to Go About Saving Strokes

THERE ARE MANY THINGS TO BE CONSIDERED IN championship golf. Continual practice, if properly directed, will naturally tend to mold a perfect swing. But I might say that, while I have won quite a number of important championships, I have yet to play a perfect eighteen-hole round. I have turned in some very satisfactory cards, but there have been poorly played shots marked up on the best of them.

Bobby Jones, Tommy Armour, Leo Diegel, in fact any good golfer, will tell you that there is no such thing as a perfectly played eighteen-hole round. You may score well, but the several recovery shots that will be the talking points of the round will be the result of poorly played shots, and even the most brilliantly executed recovery cannot wipe out the memory of the faulty shot that necessitated it.

Mental and physical ease and comfort result naturally from the least possible strain, so it is easy to understand why the easiest shot will result in the least amount. Few good golfers would think of playing one hundred feet over a tree to a closely trapped green if a chip shot to the same objective were possible.

I have found that it is always possible to play one of three shots from any lie in the fairway, usually in traps and many times in the rough. I have divided these shots into three classes.

My Number One I call the Do or Die, for it is the shot that *must* be dead to halve or win a hole in tight match competition. Number Two is the Average shot—not designed to get dead, but cutting down the element of risk to an appreciable extent by eliminating much of the hazard that must accompany the Do or Die effort. Number Three is the real Safety First shot and is worthy of any champion. In fact, if good golfers would spend more time experimenting with a wider range of shots, scoring in major events would be more consistent.

Starting with Number One, the Do or Die shot, we have a good basis for comparison. This shot is extremely dangerous and to explain just what I mean by classification of golf shots, let's assume that we find our ball in a trap guarding the green. The steep side of the trap is between the ball and the flag. The green slopes *down* to the cup. If we elect to play the Number One shot—explode right for the pin, we have a chance of laying the shot dead, but we must also face an equal chance of not getting out of the trap—or exploding across the green.

As we study the shot further, we find that by

playing a mashie-niblick, we have a chance to chip up on the green, not dead but, say, twenty feet from the flag. This will assure us of a try for a long putt and this is what I call my Number Two shot, for we have at least two chances of getting on the green to one chance of missing the shot.

I claim this is more than a fair percentage in our favor. With a mashie-niblick, we may half-top the shot, yet the force of the stroke will result in enough top-spin to carry the ball up the sloping side of the trap and it will stop *on* the green. It is hard to completely miss this type of shot. Of course, it may be played too hard, causing the ball to roll clear across the green and trickle off into another trap, but the chances are it won't, and it is on this basis of comparison that I consider the odds are two-to-one in our favor—and twenty-foot putts *are* made sometimes.

There is usually one extremely difficult hump or mound guarding each trap. The one we have elected to use in our shot classification has a tricky mound near the center of the highest part, and directly between the ball and the flag. We went over this mound with our Number One shot, veered slightly to one side, when we used our mashie-niblick for Number Two, but now we reach down in the bag and shake out our old Safety First!

When we tried Number One, we realized the danger of not getting out; the necessity of imparting enough backspin to hold the ball, for, remember, the green slopes down from the ball to the cup. The knowledge of all that might go wrong with the shot did not help us in the ever-present battle with tension. We had more confidence when we selected our mashie-niblick and chipped around this forbidding hump, because the shot required less loft, and we didn't have a worry about "cut." We also felt certain of getting within twenty feet of the flat.

Now we play old Number Three—Safety First! No possible chance of missing the shot, for we have examined the side of the trap and realize that very little over-spin will be neces-sary to make the ball climb the bank and stop on the green. We have at least three chances of getting on the green to one chance of missing the shot, so out comes our putter! We *know* that ball is going to stop on the green. The chances are it won't be close to the hole, *but* we will be out of trouble and *on* the green.

For the average player, I recommend the Number Two shot. It is much better to be within twenty feet of the cup than still in a trap, or off the green, thinking of a shot that went wrong and debating the chances of getting within inches of the flag on our next try. It will help on the next tee, too!

The same holds true off the green. Learn to use the right club to reach the green. The green may be soft; the grass may be long; or, if clipped, the grain may run the wrong way. If your ball carries to the clipped portion of the putting surface, it has a chance to roll right up to the flag. So why should you essay a high pitch, sacrificing the rhythm and simplicity of your swing in an effort to impart backspin, when you can get the same results with an *easier* shot? You would never think of playing a high-pitch shot into a stiff cross wind if a pitch-and-run shot were possible, so why tempt fate by trying a really *hard* shot when an easier effort will bring just as good, and possibly better, results?

Smart golf is winning golf! Cut down the element of chance. Horton Smith is one of the most promising young professionals in golf, because he is learning to *save* shots. He is deadly around the greens, yet there is nothing spectacular about his game. His shot work is the result of profound study and experiment with his irons. If he thinks a putter from fifty yards off the green is the right club, he uses it. If he thinks it necessary to use his deepest-faced niblick, he won't hesitate.

Taking more time with your shots may sometimes help. And, remember, you can never be sure which club to use until you have carefully studied your lie and the several approaches to the green. It is rarely possible that you will find a shot that has to be played in one certain manner.

Walter Hagen sizes up the task before him in playing from a shallow bunker. Hagen counsels against heroic measures unless circumstances plainly demand them.

After starring for eighteen years—Walter Hagen decides to get Walter Hagen, Jr., ready to keep the Hagen name high in golf in the years to come. Hagen, Sr., is giving young Hagen exactly the same swing he has used so long.

Sarazen at Sandwich BY BERNARD DARWIN

Highlights of Gene's Remarkable
Performance

THE AMERICAN VICTORY IN THE BRITISH OPEN championship is becoming so much a matter of course that you perhaps find it monotonous even as we do. Still I think there was something a little particular about Gene Sarazen's win at Princes, Sandwich, and there ought to be some enthusiasm to spare for him. Not only is he a delightful person and a great golfer, but he has been a most faithful invader of ours. It is nine years since he came over to Troon, failed mysteriously enough to qualify, and declared that he would come back if he had to swim.

He has been as good as his word, he has come back again and again and has come very near to winning, though the luck never seemed to be with him. This time he has done it in style with a score of five under fours (the best ever made in our championship) on a course very nearly 7000 yards long, and not even Bobby at his best could have been better. Doubtless he has played as well at home but he has never been so brilliant here, nor so consistent nor so entirely serene and confident. The long trail has had an ideal ending.

The story of his win is one of perfectly steady, triumphal progress. He led the field on the first day with a 70, from Mac Smith, Whit-

combe, Alliss and Davies at 71 apiece. On the second day he had a 69 and the gap had widened from one stroke to three, 140 against Alliss' 142. In the third round it was yet a little wider—Sarazen 209, Havers 213. At the end, the scores read Sarazen 283, Mac Smith 288, Havers 289. Before the championship began he was a warm favorite, and there never was any real cause for doubt. Sarazen was not in the least lucky so far as his play was concerned, but fortune did him one good turn in sending him, already the leader, out early on the final day. Experience shows that to start first and set the other fellows something to shoot at is the way to win. People very seldom come up from behind in the last round. They spurt heroically but, as a rule, the spurt just fails. The knowledge of what must be done may be an advantage to a golfer with the temperament of a Hagen, though even that I doubt, but most pursuers it kills.

Sarazen started the most crucial of rounds, the third, just after nine o'clock in the morning. He played superbly, for his score of 70 hardly did justice to his golf, and by half past eleven he had produced a record-breaking and —for all the other players—heartbreaking total of 209. It was enough, as Andrew Kirkaldy used to say of Harry Vardon "to break the heart of an iron ox." Take Alliss' case, for instance. If he kept to an average of fours he would yet be five strokes behind with a round to play. Nearly all the pursuers tailed off a little, and no wonder. Macdonald Smith who had wrecked his chances in the second round with one lethal and most unnecessary seven, did a fine 71, but he was too far behind. When Gene set out on his last lap, just after one, it seemed that there was nothing left but a march of triumph, that he could coast pleasantly home like a bicyclist down the last hill.

Then, however, there came the whispers that Havers, the last man who had kept the cup in England, was doing amazing things. So, in fact, he was, and when he played a gorgeous long second to within six or seven feet of the last hole he had that putt for a 67, which would put him within three strokes of the leader. He missed the putt, and every putt was terribly vital—but still four strokes was not a ruinous deficit from his point of view, nor an absolutely winning lead from Sarazen's.

News, of course, travels quickly over the links and I believe it was at the turn, which he had reached with perfect steadiness in 35, that Sarazen asked and was told about Havers' round. Perhaps he would have done better to have cotton wool in his ears, for homeward he did become, in his own words, a little "wobbly." Heaven knows it was not to be wondered at, if he did, for the strain must have been great. It seemed that he had got over the unavoidable bad time when he holed a great putt, slap against the back of the tin, at the fourteenth; but then there crept in three shaky, uncomfortable fives. A bad last hole might have put him in jeopardy or at least he must have thought that it might, but he played it like the bravest of the brave—too big shots and a putt laid stone dead—and 74 was good enough.

I raced away again to the far end of the course to see how Havers was getting on, but in my heart I felt something approaching a certainty that he could not do it. A 70 to tie for a championship coming on the top of a 68 was more than could be asked at fortune's hands for any human being. When he dropped two strokes to par in the first five holes, Havers practically signed his own death warrant. He struggled on well and bravely and with three holes to go his score was all fours. Two threes and a four to tie, with three long and difficult holes to play! Of course it was hopeless. Havers went out to hole his long putt at the sixteenth, ran some way past, and missed coming back. That was the end. He played the last two holes rather slackly, as well he might, and when he missed a putt for four at the home hole, he found he had missed a tie for second place. Indomitable Mac Smith had added a 70 to a 71 and ended with 288.

Of the other American players, Armour was well in the picture at the end of the first two rounds with 145—six behind Sarazen. His third round was 74 and then the leeway was too great; he eased up, played a thoroughly bad round of 83 and finished quite a long way down the list. Pursey had four steady rounds and Robert Sweeney, the Oxford undergraduate, did uncommonly well in surviving to the last day. In one of his rounds he went out in 32 and looked as if he was going to burn up the course in an unexampled conflagration, but fell away on the way home. He is, however, a fine young golfer with style and power and will make himself better known.

From the point of view of weather, there has never, I think, been such a championship in Britain. There was, save only for an hour or two on the first day, scarcely a puff of wind. The ground had plenty of run, the greens were smooth and of an ideal pace. In fact from the point of view of interest the conditions were too good—there were no very exacting shots. It was a matter of doing over and over again the straightforward and comparatively simple thing. A wind would have made the golf more interesting to watch. Incidentally, I think it would have made Sarazen's margin of victory larger for he and his game are perfectly suited to combat it. The course, as I said, was hard on 7000 yards long and yet the players never, or practically never, took a wooden club through the green except at the seventeenth hole. If the brassie is ever to come into its kingdom again, it would seem that courses will have to be not 7000 but 8000 yards long, and then everyone will lie down and die from pure weariness!

Mrs. Gene Sarazen and Gene display the British and United States Open Championship golf trophies just after Gene had been presented with the latter at the Fresh Meadow Country Club. Gene enjoys with Bob Jones the distinction of having won both trophies during the course of the same season.

Superb concentration on the shot at hand characterized the play of Gene Sarazen throughout his four rounds at Sandwich.

Back on the Crest Again BY GRANTLAND RICE

Gene Sarazen Captures First National
Open Title in Ten Years

GOLF IS THE STRANGEST OF ALL GAMES. IN almost every sport a new champion comes along, has his day, and then fades into the darkness of obscurity as some younger and better rival takes over. But golf is not like this. I can look back to Skokie in 1922, ten years ago, when young Gene Sarazen, twenty years old, led one of the greatest fields that ever gathered on one course—Bobby Jones, Walter Hagen, Bill Mehlhorn, John Black, Mac Smith, George Duncan, Abe Mitchell—the best of the tribe. He came through with a devastating 68 that took command and held it.

After that, ten years of struggle and disappointment. Year after year the stocky, hard-fighting Sarazen tried in vain to break through the golden portals of golf just once more. He could win almost any championship except the two national opens—the British and the United States. As year after year went by, these two big titles continued to flutter just beyond his reach.

The big point is that after ten years of failure in this respect, Sarazen's determination to break through became keener than ever. In fact, he trained and prepared for the double ordeal of Sandwich and Fresh Meadow in a way no golfer ever worked before. He went on

a simpler diet. He practiced more. He built a thirty-ounce driver, double the weight of his own club, to build up greater strength in his hands and wrists. He wanted strong, fresh hands to use down the stretch when tiring hands have wrecked more than one fine chance to win. As a result of all this work and study, the Sarazen of 1932 is a far greater champion than the Sarazen of 1922, where in almost every other sport he would have had to pay his toll to time.

One striking feature of Sarazen's play is that he has won his three major medal play titles in three different ways. At Skokie in 1922 Sarazen was away to an early start on the last round where he gave Bobby, Walter Hagen, John Black and others a 68 to shoot at—a 68 that left him a 288 total. The pace was too fast for the field that day.

At Sandwich in 1932 he killed off all competition with a blistering sweep in the first three rounds—70-69-70. This left him a chance to coast home in 74. He needed no counter attack here.

At Fresh Meadow he needed a 68 to win and his answer was a 66—the most remarkable finish any golf open ever knew. Gene had played Fresh Meadow hundreds of times before without any great pressure. His best score had been a 67. This included friendly matches and exhibitions. He needed the hardest sort of pressure to beat that 67 with a 66, where he knew he had to beat par to win—where he knew that he could not afford to miss a single stroke. When he left the fourteenth green, seven under even 4's, he knew the job was over, and yet he was smart enough to stick to the job in every detail until the final putt was in. For Fresh Meadow is the type of course that can blow up in your face at any given moment.

Here is one example—Sarazen had just remarked the last day that any one could lose or gain five strokes on a single nine holes. Sarazen and Cruickshank did better than this—Olin Dutra, playing magnificent golf, took an 8 on the fifteenth. On this same hole Sarazen and Cruickshank each had three's. They had picked up five strokes on one of the leaders along the length of a single fairway.

This point is brought out to show the miracle touch needed for a 32-32-34 on three successive nines where just one mistake might have easily led to a 37 or a 38.

"Golf," John Low once remarked, "is an 'umblin' game." It is more than that. It can be cruel at times in its sudden thrust. It has been hard on Mac Smith for over twenty years. At Fresh Meadow it was poison to both Phil Perkins and Bobby Cruickshank, who deserved more than many champions have earned.

Consider the case of Perkins. He leads the field with 219 strokes at the end of the third round. As he walks off the fifteenth green in the final round he is four under 4's. He finishes with a 70. On nineteen occasions out of twenty that type of golf would have left him in front by at least two strokes. It was a great finish and a game one for any pacemaker to throw into the face of the pursuing pack.

Consider next the case of Bobby Cruickshank. The wee Scot had tied Bobby Jones at Inwood nine years before. From a rather slow start of 152 for the first thirty-six holes, he had bludgeoned his way into the thick of the battle with a great 69 on the third round. And from

this point he had closed out the day's assault with a still greater 68; 137 for the last day of an open championship must be registered as one of the finest performances ever entered in the records. It was the finest last day's double round of golf ever scored.

It earned a tie with Perkins and the promise of another play-off until, faint and far behind, that drum beat of Sarazen's march was heard. There was still faint hope when both knew Gene had once more turned the corner in 32 strokes. But even that faint hope vanished, when he started home 4-4-3-4-3-3.

I have always felt that an Open Golf Championship is one of the most dramatic of all the competitions. There is a reason for this. The surviving field of the United States Open usually includes around one hundred and fifty of the greatest golfers in the world; most of them seasoned campaigners, most of them established stars. It is seldom that any one golfer can walk away from the pack. There are nearly always three or four survivors left in a headlong rush to the final green, where the galleries sense that every drive, every approach, every putt may easily decide the crown.

It has been this way through most of the championships. At Fresh Meadow there was Olin Dutra furnishing the early fireworks. A little later the scene shifted over to José Jurado of the Argentine, a fine golfer and a fine sportsman, colorful and popular with the crowd. The fine play of Leo Diegel and Wiffy Cox brought new actors to the 6800-yard stage. Then the final section of the closing climax turned to Perkins and Cruickshank until Sarazen decided "to bestride this narrow world like a Colossus."

Leo Diegel had turned from billiant but inconsistent play to the most consistent golf in the field for two years, where he never went above 75 in eight rounds at Inverness and Fresh Meadow. In these modern championships there must be consistency mixed with at least one brilliant thrust. There must be no particular weakness with any club.

Walter Hagen, hitting the ball better than

he did ten years ago, had lost his old putting touch. He was longer and straighter from the tee on a general average. But his putting stroke could not locate the pin. The marvelous putting stroke that Sarazen called to his aid down the stretch was one of the main factors in his success. The ease and smoothness of his putting stroke indicated clearly enough that every part of his machinery was well oiled, running without any friction. Coupled with the power of his long game and the accuracy of his approaches, Gene's work on the greens made his case complete. Probably no championship has ever seen anything to surpass his slashing drives and long-irons in the final round.

After the Amateur Championship last year George Von Elm announced a future program for himself as a "businessman golfer." He has collected around $7500 in prizes during the play in the winter open events, leading all the professionals in total prize money won.

Tommy Armour recently added the British Open Championship to his National Open Championship and his P.G.A. Championship.

Eight years intervened between the time when Billy Burke first began to attract attention as a young amateur until he found the pot of gold at the end of the rainbow in the Open Championship at Inverness, near Toledo.

Old Tom Stewart BY GEORGE T. HAMMOND

The Last of the Traditional Clubmakers

NOW THAT OLD TOM STEWART IS DEAD, WHAT IS to become of the sentimental golfers who loved their pet clubs as, in an earlier day, men loved their guns and dogs? There will be more heads turned out by the St. Andrews smithy—handed down to old Tom's sons, Tom, Jr., and Jack—but there's no one left to copy with care the pet mashies and favorite irons of the connoisseur.

The personality of this rugged Scot had many vivid sides. Old Tom was one of the institutions at St. Andrews.

His fame, symbolized in the little pipe which was stamped into every one of the heads hammered out at his forge, carried around the globe, and when, in his seventieth year, he succumbed to an ailment while on a brief holiday last July, he was the last of the internationally known clubmakers still active in the business. George Nicoll, whose irons are equally famous, had retired a short time before, and all the old-timers—Robert Condie, Anstruther, Willie Auchterlonie, and the others—had long ago dropped out of the picture.

Aside from the superb workmanship which went into Tom Stewart's heads, there were other sides to his fame. For one thing, he probably copied during his lifetime more different clubs and styles than any other half-dozen manufacturers taken together. And

largely for this reason, there hasn't been a new style placed on the market within the last decade but Stewart had had its counterpart years previous.

It was hard to get any two experts to agree on just what was distinctive or valuable about any one of Stewart's creations. And it should hardly need to be added that there were few duplications in Stewart's line. He was a ceaseless experimenter and considered each head a work of art alone.

In the matter of duplications, Stewart was firm. Some time ago, after Bobby Jones had won the British Open at Lytham and St. Annes, a newspaperman looked at Jones' clubs and wrote a story about them, mentioning the predominance of Stewart heads. With native shrewdness and enterprise, Stewart then ran a facsimile of the story in his advertising and stamped R.T.J. on heads of the same models.

But when an order came from America for a set of R.T.J. heads drilled for steel shafts, Stewart refused to furnish them. "I will not make heads drilled for steel shafts," he said, "until steel shafts have been legalized by the Royal and Ancient." And he had exactly the same theory about making out of stainless steel duplicates of his Coventry metal heads.

For year after year Stewart's forge, about a quarter of a mile from the Old Course at St.

Andrews, near the railway station, turned out between 3000 and 5000 heads per month. Business had been steadily more prosperous. Rival firms would try to get one of Stewart's men to work for them, so they might speak of having a "Stewart foreman" in their shops.

Although well along in years, Tom himself was a steady worker at the forge, dividing his day into three working periods. He would begin at six in the morning and work till nine; then take an hour off and resume again from ten till one. After lunch he went back to the job from two till six, when he called it a day. In busy times he would personally go over the orders and divide up the shipments so that everyone would have some of the limited number turned out.

It took this devotion to his work to build up the great reputation, but old Tom was far from a drudge. Invariably, the forge was closed when a big match was on at St. Andrews. When Bobby Jones won the British Open over the Old Course, the smithy was closed for two days. "I saw Bobby play every shot," said Stewart proudly. He kept an interesting scrapbook of clippings and pictures of his favorites.

And of all the great golfers who came to St. Andrews, or corresponded with him, four had his highest admiration. They were Jones, George Duncan, Jim Braid and Jock Hutchison. Nothing would please old Tom more than to welcome some visiting American, doff the well-worn apron and go out to the Old Course to show just where some of these players had made a shot that was historic. Duncan's long standing record of 70 Stewart knew by heart.

Tom had unbounded enthusiasm as a player. For more than forty years, he played a round of golf four times a week on the Old Course, and as recently as last May he scored an 89, going out in 42 and coming home in 47, in windy weather. Through his broad Scottish burr, Stewart would rather have talked about his last round of golf than anything else.

The extraordinarily large hands and fingers, which no one who met him ever forgot, helped to make him a first-class player when he was in his prime. He was a massive figure, weighing 190 pounds, and oversize in every dimension; a legendary figure of a smithy. For headmaking is more of a blacksmith's job than a clubmaker's, which accounts for the small number of experts in the line. In this country there were never any noted fashioners of individual clubheads, except of wooden clubs, which with a rasp and knives could be modelled at the bench.

His curious antipathy to having his picture taken, an obsession which few of his friends cared to cross, may have been due to his realization of his almost grotesque proportions, especially the Stone Age fists.

Aside from his business correspondence, which brought letters postmarked from every country in the world, Stewart had many friends who kept him posted on affairs of the realm. Reports came to him from the far-flung points, telling him how the young fellows who had caddied for him had secured jobs as pros.

The top-notch amateurs were always requisitioning some replica of a pet club, and two years ago Stewart made a perfect copy of a spade mashie for Frank Craven, the actor-playwright, in less than two hours, doing most of the work himself.

The passing of old Tom Stewart closes a well-defined period in golf history, when consecrated craftsmen supplied the implements for the game in the true spirit of its traditions. An article in an American trade paper a short time ago intimated that Stewart had lost much of his business because he had refused to make heads for steel shafts. It drew this reply from the St. Andrews sage. "That's hitting below the belt. My business is greater than ever, but I will always follow the R. and A. edicts. Why should people make guesses at things they know nothing about?"

Tom Stewart's interest was golf, and he prided himself on knowing all about that. To fill his niche we have now only monotonously clicking machines, fire-breathing open-hearth furnaces, and a hundred robots. At their passing no retrospective picture will be penned, for personality has gone out of clubmaking. Tom Stewart is dead.

The Left Is in Charge BY ROBERT T. JONES, JR.

Citing Certain Reasons Why the Left
Arm Should Dominate the Swing

THE MORE I PLAY AND STUDY THE GAME OF GOLF, the more firmly do I become convinced that the left arm must dominate in any sound swing. I know full well how difficult the average player finds it to bring about this state of affairs in the swing, but nevertheless, I haven't the slightest doubt that this is the objective toward which he must aim, if he is to acquire a sound swing.

The backswing is merely a means of getting into position, and is not itself directly concerned with hitting the ball; still it is an important part of the swing, and I think the more reliable play is made possible by asserting left-hand control from the very moment the club leaves the ball going back. I have been experimenting a good bit lately along these lines and I have found on every occasion, even when playing very short shots, that my results are uniformly good when, and only when, I swing the club back with my left hand, allowing the right to grip the shaft only very lightly.

The value of a leisurely backswing has been adequately and rightly stressed. One reason why it is so important has to do with the left-hand control, for the right hand is naturally a fast-mover, and it is safe to say that most quick backswings are caused by too much right

hand. In its backhand position, in order to swing the club back, the left hand must push and the left arm must extend itself. Its motion, therefore, must be slower than that which could be accomplished by a quick pick-up with the other hand.

The magnificent breadth of arc to be seen in the swings of most expert players has caused general admiration. Only one thing can make this wide sweeping arc possible, and that is a left arm extended to the utmost. Obviously, if there is any bend in the left elbow, the path of the clubhead must be contracted by that much. And certainly the most effective way to assure a full extension of the left arm is to force it to do most of the swinging.

In starting the club back, the first movement should never be performed by the wrists alone. It is a common mistake to originate the motion of a swing by rolling the wrists so that the clubhead swings in sharply around the knees, or by an abrupt pick-up with the right hand. These mistakes are both fatal, because they immediately place the left hand at a disadvantage in such a way that it is almost impossible for it ever to assume control.

The best motion at this point is a straight push backward with the left arm, involving a direct turn of the hips and shoulders. If this is done correctly, the clubhead will actually be the last thing to move, and it will in the end be dragged away from the ball, lagging behind the hands. This motion not only preserves, or rather assures an extended left arm, but it also encourages a free hip turn, a thing which is most difficult for the average golfer to achieve.

Two action photographs showing how Bobby Jones keeps his left side in complete charge of the swing.

Memories of Freddie Tait BY BERNARD DARWIN

What Would We Not Give to Hear His Pipes Again?

IT IS PLEASANT TO BE ASKED TO WRITE SOME memories of Freddie Tait, because he fell in the South African war now over thirty-two years ago, and one naturally begins to be afraid lest he be forgotten. To be sure, his name remains among that of the ancient and unquestioned heroes, but to most of the golfers of today he can be no more than a name. Let me try then to set down what manner of man and golfer he was, and try to explain the secret of his extraordinary fame.

In his day and in his own Scotland he was a national hero. I do not think I have ever seen any other golfer so adored by the crowd—no, not Harry Vardon or Bobby Jones in their primes. It was a tremendous and to his adversaries an almost terrifying popularity. He was only thirty when he was killed; a brave young man, like many others who were killed, a very good specimen of the plucky, cheerful, open-airish regular soldier; a thoroughly friendly creature, who made friends with all sorts and conditions of men, but not in any way possessed of an outstanding mind and character.

He was just a thoroughly good fellow who played a game very skilfully and in a cheery and chivalrous spirit. Yet, when he died, it is hardly too much to say that Scotland went into mourning, and his old friend John Low wrote a full-sized biography of him that was widely read. This is a remarkable state of things, and there was some remarkable quality about this otherwise ordinary man which, in the language of the theatres, "got across," so that he had only to step onto the links for everyone to follow him.

There was one thing about him that appealed intensely to the Scots, namely, that Freddie was above everything else a Scottish golfer. Discussion simply ceased for him when any other course was compared with St. Andrews. He stood by the old course and in the old ways. He liked the thrust and parry of match play and regarded score play as no more of a game than rifle shooting. He loved in particular the foursome, and, when he played in one, was always most particular to consult his partner on any possible point of tactics. Moreover he had, as it seems to us, that almost parochial sort of patriotism which wants above everything else to see the Englishman beaten.

These were some of the things in his character that made the crowd love him, but there was further something in his manner of playing that drew them to him as a magnet. He had beyond question a wonderfully gay and gallant way with him, when playing a big match, a cheerful and brave and confident, though never a swaggering, way. Attraction is always apt to be mutual and perhaps the crowd loved Freddie because he loved the crowd. He never "played to the gallery," for there was no touch of self-consciousness, and he did not show by the movement of an eyelid that he knew the crowd was there. But he liked the tramp of the feet behind him and the squeezing his way through the serried ranks around the putting green. He liked the feeling of being in the ring because it inspired him to fight his hardest and best.

His actual shots, too, made a great appeal, because his game combined two qualities not always found together. He seemed to be hitting the ball almost gently, at any rate not nearly as hard as he could, to be playing "well within himself." At the same time he could, if need be, pull out a colossal shot and some of his recoveries were historic. To talk overmuch of a golfer's recoveries is often to give to those, who have never seen him, a false impression.

Many people, I fancy, think of Tait as a wild and terrific hitter, with an exaggerated "St. Andrews swing," who was constantly off the course and as constantly saving himself. This was not so. Though a St. Andrews golfer he had not the typical slashing style of Fife; his swing was not noticeably long; the club was taken back slowly, under very obvious control, and he seemed to be steering it to the very end of the follow-through. Now and again he could, it is true, play a surprisingly crooked shot, and, in that regard, it must be remembered that he often had leave from his regiment only a day or two before a championship, and was apt to be rather short of practice. When he did play that wild shot he could and did make noble amends, but in his best game there were no recoveries because none was needed.

As quite a young man, Freddie had a great reputation as a driver, and he made one vast drive on frosty ground at St. Andrews which was said to have disproved the theories of his father, an eminent professor of physics, as to how far a ball could go. Later he kept these mighty swipes for emergencies and made accuracy his aim from the tee. I ought to add here that he had no truck with any such innovations as the overlapping or Vardon grip and held his club in the old-fashioned way with the right hand noticeably underneath the shaft.

In my recollection the most interesting parts of his game were his iron play and his putting. He was a thorough master of all iron clubs, but, as befitted one brought up among the banks and bracs of St. Andrews, he liked best the pitch and run and could play it in every conceivable form, varying with the nicest artistry the height of the pitch and the length of the run. He must have been very strong in the forearms (incidentally, he was a fine gymnast), for he could send the ball very far with very little apparent effort. Mr. John Low says of him that he "hardly ever used the half or three-quarter swing at all; every iron shot was a development of the forearm stroke and his whole

Lt. Freddie Tait in formal uniform. This picture was made just before his untimely death during the Boer War.

approach play a glorification of the so-called wrist shot."

His putting was done with a decidedly lofted cleek, so that the ball, when he struck it, leaped perceptibly in the air. He perhaps counteracted this loft a little by standing somewhat in front of the ball, but it was a very free style, and never was there a putter who so regularly obeyed the maxim "never up, never in." He was always going for the hole and his reputation as a lucky player was, I think, due to this persistent boldness. Fortune favors the brave at golf, and there never was a timid putter yet who got the name of being lucky. How clearly I can see him now thrusting out his right foot in a most characteristic gesture as the ball hits the back of the tin and drops at the end of a long putt.

Freddie never won the Open Championship though he was several times near the top of the list. I doubt if he ever had the mechanical accuracy quite to keep up for four rounds against the best professionals—and Vardon, Braid and Taylor were his contemporaries. He had it in him to beat any man in a match and his two chief triumphs were his victories in the Amateur Championship of 1896 and 1898. They were won in his two distinct manners, the first by absolutely faultless golf, the second by a series of heroic recoveries following on wild shots.

I was not at Sandwich in 1896 but I did see him win at Hoylake two years later and never shall I forget his beating John Low in the semifinal at the twenty-second hole. I was a partisan of John Low that day and it certainly did seem to me that he was fighting not against a mortal man but against the devil that was in his jerkin. Two vast wooden club shots did Freddie lay so near the hole, if not positively dead, that he holed the putt. One was at the sixteenth over the cross bunker. One, even more crucial at the twenty-first, and in each case his wretched adversary had played faultlessly, whereas Freddie had made some mistakes that deserved to be fatal.

Moreover, at the twentieth he holed a great racing putt over a ridge and furrow green.

That putt really was lucky, I believe, for Freddie looked a beaten man. Over those brassie shots he took plenty of pains, addressing the ball very deliberately, but he just went up to the ball and hit that putt as if in despair.

His two chief rivals were the two giants of Hoylake, Harold Hilton and John Ball. Hilton was nearly always beaten. That great little man simply could not play against him, and Freddie took perhaps some unchristian pleasure in crushing him. I remember particularly the Amateur Championship of 1898—the first I ever saw. Hilton was Open Champion, in great form and on his own Hoylake. He had to meet Freddie Tait in the fourth round and all Liverpool was coming out to see the match. At lunch time I saw Freddie assiduously practicing putting in front of the clubhouse. "Is it going well?" someone asked him, and he answered with a victorious ring in his voice, "It will be this afternoon." It did; so much so that he won by six and five and the poor Open Champion crumpled sadly beneath the attack.

The other Hoylake champion, John Ball, had something the best of Freddie. He could and did generally beat him and only the most pervid of Scots—I am English—will deny that John Ball was the greater golfer. Their most historic match was at Prestwick in 1899—Freddie's last championship before he sailed for South Africa. He was at one time in the morning five up but he pulled down to three at luncheon and was finally beaten after a desperate struggle by John's driving a three at the thirty-seventh hole.

One must be allowed to be a little obstinate about the heroes of one's youth and I shall always maintain that this was the greatest golf match I ever saw, not by any means the most perfect in play, but the most nearly divine in point of god-like thrusts by either side. The Hoylake supporters in a body retired to the clubhouse after the thirty-sixth hole. They could endure no more and waited, with their heads presumably buried in cushions, till someone came to tell them what had happened.

It was in that match—at the thirty-fifth hole —that two much quoted shots followed one another from the big Alps bunker, Freddie playing the ball out of a deep puddle on to the green and John Ball following with an equally great shot from hard, wet sand close under the face of the black wooden sleepers. I can still see Freddie's ball rocking on the little waves that he made in the puddle as he waded in. I can hear a Scottish friend next to me crying out in an agony, "Wait until it settles, Freddie, wait till it settles." I don't think he had the least notion that he was speaking above a whisper. Yes, that was a day of heroic emotions.

The ball that floated was of course a guttie and Freddie never played with or heard of another kind. He was dead and buried before the Haskell caught on. As far as it is possible to form a judgment he would have been exactly suited to the rubber-cored ball, even though his sturdy, conservative soul would have hated it. It would have responded to the full to his restrained and almost persuasive stroke. How he might have fared against the champions of today is a futile inquiry, but he was a very great golfer with a certain exciting quality in his game that has never been surpassed. If he had lived he would have been sixty-two today, no longer a champion but still, if I mistake not, a formidable player and a great partner in a foursome around St. Andrews.

Let me end with the late Mr. Andrew Lang's words about him. "I never heard a word said against him except a solitary complaint that, in the lightness of his heart, he played pibrochs round the drowsy town at the midnight hour. What would we not give to hear his pipes again?"

Alan F. MacFie won the first British Amateur Championship in 1885. He is now a perennial spectator at almost every event played on the British Isles.

The Art of Good Putting BY ROBERT T. JONES, JR.

Building the Foundation
for a Consistent Style

IT MAY BE SET DOWN AS A FUNDAMENTAL THAT there is no possibility of putting well without a rhythmic stroke, directed by relaxed muscles, which can receive and execute the most delicate impulses. This means, for one thing, that the proper address for putting calls for the sacrifice of everything else to a position and feeling of comfort. Anything which works contrary to this purpose is a serious handicap, and one consideration which leads to such an end is the practice of trying studiously to imitate the method of another player.

I can speak of this practice with a background of considerable experience, rather sorrowfully gained. I don't believe anyone has ever undergone more worry than I have in trying to develop a reliable method. I can recall trying at different times to imitate the styles and methods of nearly all the great putters. I have even gone to the extent of trying to look like them and to affect the same mannerisms. But in the end, I became thoroughly and unalterably convinced that my attempt thus to imitate was in itself my most serious mistake. It was only when I gave up the practice entirely, and set about trying to accommodate myself to a completely comfortable position, permitting a smooth rhythmic swing, regard-

less of everything else, that I began to make headway. Now I give no thought to the placing of my feet, the inclination or the facing of my body, or anything else, except to be sure that I am comfortable as I start the club in motion.

For example, I would never consider for a moment advising one to keep his head still or his body immovable. Whether or not the best putters do keep their heads or bodies absolutely still while making the stroke, has nothing to do with the case. The point is, in trying to do these things the player is almost sure to set up tension, and the mere thought of consciously trying to keep the head or body absolutely still means introducing an outside distraction. My advice is to forget these things entirely, and to allow them to take care of themselves. If the motion of the swing suggests the necessity of a slight body movement, then by all means let it move. The feeling of ease is worth all of the mechanical precision that could be crowded into a dozen strokes. Rhythm and smoothness are the two things mostly to be desired and attained.

Along somewhat more specific lines, in my own particular case, I find that it is an aid to comfort to stand with my feet quite close together, just as I would normally, if I were not playing a golf stroke; to permit a slight bend in both knees, and to keep my arms close to my body. Possibly, since the word "keep" suggests the exercise of restraint, it may be better to say that I refrain from extending my arms away from the body.

While my arms are near my sides, there should never be a consciousness of purposely trying to "keep" them there. Inspection shows that my right forearm touches lightly the front of my trousers. At the same time the left is free from the side. I am careful to see that this situation exists, and that this arm remains entirely free. If the left elbow presses closely against the left side, no end of trouble can and most likely will result. In such a position, it produces or encourages an almost irresistible tendency to yank the putt off the line to the left. Whenever I begin to pull my putts, and experience a feeling of tightening in the left wrist, as I hit the ball, I immediately turn this left elbow even further out, until it points almost directly toward the hole. This helps not only to correct the tendency toward locking, but also encourages stroking along the proper line.

The correct mental picture of the putting stroke itself is that of a sweep. I like to feel that instead of driving the ball toward the hole, I am merely sweeping it over the turf. The two essential factors in, and characteristics of, this kind of stroke are a marked flatness of the vertical arc on which the clubhead is swung, and a good alignment, which prevents cutting across the ball. As to the former, the head of the putter should never rise abruptly from the turf, either in going back or in following through after impact.

The conception of the stroke as a swing rather than a hit tends to prevent a pick-up with the right hand, which is the chief cause of cutting. If one swings the club back mainly with the left hand, there will be little danger of lifting. Furthermore, the head of the club will be taken back along an inside horizontal arc, whence it can most easily be directed along the intended line in the forward swing.

Numbers of players encounter trouble in putting because they fail to employ a backswing long enough to allow a smooth stroke without hurry or snatchy effort. The inclination is very strong, especially when trying to hole a difficult five- or six-footer, to lapse into the error of feeling that the shortest possible backswing offers the least danger of turning the clubhead away from the correct setting at impact. It sounds reasonable enough, to be sure. But in my own case, I have disproved entirely the logic of the feeling, in terms of results.

I find that troubles only multiply when I shorten my backswing. I begin to stab, jab, and cut with the clubhead, and very shortly, any semblance of what is ordinarily called putting "touch" vanishes. An ample backswing leisurely and free, made from a thoroughly comfortable position, not only improves my putting stroke mechanically, but also helps to keep me in a better frame of mind, where I am able to concentrate on hitting the ball correctly, without worrying about irregularities and hidden rolls in the green, once I have given those things due consideration, and settled to the task of playing the stroke.

The putting stance used by Bobby Jones. Notice the vertical line, formed by the shaft between his left eye and the ball.

"Nipper" Campbell Takes the Stand

BY JAMES RESTON

One of the Famous Veterans of Golf in This Country
Discourses on Its Various Phases

I HAD THOUGHT OF GOLF ONLY AS A VERY ENJOY-able game until I met Alec "Nipper" Campbell. To him it is something entirely different. It is something by which to live materially and spiritually. It is his philosophy.

Golf in the United States was still at the lisping age when, in 1899, Alec came from St. Andrews to be professional to The Country Club at Brookline. A nineteen-year-old boy, a kind of a golfing engine, he was brought to Boston by Mr. G. H. Windeler, one of the fathers of the game in America. Today, Alec Campbell, waggish and whimsical, is the professional at the Moraine Park Country Club course, which he built, in Dayton, Ohio.

Though the glamour of his competitive days has slipped away, Alec brings the enthusiasm of a boy to the game, a contagious enthusiasm which beggars description. In mid-winter he seldom misses a day at the course. At fifty-three, lithe and small, he walks hatless across two miles of frozen ground to the course. Once there, he works in his shop or wanders over the course, club in hand. Alone, contented, his is another world.

What, then, after thirty years in competitive golf in America and Britain, has this man to say of the game?

On the difficulty of teaching:

"Y'know it's hard to teach the game. Man's like a narrow-moothed whiskey bottle. He can only tak a word or two at a gulp. Ye have to tak it slow. But the American's a guid pupil. He's studyin' the game. Tak the Governor! [Former Governor of Ohio James M. Cox, Democratic candidate for the presidency in 1920.] There's nae nonsense wi' him. He'll see ye doin' somethin' an' he'll ask ye how ye did it.

"An' when ye tell him, he'll work at it till he masters it. He may have to change it to suit his style, but he gets the notion an' he uses it. I'm no tellin' ye he's the average, for he's no', but the Yank's workin' along the same lines, thinkin' his way through. An' that's why he's doin' sae weel."

Are there any new ideas regarding the golf swing or the ways of teaching it?

"It's the ways o' sayin' 'em that's new: no' the ideas. The auld caddies on the ither side knew 'em all before a lot o' these people touched a club. But that's no' tae say the new ways o' sayin' and describin' things is no good. A man can understand 'keep your chin back o' the ball' when ye'll jist muddle him by tryin' to describe swayin' to him. But this 'forward press' business they're bletherin' aboot is as auld as the hills. Only we called it the 'delay.' An' the 'drag' they talk aboot is no' much different. They're a' done for the same purpose —to make ye start the club back richt."

What is the most important fundamental?

"The grip. An' I'll tell ye why. The golf swing's the same as onything else. Start it richt, an' chances are ye'll end it richt. But if ye're wrong at the start, ye're a goner. If the grip's guid, the first foot o' the back swing'll be guid, an' there ye are. Now I'm no' sayin' that means the overlappin' or the interlockin' grip. When Sarazen was a bad gripper, it was nae because he was lockin' his fingers. It was jist because he did nae have his hands the gither."

Why have the British golfers slipped?

"They've no' got a model, an' they're no' takin' the pains wi' it. The war hurt 'em. They're no 'footerin' wi' it the way they used to."

How about Sarazen's proposal to enlarge the golf cup to eight inches?

"Y'know, I had Nancy, ma wife, save me some tin cans an' I tried 'em oot. I had 'em in the greens there. The only thing I like aboot 'em is the sound. My, they've got a grand sound!

"They'll hang Gene if he talks aboot 'em on the ither side.

"If they really want to give 'em a try though, let 'em play a tournament wi' 'em, an' have the pros play thirty-six holes to the eight-inch cups an' the amateur to the four-inchers; an' then let 'em change on the last thirty-six an' see what happens."

Have there been many changes in golf course construction in the past twenty years?

"They're jumpin' frae pillar to post on the course buildin'. For a while they were tryin' everythin'. I was lookin' for 'em to run ventilation shafts up the trees afore long. But they're gettin' more sensible in their auld age. When I

first came to America, all the par-four holes were bunkered in back. The Chicago Golf Club course is an example. A fine course, but it penalizes the bold player. We've learned to stop that, to give the man wi' courage the advantage. That's why ye see nae bunkers in back o' my two-shotters at Moraine.

"They're only learnin' how to make bunkers. Ye see so many that are nae bunkers at a'. A bunker should be put down only where it'll make ye play a grand shot in order to save a stroke. Otherwise, it's meant to cost ye. These things ye can slap the ball out of are nae bunkers.

"There was a tendency to build courses only for the best players a while ago. An' that's no richt. Courses should be built specifically for the average club member with tees so situated that you can push the scratch player back. The best course is the one that's built into the landscape ye've got."

What did the steel shafts do to the game?

"Plenty. They changed the correct use of the club from a *swing* to a *hit*. We slug the ball now. They give more distance with the wooden clubs. But there's nae comparison through the fairway.

"The steel shafts changed the professional's life entirely. Once he was a craftsman, a mechanic. In the old country he learned the trade jist like a carpenter, an' often he went before a notary an' signed a contract before he got the job. It was part o' his work to season hickory, to cut the heads richt oot o' the block, an' to know how to balance a club.

"Everything's ready-made now, an' when there's any repairin' to be done, back it goes to the factory. Club-makin' is a lost art. An' do ye see what that has done to the pro? He has nae anythin' to do wi' himsel'. He sits aroun' the shop when he's no' teachin', because he's fed up wi' playin'. What's to become o' him? What's he to do when the tournament days pass? He'll be sick o' the game an' he'll have naethin' to fa' back on.

"Wi' me it's different. I'm always experimentin' wi' somethin': a new clubhead, or some new kind o' grass for the fairways, or the rough. An' that's anither thing. The pro's goin' to have to learn how to take care o' the course. It'll be part o' his job in the future.

"There's nae question, the pro killed the goose that laid the golden egg. He made pennies and lost dollars when he boomed the steel shaft. He made some money all at once, but now that he's got a' the racks jinglin' wi' steel, he's no gettin' any repairin' to do, and he can't re-sell the same members on the fact that they should throw away their one-hundred-dollar sets jist because he proved that he was wrong."

What is the future of golf?

"It's jist beginnin'. The boys are swingin' golf clubs in the streets in these days instead o' baseball bats. Public course golf should get to a greater number o' people a' the time. I think maybe we'll have more golf at the golf courses in the future an' less social life."

Alec's is an interesting history. Raised on the sea-born turf at Troon, he accepted golf as he did the mist of Scotland's hills. It was part of the landscape. It was more important than school and far more interesting. So every day he walked for a mile along the beach to the course by the sea, and this he did from the time he was old enough to carry the sticks.

Every night he visited the burn at Black Rock (the second hole on the Troon course), for there he had concealed in the mouth of a drain a piece of fishing net ("which ol' Mr. Cameron, a fisherman, gied me") which yielded its weekly supply of gutties. Then, with only the plover and the wild duck for companions, with fishing nets laid out to dry upon the fairways, he played with a sense of possession.

These nightly rounds bore fruit. One of the dramatic stories in Scottish golf history concerns fifteen-year-old Alec Campbell, a "wee laddie with an amazing short game," who beat the best players in his section of the land in the first tournament he entered. All Scotland heard of this feat, and everyone was astonished. But not Alec. "I told ye I'd win, Mither,"

he shouted as he rushed into the house after beating Stewart Garner, two and one, in the final. His mother gave him "tuppence" (four cents), "an' I went to Troon on a jaunt!"

Four years serving his time, a year of which he spent in worshipping Harry Vardon, and a few months as a journeyman at St. Andrews, elapsed before he came to the United States in 1899. And this boy dreamed. He did not realize then how the small man was handicapped by the guttie ball. But always it managed to beat him.

Fortune robbed him of the United States Open title in 1907 in one of the strangest cases in the history of the game. Playing at the Merion Cricket Club course in Philadelphia, Alec was leading the field as he stood on the fourth tee on the last round. He was using a new ball which had just been invented, the "silk-pneumatic" ball, and the "Nipper" was being paid to play with it. When he hit his drive on the fourth, part of the air gave out of the ball and it fluttered into a trap. A comparatively easy hole, the fourth cost him a seven. His nerves shaken by his misfortune, he took fives at the next two holes, dropping strokes to par at both. At the finish, he was two shots behind Alec Ross, now professional at the Detroit Country Club.

It is impossible to estimate the influence of Alec Campbell on the game. For example, the shy, quiet lad "who lived jist aff the twelveth fairway" at Brookline, the boy who watched Campbell's every movement, was no other than Francis Ouimet, who was to come to Alec, in his famous match with Vardon and Ray, for encouragement and counsel.

His swing is still a picture of studied ease, a "fast-and-faster" swing with great flexibility of the wrists. "Ye can niver turn awa' frae that ba' too far on the backstroke," says Alec, and his own swing demonstrates this point. But it is not the swing nor his knowledge of the swing that marks this man. It is the man himself and his knowledge of other men.

Think Before You Putt BY JERRY TRAVERS

A Putting Master Points Out the Necessity of
Studying the Shot Well before Stroking the Ball

THERE ARE TWO T's IN PUTTING—TECHNIQUE and Thought. A well-grounded putting technique is essential, of course, but you must have more than that. In theory, anyone who has learned to putt a ball successfully under a given set of circumstances should be able to repeat the performance over and over again without once missing, so long as the circumstances remain the same.

That's technique.

But alter the circumstances in some way—a different slope, a different angle, a different texture of turf or a different type of club—and the golfer must plan a program of action which will provide for and overcome the abnormality.

That's thought.

A good putt, the kind of long, curling, perfect putt that makes the gallery gasp, can only be the product of science and skill. It means that the golfer who made it has studied out his shot beforehand, that he has made every bit of technical proficiency he possesses count to the utmost.

The truth of this was brought home to me the other day in a chance conversation with an old friend, H. L. Edwards, of Dallas, Texas, himself a winner of many championships in the early days, and a lifelong lover and keen observer of the game.

"You know, Jerry," he told me, "I learned my greatest lesson in putting as a spectator when the Open Championship was being held at the Myopia Country Club in Massachusetts away back in 1908. I was standing behind the twelfth green, a mighty tricky and difficult green, as the great and the near-great went by. They were all there—Alex Smith, Willie Smith, Willie Anderson, Georgie Low, and others.

"One by one they pitched mechanically up to the green. One by one they stepped nonchalantly up with their putters, casually glanced at the lie, gave the ball a tap—and missed by a mile! One after another, they took their second, then their third putts, ruefully shook their heads and walked away.

"Then down the fairway came Walter Travis, greatest golfer, beyond all doubt, of the day. I watched him pause for his approach shot, saw it sail, straight and high, for the green. But it was a trifle too strong and it came to rest several feet behind the cup. From that angle the green's bad features, its speed and its downward, irregular slope, were accentuated. I watched Travis to see what he would do.

"Slowly he walked out on the green and carefully he picked out the spot where the ball, if propelled at just the proper speed, would come almost to a dead stop before, yielding to gravity from a new quarter, it would turn down the next slope toward the cup.

"I saw him walk back and address the ball. He called his caddie and ordered him to stand on that special spot he had picked out so carefully. For a moment he eyed the caddie's feet intently, then motioned the boy away and played. The ball, perfectly judged, wended its way down the slope, turned at the exact spot —and rimmed the cup.

"Travis tapped it into the cup and stalked away, one of very few indeed to hole out in two putts. Technique, plus thought, had enabled him to pick up a valuable stroke where his more careless opponents had been willing to leave too much to chance. And it isn't necessary for me to point out that a single stroke can win the National Open!"

It happens that this anecdote illustrates, almost exactly, the formula I would recommend for thoughtful and effective putting. I propose to deal here with the mental side of putting almost exclusively.

We will assume that you have already acquired the necessary mechanical proficiency, the grip, the stance and the stroke. These are things you can learn from any good instructor, or even a textbook, if you practice enough. It is when you come to apply them that you must think, and think, and think.

In putting, as in no other department of the game, the physical circumstances surrounding a shot are a largely determining factor. Rule One, therefore, is "Look Over the Ground."

First study the green itself. Which way does the grain run? Study the grain's effect on your ball and make due allowance for it. Experience is the best teacher here—once you've learned how to determine the grain.

Now, study the grass. Is it long or short, thick or thin, wet or dry? From this you'll be able to tell whether it is fast or slow or just average, and from this you'll be able to judge the speed you'll need to carry to the cup.

Next, go back to the ball. Stand squarely behind it and in your mind's eye trace out the line which the ball must follow in its course from the club to the cup. Is it a straight line? Or are there swells and slopes which will make it necessary for the ball to change direction a little, here and there?

If you must allow for a change of direction, try to determine (as Travis did) the exact point at which momentum must give way to gravity. For remember, if momentum overcomes gravity at this point, all is lost. The ball will veer, yes—but it will veer away from the cup. Keep in mind, therefore, that the distance you must putt is not necessarily the distance to the hole but the distance to the spot where the ball will cease traveling under its own power, the point at which gravity will take up and finish your task.

Now, address your ball. If you've gone through all these preliminary steps carefully and intently, you've virtually called your shot. Every scientific factor has received full attention. Like a trained artillery officer, you've laid your plans for a direct "hit." All you've got to do now is to make the mechanical, the technical, motions perfectly. That, of course, requires concentration. And there's a special way of doing it.

You must think that ball right into the cup! Close your eyes for a moment and try to visualize it as it starts its journey, in just the right direction at just the right speed, and rolls unerringly along until it reaches its objective with a gratifying "plop."

Now, with this pleasing picture still fresh in your mind, you're all ready. Go ahead and putt, trying to make the actual execution as much like the ideal as possible.

Try this method and keep on trying. Soon you'll find that the procedure I've described will become second nature to you, that it will be just as easy to putt carefully as carelessly.

Craig Wood Tells How He Did It

BY MAXWELL STYLES

Big Prize Winner of the Winter Season Explains Improved Game

CLOSE FOLLOWERS OF GOLF HAVE BEEN WONDERing for the past few seasons just why it was that Craig Wood had not previously come through to win one or more of the big tournament competitions. Tommy Armour, for instance, has been heard to remark that Craig appeared to have everything needed to return him a winner. During the past winter season, he came through to fulfil the expectancy. He was the terror of the professional tournament trail in California, winning no less than three important competitions in succession.

It occurred to this writer to seek out the blond giant and inquire of him to just what he attributed his success in winning, where heretofore he almost invariably finished back in the pack, sometimes close, but rarely a winner, in spite of the fine game he possessed. Wood has for some time been rated among the real long drivers, the boys with the extra big wallop. And strangely enough, he attributes his success to a voluntary curtailment of distance, not through an effort to shorten his swing or restrain his hitting power, but through the use of a brassie, with more loft, from the tee, instead of the straighter-faced driver. To that he

adds that he suddenly found himself with a marvelous putting touch.

Wood explains that he came to this decision in time to try the idea out in the Miami Biltmore Open late in November, before starting on his trip to California. It helped to steady his game there, and as he persevered with it, the plan reaped its reward later in California. For certainly when he showed up there, his entire game reflected a slow deliberate confidence that was evident to all.

"I suddenly realized," Wood explained, "that golf is simply a game of targets. Each shot should be played with some definite objective in mind.

"Any definite objective is a target. Therefore, every shot in golf should be played as a shot at some clearly defined target. All players realize this when they are playing a shot to the green. A narrow opening between bunkers, or the pin itself, may be the target. But what many of them forget is that the shot off the tee should, also, be aimed at some target down the fairway.

"Too many players—and I was one of them —seek only to gain distance off the tee. They think that as long as they belt one out from two hundred and twenty-five to two hundred and seventy-five yards, depending on the average distance gained by the individual, and providing that the drive stays on the fairway, the tee shot has been a success. That is not true. The tee shot is not a perfect shot unless it is so placed as to open up the hole for the second shot.

"What I mean to say is that, if the player selects the proper target for his drive, and hits it, then he has a bigger target to shoot at on his second shot. The second shot is usually the shot that determines whether the player is to putt for a birdie or have to fight for a buzzard. If the target for this second shot is a small target, with bunkers or other obstacles barring the path to the pin, the odds favor the chance that the player will be playing out of trouble with his third and having little chance for his par. But if, when he takes his stance for his second shot, the player is faced by the easiest possible route to the green, by a target that is big and wide, the chances of securing a par or birdie increase tremendously.

"Whether the player is to have the small, hard-to-hit target for his second shot, or the big, hard-to-miss target, depends entirely on whether he hit the correct target with his tee shot. Some holes play better from the right-hand side of the fairway than from the left, others present a better route of approach from the left. In some instances the middle of the fairway is the correct spot.

"I emphasize the phrase 'in some instances' because too often the player believes he has played the correct tee shot every time his drive splits the fairway. He thinks that he has had a better drive than his opponent who may be off to the right or left. Sometimes he is right, but more often he is wrong, because only a few holes play best from the center position. Frequently it is better to be on one side of the fairway with the green well open in front. The design of the hole demands it.

"That is one of the secrets of the success of Bobby Jones. Bobby is a marvelous player from every angle, but one thing that stands

out in my mind about Bobby is that he is always able to select the right target for his tee shot, and hit it.

"Gene Sarazen is the exact opposite. Sarazen is one of those devil-may-care players who gets up on the tee and socks it out. Gene doesn't seem to care whether the ball winds up on the fairway or in the rough. He is the exception that proves the rule in my theory. But we must remember that Sarazen can play shots out of the rough that no other man living can play. In fact, he plays quite as well off rough ground as he plays off fairway. And if he misses the target with his second, and lands in the bunker, again we find him the greatest of all bunker players. Sarazen is one in a million who needs no targets to shoot at for the reason that he probably will be putting for his par regardless of whether his shots from tee to green have been played off fairway, rough, or concrete.

"Macdonald Smith, Denny Shute, Olin Dutra, Paul Runyan and Walter Hagen—the way Walter is playing today—are other outstanding examples of players who carefully select definite targets for their tee shots, and hit these targets with regularity."

Having emphasized his point that targets should be there, and hit if possible, Wood then launched into a discussion of how the player best may hit these targets.

"The lofted wood club is the answer," he said. "It is very difficult to control a ball that is hit with a straight-faced club. Only a few players can do it. The straight-faced club gains distance but it loses accuracy. I was hitting a ball twenty-five to thirty yards farther with a driver than I am now getting with my brassie. And yet I have found that by sacrificing twenty-five yards for every drive I have cut my score from one to two strokes a round, or five or six strokes for a seventy-two-hole tournament.

"Five or six strokes in seventy-two holes mean the difference between victory and a place back about ninth or tenth. To me those strokes meant the difference between my rather mediocre showing of the past and my three victories in California this winter. I am hoping that they may mean the difference between my previous showing in national competition and a future Open Championship.

"I know that what has helped me will help others, for I was one of the outstanding examples of the big, strong fellow who thinks he is tops, if he can sock his drive out past all his competitors, regardless of where this drive may happen to wind up. I did a snappy about-face, took my sacrifice of twenty-five yards, straightened out my tee shots, so that they began hitting the targets at which they were aimed, and immediately began to make money."

Craig Wood and Gene Sarazen are shown driving during the recent British Open Championship at St. Andrews. On one hole Wood smacked a drive that was paced off at more than 400 yards.

Hilton of Hoylake BY BERNARD DARWIN

The Only Englishman to Win the
United States Amateur Championship

THIS YEAR'S AMATEUR CHAMPIONSHIP AT HOY-lake will be the first Championship there for eight and forty years to lack both the two great Hoylake golfers, John Ball and Harold Hilton. That is in some sort a *memento mori,* a rather sad and solemn thought if we are allowed— and I suppose we are not—to take games and its heroes either sadly or solemnly. And they *were* heroes, those two.

Just before I got a letter asking me to write something about Mr. Hilton, I had had the pleasure of seeing him again. I went down for one night and a round of golf to Cooden Beach in Sussex, where he now lives, and we had long talks together. It made me feel rather old because we talked mostly of golfers who to the others in the room were little more than names.

When Mr. Hilton got out of his chair in de-scribing how Johnny Laidlay had played a par-ticularly long stealing run up at a particular hole, held an imaginary club in a delicate, caressing grip, threw himself into an attitude and said, "You know how he played them," I did know and I could in my mind's eye see the whole scene. The rest listened full of interest as people always will listen to Mr. Hilton when he talks about golf, but they could *see*

nothing: for them he might as well have been talking of the now legendary Allan Robertson.

It must not be thought from this that Mr. Hilton lives in the past of golf. He is not very strong nowadays, though he is but sixty-four, and save for a little putting he plays no more, but he is as eager, as keen and interested in all the young golfers (and no man was ever kinder to youngsters) as he ever was; he can see as quickly as ever he did what they do wrong, and what they do right, and is as ready as ever to demonstrate it with that backhand move-ment of his left hand, a movement so charac-teristic that I think the mere mention of it must recall him to any who ever met him.

This is not a statistical article: it is rather, in a very humble way, a personal sketch. Still, as the years go ruthlessly on and make dim the brightest records, I had better set out Mr. Hil-ton's victories. He won two British Open Championships, at Muirfield in 1892 and at Hoylake in 1897; and he was within a painful inch (it hurts me to think about it) of winning two more. He won four British Amateur Championships—1900 at Sandwich, 1901 at St. Andrews, 1911 at Prestwick, 1913 at St. An-drews—and he was thrice also beaten in the final. He won one American Amateur Championship; namely, at Apawamis in 1911.

The number of his lesser victories, especially in score play, is as that of the sands of the sea. Till Bobby Jones appeared, it might safely be said of him that Mr. Hilton was the greatest of all amateur score players. Even now I would say that no golfer, amateur or professional, that ever lived has *known* golf as he has. To me he stands unrivalled in his power of observation and inference, in his understanding of how certain results follow from certain causes. Assuredly, too, because he is a highly strung man with the temperament of an artist, nobody has seen more deeply into the golfer's heart nor better understood his mental as well as his physical difficulties.

In one of our talks the other day at Cooden, we were discussing the fighting qualities of various golfers and somebody said to him, "You could fight pretty well too, couldn't you?" His answer was one worth remembering, "Sometimes—when I could see the humor of it all." That was a general truth, for we could all of us fight better, I suppose, if we could see the fun of taking three putts from a few yards or plumping a short pitch into a bunker in playing the one off two.

It was certainly a personal truth because Mr. Hilton, like all highly strung players, could suffer acutely enough over his golf. The particular instance he gave was of his match at St. Andrews in 1913 against Heinrich Schmidt, the young American who flashed into our golf that year like a meteor and nearly frightened us out of our wits. I don't know whether "meteor" is exactly the right word, because Mr. Schmidt took longer over the game that summer than anyone I ever saw, but I will let it stand: at any rate there is no doubt about the fright he caused.

The two had a dour match and going to the seventeenth, the famous Road Hole of many and sinister memories, they were all even. Mr. Hilton had the best of the hole; he was nearly on the green in two and had to play a short run up. He played it with his putter, played a trifle too gently and too near the Road bunker and behold! the ball took a malignant curve to

One of the world's truly great amateurs—Harold Hilton, of England. He won four British Amateurs, one British Open, and one United States Amateur Championship.

the left (it is an ancient booby-trap at that hole) and swung right into the bunker!

Now to putt into a bunker is not in a sense an amusing thing to do, but, just as Mr. Hilton was feeling rather miserable, he heard a Scotsman in the gallery exclaim "Good God" in tones of solemn anguish. That made him laugh; he played a fine bold shot out of the bunker, got his half, won the match by holing a long putt at the nineteenth and ultimately won the championship. The solemn Scot and his own sense of humor changed between them perhaps the course of golfing history.

That was an example of Mr. Hilton's fighting powers in match play, but his general reputation has always been that of a supreme score player, who was apt to fade away a little in a match. I do not think that reputation is at all fair to him. It comes from just one fact which is undeniable, namely that he could never do himself justice against his great rival and contemporary, Freddie Tait. In an Open Championship there was only one in it, Hilton; in a single combat between the pair, there was only one in it, Tait. Freddie had what I suppose would be called today the "Indian Sign" on Hilton. He thought he could beat him and he went out—perhaps a little truculently—to do it.

I remember one battle between them at Hoylake in 1898, when Hilton was the holder of the Open Championship and was playing the best golf he had ever played in his life. The whole of Liverpool came out to see it and they saw a sad débâcle. Their own man got a good start, too; he was one up, I think, at the second hole; then he began to make slips and Tait began to hole long putts with a light of victory in his eye. In less than no time it was all over.

That was a collapse; as a rule the matches were close enough, but Tait won them; he won them so steadily that Hilton never won an Amateur Championship till Tait had gone with his regiment to the South African War in which he was killed. Yet apart from that one insuperable weakness, I always will maintain that Harold Hilton was a good match player, who could spurt and cling on and recover from disaster as well as any other man. Did he not lose a whole winning lead of five holes to John Low in 1901 and then come away with two such full wooden club shots up to the pin at the thirty-fifth and thirty-sixth holes respectively as could never be surpassed?

Still he was greatest with a card and pencil, perhaps because his astonishing accuracy with wooden clubs seemed to make as nearly as might be impossible any of those major disasters that wreck a card. By the irony of fate, he would, humanly speaking, have won one more Open Championship, if, for a single shot, he had stuck to his wooden club. That was at Prestwick in 1898, when Harry Vardon was at his prime.

In the second round Hilton came to the short fifth over the Himalayas with a fine score. He could easily have played the shot with his trusty spoon—there never has been a better spoon player—but some imp of fate induced him to take a long-iron that he did not know well. He pulled the ball around into a horrible place in the face of the big sandhills and took eight to the hole. Eight to a simple par three hole, and yet, in the end, he was just —and only just—beaten by Harry Vardon and Willie Park. Probably he learned a lesson as to trusting to his spoon, but at a cruel cost.

He was the most accurate of all the wooden club players of his day and yet a first sight of him would hardly have conveyed it. Imagine a short man (he is five feet six inches in height) with a long club placing his feet with meticulous care in regard to the line and then rather sitting down to the ball. The waggle is careful and restrained; then suddenly all is changed; he seems almost to jump on to his toes in the upswing and fairly to fling himself at the ball.

There is no doubt at all that he is on his toes at the moment of hitting and the follow through of body, head, arms and all is of unrestrained and glorious freedom. In old days when caps were smaller, his cap always fell off as the club came through. Here is a swing of fascinating vigor and dash, hardly at first sight one which would tend to deadly accuracy. Yet the fact remains that it did, and not merely to accuracy but to accurate jugglery. He could play all manner of antics with the ball, and, when one sees Kirkwood's amazing tricks, one thinks that there was once an amateur who could fully have equalled them.

I have said little about his iron play, although it was very fine, especially in any stroke which called for much backspin. This is because his mastery of wooden clubs was so intensely interesting. It was with them, I think, that he had spent the greater number of those happy solitary hours of practice at Hoylake. He began his golfing life with a slight natural "fade" on his wooden club shots. Then finding that he wanted more length he acquired the "draw," and given a wind on his right shoulder, could hit an extra long ball with plenty of run.

Yet he never quite forgot his old shot. In 1911 at Prestwick, the ground was like a brick and the rough at the sides of the course very thick. Playing in the international match before the championship, he found that his drives with a draw on them were all finishing in the rough. Instantly he changed over and began to recultivate his fading stroke which he had not played for years. He had just about one day in which to make the change and he won that championship by means of keeping his necessarily rather shorter drives religiously on the fairway. That is surely an instance of real mastery of the game.

A master of the game—that is what Harold Hilton is. He has a natural quick and logical mind and remarkable powers of observation; and he might have devoted them to plenty of other things, but he chose to devote them to golf, and if any man can be said to "comprehend its mystery" he is the man. But I am suddenly afraid I may have made him out too serious or priggish about his game. That would be utterly and absurdly wrong, for he chuckles and bubbles over the ridiculous side of it and is altogether the friendliest and most companionable of creatures. I said before that he was very kind to young golfers. Well, we were all young once, and I shall never forget his friendliness to one juvenile golfer, who first set reverent eyes on him at Hoylake thirty-five years ago.

Dr. Nicholas Murray Butler, president of Columbia University, plays golf at almost every opportunity he can get when his academic responsibilities permit.

Charles Evans Hughes, Chief Justice of the United States Supreme Court, is a frequent player in the Washington vicinity.

The First Move in the Golf Swing

BY ROBERT T. JONES, JR.

A Turn of the Hips Must Inaugurate the Action Both in the Backswing and Downswing to Produce Timing and Power

I HAVE OFTEN BEEN ASKED IF I AM CONSCIOUS OF making any first move in starting the golf swing, or whether there are several parts of the body that start together. In my own case I make a point of starting the action of the swing with a definite turn of the left hip. I get the hip under way before my hands have made any effort to swing the head of the club. Naturally as the left hip starts the hands and clubhead move at the same time, a short distance at least, before the left hand starts taking the clubhead farther back.

There is an important reason to my mind for this starting move, and that is to be sure the left hip has gotten under way before anything else can happen. If this is not done—if the hands start the swing first—there will be a tendency or a temptation to leave the left hip behind, in other words not to make a full body turn, which is one of the most common faults in golf.

Many of the best of the old-time instructors used to say, "Don't leave the left shoulder behind"; others would advise starting the swing with the turn of the left knee, but if you turn the left hip you will find the left shoulder and the left knee will turn with it, in fact the entire left side will turn with it. It is quite possible to turn the left shoulder and the left knee without moving appreciably the left hip, which is the central guiding section of the body. In my own case, I want to be sure that that left hip is turning toward the right. If it does that, it will then keep its place in the backswing.

Briefly stated, the reason for starting the action, as I have outlined, is to develop a proper co-ordination between the movements of the body and arms. If the body starts first as it should, and I am speaking now of the middle part of the body, it is easy enough to complete the body turn needed, and then have the hands and arms complete the action of taking the club back. But if the hand and arm action comes first, it is very difficult indeed to effect the necessary body turn, and therefore to develop the proper co-ordination between body and arms.

In other words, a full body turn is necessary in a well-made golf swing, supposing of course that reference is being made to a full stroke.

Unless this body turn is made, the player can never come to a feeling of full power at the top of the swing, for the simple reason that there will be tension in the left side, meaning that a feeling of freedom and power in the wrists will be lacking. Therefore, the simplest and easiest assurance of getting this feeling of power at the top of the upswing is to see that the movement of the left hip around toward the right is the initial move of the backswing.

And just as the hip or middle of the body movement starts the backswing, so does a similar movement in the reverse direction start the downswing. Just as failure to start the body first, in taking the club back, almost invariably results in failure to develop the proper co-ordination between the body and arms on the backswing, so failure to start the hips first coming down, makes it impossible for this co-ordination to exist in the downswing. The player, feeling a lack of power, unconsciously tries to supply it through a thrust of the shoulders. He swings them around too quickly for the arms to develop proper co-ordination.

Virginia Van Wie, of Chicago, who this year became the fourth golfer to win three successive championships.

Miss Helen Hicks, who was defeated by Miss Van Wie in the Nationals at Exmoor, Highland Park, Illinois.

Miss Edith Cummings, of Chicago, the former Women's National Champion.

The Supreme Match Player BY BERNARD DARWIN

The Man Who Won Eight British Amateurs

CHRISTMAS DAY OF LAST YEAR WAS THE SEVentieth birthday of that very great golfer who was first known as Mr. John Ball tertius, then Mr. John Ball junr. and is now Mr. John Ball. It is almost superfluous to add that he was born at Hoylake in Cheshire, for he was a very small boy when that famous course was first laid out and the names of the links and its supreme hero have been inescapably intertwined ever since.

Mr. Ball's chief victories (his minor ones are innumerable) may be baldly set down. He won the Open Championship once—in 1890— being the first amateur ever to do so; he won the Amateur Championship eight times, in 1888, 1890, 1892, 1894, 1899, 1907, 1910, 1912, that is to say five times with the guttie ball and three times with the rubber core. That is a remarkable record, but it does no more than bare justice to Mr. Ball's powers and certainly cannot convey—I fear no words of mine can do so—the almost idolatrous hero-worship with which he is regarded.

It is one of the consolations of growing old that one has seen some things which younger people never can see, and for my part I am profoundly sorry for those who never watched Mr. Ball playing a big match before a big crowd at Hoylake. The hero himself, always with a boutonniere presented by some admirer; the bodyguard of rosetted stewards; the fishermen in their blue jerseys carrying the rope with the air of men performing a sacred rite; the tramp of the prayerful crowd behind that rope; the very errand boys on the road neglecting their work to hear how "John" was getting on—I have seen many scenes of enthusiasm in my wanderings over many links but never one like that. It possessed some quality of its own—touching, exciting, bringing a lump to the throat—which no words can depict, and we shall never see its like again.

A few great players of games have above all others this faculty of inspiring hero-worship, and it is characteristic of them that they become legends in their lifetime. They may not say much—and indeed Mr. Ball is a man of few words—but about what they do say there is something characteristic, so that their sayings pass into oft-recounted stories. What a number of stories there are at Hoylake about Mr. Ball! One of the most characteristic is of a medal competition years ago now, played when the wind at Hoylake was blowing as it can blow there. His score was strokes and strokes lower than anyone else's and his explanation of this was that "he happened to be hitting just the right sort of ball for the day."

Another, which I always like, is of a match which he played against a young golfer who was clearly overawed by the importance of the occasion. Mr. Ball soon had a lead of three or four holes and then he turned to a friend and said "I think we'll finish it at the Dun." The Dun is the sixteenth hole, quite near the clubhouse, and sure enough the young gentleman was allowed to get a hole or two back. Then, when it came to the Dun, Mr. Ball hit a great brassie shot right home over the cross bunker and finished the match by 3 and 2.

It was in that same match that, at the third hole (the "Long"), his adversary put his tee shot into a bunker. "He's in the bunker," said one of the Hoylake supporters. "You didn't see, did you?" "No," answered Mr. Ball. "Why should I? It's my business to get a five."

There are other legends dealing with his invincible and almost obstinate modesty. On one occasion when he had won a Championship, tremendous preparations were made by the Hoylake crowd to receive him at the station. The crowd waited and waited and no hero ever arrived. Mr. Ball, with an instinctive knowledge of the terrors awaiting him, had got out at an earlier station and walked home unperceived across country.

On the occasion of another victory the Royal Liverpool Golf Club had his portrait painted and hung, where it still hangs, upon the stairs. It is alleged that for several years Mr. Ball steadily refused to pass it, and confined his visits to the clubhouse entirely to the ground floor.

Those little legends may give perhaps some notion of the man, silent, retiring, shrewd, resolute, a dour and a bonny fighter. It is curious to know that for the first year or two after the founding of the Amateur Championship, Mr. Ball was the despair of his Hoylake friends because he seemed never to be able to do himself justice in a big match. Then he came into his kingdom and from that moment he was known as the man for an apparently lost cause, who would emerge incredibly victorious from the most forlorn of hopes.

He was a supreme match player and it is worth noticing, from one of the small stories I told, that he did it by playing, as we now say, "against par." It was his business to go faultlessly down the middle and let the other man make the mistakes, and the more intense the crisis the more closely he stuck to business. He was, I think, rather a lazy starter, inclined not to bother himself over much, but there never was a fiercer finisher, and there was something about that relentless concentration that seemed to paralyze the enemy.

As he grew older he won his matches chiefly by lethal accuracy, but, when he had been younger and longer and stronger, it was not so

The incomparable British Amateur, Mr. John Ball of Hoylake, who has won eight British Amateur Championships.

much this mechanical precision that was feared as his power of putting in some irresistible thrust. Mr. Horace Hutchinson used to tell me pityingly that I was too young to have seen the real and greatest John Ball, who was always likely to let loose a knock-out blow at a critical moment.

I sometimes think that players with unsound methods are unjustly criticized for lack of nerve and conversely that those with a sound method are too loudly praised for indomitable courage. Undoubtedly a smooth swing that will continue to function, despite the player's agitation, is a very present help in trouble. Mr. Ball had a splendid nerve and he also had a swing travelling in so smooth and well-oiled a groove that nothing apparently could disturb it. Thus he was twice armed, and almost invincible.

The comparative beauty of different players' styles must always be a matter of opinion. I can only say that everybody is agreed that Mr. Ball's was a beautiful swing, and to me it was the most beautiful of all. Personally I should get more aesthetic ecstasy from watching him than from Bobby Jones and Harry Vardon put together, and it is hardly possible to say more than that. It is not possible to put the rhythm of a lovely movement into words and Mr. Ball's swing had a quality which, as the reviewers say of a book that puzzles them, "defies analysis." If one tries to take it to pieces, it may appear both unorthodox and unlovely.

He held his club with what is now rather disparagingly called a "palm grip"; but this was deceptive, for though the right hand seemed far under the club, yet the grip was really a light one with the fingers playing a far greater part than appeared. The feet were noticeably wide apart and the legs stiff; that sounds unattractive but it was not; it merely suggested the firmness of a rock.

The ball, especially in Mr. Ball's younger days, was very far back, almost by his right toe, but his pivot was so big and free and supple that there was not the faintest look of strain or effort as there might have been with another. As he grew older and just a little stiffer, he had his feet closer together, and the ball more forward, but it was in his earlier style that he hit his most fascinating shot, the ball starting very low, then rising gradually and finally falling almost dead. It was, I think, a peculiarly "guttie ball" shot and no one had it in greater perfection.

Mr. Ball was always a fine driver and in his youth a very long one, but it was his cleek and iron play that was his strongest point. It has often been said that it was J. H. Taylor who, when he first burst on the world, showed golfers a new standard of accurate iron play up till then believed unattainable. No doubt he had a great effect, but I believe Mr. Hilton to be right in saying that it was Mr. Ball, a few years earlier, who had first opened men's eyes to the possibilities of long and accurate iron play right up to the flag. At any rate he was superbly accurate, and he seemed to have an almost unique power of stopping his backswing at any point he desired and so had a wonderful control over every sort of "half-shot."

One extraordinary quality he undoubtedly possessed, namely that of playing high lofting shots with very little lofted clubs. If he could, he preferred to pitch just over a bunker and let the ball run, but he could loft as high and stop as dead as any man. Yet he hardly ever used a really lofted club; indeed, he once lost the final of a championship at St. Andrews by pitching into the burn at the nineteenth hole, because he used a mashie to which he was unaccustomed. A medium iron was his normal pitching club, and it was only in dire straits that he used a niblick in a bunker. Yet no one could get out of any horrid place better, and it is one of his complaints against modern greenkeepers that, with their raking and trimming, they make the bunkers far too easy.

One comparatively weak joint there was in his harness; he was not entirely trustworthy over the short putts. Great players are easy targets for criticism on the green, and it was sometimes unfairly said of him, as of Harry Vardon, that he "could not putt." He was to my mind a very good approach putter (so was Vardon) and his only failing was that he had occasional bad days at the quite short ones.

I remember watching perhaps the most celebrated of all his matches, the final at Prestwick in 1899, when, having been at one time five down to Freddie Tait, he won at the thirty-seventh hole. That was one of his bad putting days and on every green his caddie produced for him a choice of three weapons, a swan-necked iron putter, a driving cleek and some sort of iron. It was, I think, with the iron that he holed the winning putt for a three at the thirty-seventh.

As I said just now, Mr. Ball is a good conservative and does not like some new ways. He likes bunkers that make you, in his own words, "scratch your head" and I have heard him call the modern ones "geranium beds." He does not profess to understand (I don't think he tries very hard) the whole numbered series of to-day's irons; I heard him chuckle with unchristian malice last year when a young gentleman

took an eight-iron to play a simple running shot and left the ball halfway to the hole.

When he comes to Hoylake (as he still does sometimes, though he now lives in Wales) to play a foursome, it is with a limited and old-fashioned armory that he goes out to fight. He does not come as often as his friends would like, but when he does it is a very great occasion. Last year he watched the Amateur Championship there on one or two days. On one of these days I met a young man who was helping to marshal the crowd; he was pale and agitated and was clearly recovering from a shock. "O Heavens," he exclaimed, "I've nearly done the most ghastly thing I ever did in my life. I saw an old gentleman where I thought he ought not to be; I was just going to shoo him away when I saw it was John Ball."

Poor young man! He was indeed saved just in time from a dreadful act of profanity, for if there is a golfing shrine upon earth, it is Hoylake and its deity is John Ball.

His Highness the Prince of Wales, during a recent round in England, shows that he is, as usual, the last word in sartorial splendor.

The Masters Fixture BY GRANTLAND RICE

*The Augusta National Tournament Marks
the Beginning of a New Spring Tumult*

THERE IS ONE POINT YOU CAN GAMBLE ON, AS far as anyone can look ahead. The Augusta National's annual Masters Tournament is on its way to become one of the big fixtures of golf, presenting Bobby Jones again next spring in his second start since 1930, playing informally as the host at the course he conceived, designed, and built.

The opening act was an amazing success. There were automobiles parked around the club from thirty-eight states and Canada. Eighteen thousand more words were telegraphed from the Augusta battlefield than from the last United States Open. Thousands of people came from all over the country to see what the mop-up star of 1930 could do against a fast moving field of young stars and veterans, after four years rest from the wars.

The fact that Bobby Jones finished back of twelve competitors, ten strokes back of Horton Smith and nine strokes back of Craig Wood, the two young leaders, will only pack on new interest for the second act next spring. Supporting Georgians and thousands of others believe it will be another story next time. Maybe it will and maybe it won't. A year is a long time in sport.

The contesting field drew a big kick out of playing a new type of course where so much versatility and variety in stroke making were needed on so many holes—where long spectacular shots were needed to get home on the four big holes of the course, ranging from four hundred and eighty to five hundred and twenty yards.

The big crowds suffered heavily as Bobby's short game slipped away from his control, but the session was packed with thrills. There were no dull moments. Jones and Hagen, winners of twenty-four national crowns, tied with Denny Shute for thirteenth place and yet this trio also furnished rushing galleries a full assortment of brilliant shots.

Hagen was hitting the ball better than ever. Jones was just as good up to the shorter thrusts as he ever was. Neither could find a putting touch. In turn they tightened up their chip shots and their shorter pitches.

It was a new and better Horton Smith, stroking the ball in flawless fashion, who led this able field, with Craig Wood at his heels; Billy Burke, Paul Runyan and Ed Dudley in close pursuit. The tall and slender Joplin Pine carried his old smooth putting touch, and he was much sounder from the tee and with his iron play up and down the fairways than he had ever been before.

The Augusta National happens to be the type of course that lends itself to the spectacular side, where nerve-wrecking gambles keep the gallery keyed up. And I have rarely seen any gallery more keyed up for four days than this invasion from thirty-eight states, Canada and England, happened to be.

The crowds by early spring dusk were limp from excitement and overworked nerves. The gallery range was from young girls and boys of twelve and fourteen to gray-haired men of eighty and eighty-five, including George Wright, who retired from competitive sport in 1878, just fifty-six years ago, and who a short while later brought over the first sets of golf clubs known in this country. There were Devereux Milburn, the greatest of all polo backs, Eugene Grace, president of Bethlehem Steel, Herbert Jaques, president of the United States Golf Association, Judge Henderson and Mr. John Herbert, both over eighty, who were pioneers in college football at Yale and Rutgers more than sixty years ago.

Too many expected miracles from Bobby Jones after his four-year lay-off from hard, grim competitive golf, but that, in a human measure, was to be expected. Almost everything happened. Craig Wood almost holed a hundred-to-one shot through a hundred or so pines hiding the green, and Ross Somerville got a hole in one at the short seventh. [Now the sixteenth—Ed.] Horton Smith had to hole a twelve-foot putt to take the lead on the seventy-first hole, and he did.

On his last nine holes, Ed Dudley had reasonable putts for eight birdies and not a one of them dropped.

It was that sort of a tournament. Mr. Herbert H. Ramsay, former president of the United States Golf Association, who also put on a swell job of broadcasting, pronounced it one of the greatest golf shows he had ever seen. And he has been in the thick of many big championship wars.

The general opinion was that Bobby Jones and the Augusta National had started a feature which is sure to be one of the big fixtures of the game and that 1935 would be an even greater production, with just as much general interest and just as much emotional excitement.

The reaction of the big field was that the course was a most excellent test of golf, and an ideal setting for a big tournament. Measuring around sixty-seven hundred yards in length, it gives plenty of room for the big hitters, and yet skill and courage in playing up to the greens are always important factors in low scoring. In a scenic way, the layout keeps pretty close to par figures, anyway you take it.

Next time Bobby hopes the crowd at large will figure him as one of the contestants trying to win—not almost sure to win. "There never was anyone invincible in golf," he said, "and I don't believe there ever will be."

Walter Hagen draws this studious gaze of the galleryites as he hands in his card at the end of his first round, during the recent Masters Tournament.

James A. Farley, who managed the presidential campaign of President-elect Franklin D. Roosevelt, and Senator Huey Long, of Louisiana, were found in discussion on the golf course of Warm Springs, Georgia. Mr. Farley appears to be doing the golfing; Senator Long, as usual, is doing the talking.

One of the most skillful shotmakers in the ranks of the radio stars is the jolly singing troubadour, Frank Crumit, who sometimes shoots rounds in the 70's.

Gene Tunney with his good friend Dr. William Lyon Phelps, of Yale University, just before teeing off for a round over the rugged Yale course. Dr. Phelps remarked that "Gene can take my place before a class in English much better than I could take his in the ring."

Six of the most enthusiastic golfers on the Pacific coast are, from left to right, Ty Cobb, Frank Craven, Chandler Egan, Oliver Hardy. Guy Kibbee, Harvey Hicks.

Mr. A. D. Lasker, the Chicago philanthropist and advertising magnate, made an offer some years ago to give anyone $500 to break par on his private course. Tommy Armour finally cashed in on it last summer.

Public Entertainer Number One Al Jolson is shown with his wife, the vivacious Ruby Keeler, just before a round in the Hollywood hills.

Man of Destiny BY BERNARD DARWIN

Lawson Little Rules British Amateurs

I AM BIDDEN TO WRITE ABOUT THE CHIEF EVENTS in the Amateur Championship at Prestwick. I will do my best but my trouble is that everything else seems very faint and far away while in front, dwarfing everything else, looms the colossal figure of Lawson Little.

No doubt you have heard long ago of all the wonderful things he did in the final at Prestwick and his ten under fours (or thirteen over threes) for twenty-three holes, his twelve threes—more than fifty per cent—in those same twenty-three holes, his ten under an average of two putts per green and so on. These are eloquent statistics and I could easily provide some more, such as that if Little had given Jimmy Wallace, his poor adversary, half a stroke a hole he would still have been three up. But no statistics can convey the immense impression that he made on us who saw him. I am quite sure I have never seen such golf in my life, and I am equally sure that, as long as I live, I shall never admit that anybody else has played such golf again. The power and accuracy of the long game, the delicacy of the short pitches and runs among the puzzling lumps and bumps of Prestwick, the murderous putting were all equally striking. Perhaps most impressive of all was the unhasting, unresting relentless power of going on and on. Here seemed to me the beau ideal of golf played against par and not against a human adversary. I am sure that Little knew that Wallace was there because, when he was leading by untold holes, he conceded him one or two rather long putts with a gesture as generous and pretty; but regarded purely as an enemy, I do not believe he paid the least attention to him. He bent his whole mind to the task of playing each hole as well as it could be played and the more terrifyingly and brilliant grew his score, the less he was frightened of it and the more he concentrated on the hole immediately before him.

Though all hope of a match had vanished long before, most of us expected that Little would be a little more human after luncheon, might perhaps make a slip or two and allow Wallace to win one hole. On the contrary he was better than ever. When he began the second round by holing a twelve-yard putt for three, we smiled and when he holed another at the fourth we laughed aloud. It was too ridiculously good. When he was in the pleasant position of dormie fourteen and was about to play a blind short hole over the towering Himalaya, a Scottish friend said to me, "I expect the fellow will do it in one." He was not so far wrong, for the ball went straight as an arrow for the hole, very nearly pitched into it, and lay a few yards beyond. The champion's last shot was as good as his first and there were no worse ones in between.

Truly a mighty golfer! A Juggernaut that trampled down everything before him. The moment the American Walker Cup team had played their first practice round at St. Andrews, the wise men agreed that of all that formidable side, Lawson Little was the most dangerous. They never had any cause to change their view. He was magnificent in the Walker Cup when he walked all over Cyril Tolley and right through the tournament at Prestwick. He played so well that only once was he hard pressed, when Leslie Garnett took him to the nineteenth hole in the semifinal. If ever it was true that the right man won, it was true of Lawson Little.

Let me say one word for poor James Wallace, the artisan golfer from Troon and a most gallant and modest player, who was Little's victim in the final. On Friday night he was a national hero on the pinnacle of fame; at a quarter past two on Saturday he had become the man who had lost more holes in a final than anybody else in history. There have been players who have got through undeservedly into finals, but Wallace was not one of them. He had had the hardest of all rows to hoe; he had beaten no less than five Walker Cup players—two Americans, Chandler Egan and George Dunlap, three British: Cyril Tolley, Eric Fiddian, and the best player in this country, Jack McLean. He ran into a tornado, the magic deserted his putter and down he went with a crash, but what he had done before that crash ought to be remembered forever in his favor.

Lawson Little leads the way from the fifth hole which he had just taken despite stymie at the hands of Jimmy Wallace, the other finalist in the British Amateur.

Little is an interested observer in the progress of one of his booming drives.

Using Your Hands BY ROBERT T. JONES, JR.

Their Responsibility in the Swing

JUST AS A CHAIN IS NO STRONGER THAN ITS weakest link, a golfer is rarely any better than his hands. Although a great part of the power of his stroke originates in the center of his body, this power is of no use unless it is transmitted, and a critical point in this transmission is in the hands and wrists.

Dead hands or wooden wrists directly produce as many golfing mistakes as any other one single detail. Besides the important businesses of timing the stroke and of supplying a considerable clubhead acceleration in the climactic stages, active hands are needed so that the head can stay down, so that the right shoulder may not come up, so that the left arm may remain straight, and so that the iron shots may be struck downward. Disregarding whatever contribution they may make in the way of power and length, it is enough to say that they are directly charged with the responsibility for a clean, solid contact.

One of the greatest difficulties besetting the average golfer is to maintain a positive grip upon the club without destroying the suppleness of his wrists and the usefulness of his hands. A tight grip means wooden wrists, and yet the club must not be allowed to turn in the hands. How is he going to do it? It is like the steak that must be thick, but not too thick, rare, but not too rare.

A great part of the answer is had when we say that the club is held mainly by the fingers, even though at certain points it may touch the palm. For it may be held quite firmly there without in any way hampering the movement of the hand or wrist, whereas when held like a baseball bat, the muscles of the forearm become taut.

It is never necessary to squeeze the clubhandle with any part of the hand. When you ground the club behind the ball, you should merely be conscious that you are holding it, that you feel it. When you begin to move it, your grip will tighten up naturally. But when you begin to move, start the action with the left hand, and feel the pressure mainly in the three smaller fingers of that hand, and then keep the feeling all the way through that these three fingers have the club under control.

This grip is definitely helpful in securing a complete cocking of the wrists at the top of the swing. At this point, when the motion is changing direction, the body begins to unwind before the club starts down, and the cocking is completed by the little tug of the clubhead on the hands as its movement is stopped and reversed. If the club were held in the palm, this would be a dangerous point, for either the tug would have to be resisted by a tight grip and a solid wrist, or the hold upon the club would have to be relaxed. But with the positive finger control the entire action can be handled smoothly as a slight opening of the hands takes up the shock without for an instant relaxing the grip.

So far as the right hand is concerned it will be best to keep the grip throughout as light as possible. This is mainly to avoid a natural inclination to pick the club up from the ball or to hit from the top of the swing. Many persons have asked me about the whiteness of the index finger of my right hand as I waggle the club, inquiring if this did not indicate a tight grip. As a matter of fact very little gripping is done between the index finger and thumb here. The whiteness is due to pressure on only one side, as the hand is set in against the club.

Here's a close-up of the grip used by Bobby Jones. It will be noted that he laps the little finger of the right hand over the forefinger of the left.

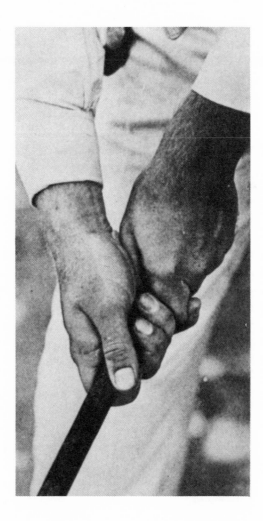

Meet the Silver Fox

BY CLARENCE BUDINGTON KELLAND

Tommy Armour Has One of the Shrewdest Heads in the Game

TOMMY ARMOUR HAS A MOUTH LIKE A STEEL trap, a nose like a ski jump, hands like the fins of a shark, and eyes which indicate he would enjoy seeing you get a compound fracture of the leg.

He also plays golf.

He is, in addition, a businessman.

Although it is a fact that Tommy came to this country as an amateur, he had all the qualifications necessary to elevate him to the top ranks of the professional, and among these was an acid gift of salesmanship. There are few more entertaining sights than to see Tommy go to work on a new member—or even a visitor to the shop. The first time I ever watched his methods, they were turned loose on me. I am able to speak from sad experience.

You come into the shop and meet Mr. Armour. He does not fall on your neck in raptures of joy. There is little if anything of the effusive in his make-up. Instead of that, he peers at you with basilisk eyes calculating the strength of your sales-resistance and estimating your possibilities as a customer and as a human being. He snaps off a couple of Scottish consonants and then walks over to your golf bag and picks out your driver. You watch with

interest. He waggles the club; he grips it; then he holds it out in front of him with a gesture so eloquent that you begin to shrivel inside your clothes and to wish you had gone to Chicago instead.

He never so much as glances at you again, but his tanned, angular face takes on an expression of such utter scorn—mixed with a trifle of sorrow—that you feel exactly as if you had been caught stealing a blanket off the baby's bed on a cold night. He puts your driver back in the bag gently—so gently!—and then walks away with dragging step, as if there were things in the world too terrible for the human mind to consider.

If you turn then and run you may be saved; but if, as ninety-nine men out of a hundred will do, you ask what's the matter with your driver, you are lost.

"Nothing," says Tommy. "Nothing at all."

"It's a darned good driver,' you say.

"What do ye play around in?" Tommy asks.

"Ninety," you say.

"I wonder at it," says Tommy, with just the hint of a side glance at your golf bag.

By that time you are convinced that you are unclean and unfit for human society. You are marked as an outsider, a Pariah, a leper, by that golf club. You know no gentleman would play with such a tool, and that to go out on a golf course with it is a more shameful thing than teeing up your ball in the rough.

"What's wrong with it?" you insist.

"Look at my one," says Mr. Armour, and you find yourself with a club in your hands. He never says, "Take a look at mine," it is always "my one." Then, saddened by so much inefficiency in the world he says pitifully, "Who sold you such a set of clubs?"

That will be about the finish. Presently you walk out of the shop with three new woods, a full set of irons and a putter—and a date to take a number of lessons from Mr. Armour at an unpleasantly early hour when you really want to sleep.

They say he is the greatest iron player of all time. Maybe. Me, I say his chief claim to fame is salesmanship.

It has been my privilege to play with him daily for weeks at a stretch. Once I played nine successive rounds with him over the exceedingly long and difficult South Course at Boca Raton. His highest score for that series was sixty-nine. And it was all under greater pressure than he has ever been in an open championship, because I was his opponent, and we were playing five dollar Nassaus with me getting a stroke a hole—and his endeavor was to make a better and nobler and wiser man of me. He did.

Tommy never says an unkind thing to any-body accidentally; if he drops acid on you it is because he wants to. He never flatters, and he never falls on anybody's neck. But if he likes you you find it out. I wouldn't know just how you find it out, because he doesn't tell you, or show you. But in some mysterious, dour, ingrowing way he lets you know you are in— and then, if you are a member of the lodge in good standing, you feel honored. For, among a number of things, Tommy Armour is a gentleman, and a judge of human critters, and a sportsman, and a conversationalist, and a drinker of beer. He makes observations. He is temperamental as a soprano with a frog in her throat, but at the same time he keeps both his feet on the ground. And, in spite of his being dour, sour, acid, vertiginous, and endowed with special and painful brands of poison, he is the sort of companion you would travel miles to sit with.

Tommy Armour is a great golfer—a superlative golfer. But he is something more than that —he is a personage. He has what it takes to stand out from the herd. There have been moments when I would like to shove an icicle through his cold heart; there have been moments when I wish his confounded Scottish consonants would split splinters off his front teeth; but for all that, at any time, I will take a long train ride to spend an evening with him. And I'm pretty choosy about whom I get shut in a room with alone for more than fifteen minutes.

I guess I like him.

". . . a mouth like a steel trap, a nose like the take-off of a ski jump, a pair of hands like the fins of a man-eating shark, and a couple of saturnine eyes that view the world with dour humor."

Check Your Heel-and-Toe Balance

BY ROBERT T. JONES, JR.

Should Your Weight be on Your Heels or Your Toes?

ABE MITCHELL ONCE WROTE THAT IN ORDER TO play good golf the player "must move freely beneath himself," which statement represents a graphic way of stressing the importance of correct use of the feet and legs.

A perfect balance is, of course, essential, but the thing that escapes most players is that this balance must be flexible and mobile, a balance of motion rather than of a body at rest. What we most want to avoid is any tendency on the part of the player to set himself firmly as though he would anticipate the attempt of some outside agency to move him from his feet.

I have often tried, and I think it is of the utmost importance to do so, to lay emphasis upon the necessity of alertness in the attitude when addressing the ball. This one word implies a lot with respect to the first position, and is certainly one which the golfer should keep in his mind. To be alert, one must be ready for action, or for movement, in any direction, and muscles and limbs must be free, not set to take a shock standing still.

He may not be literally "on his toes," but he will certainly not be "back on his heels."

So in golf the alert posture is fairly erect, with the weight about evenly divided between the two feet, and the knees slightly bent. But above all, in order to obtain the proper mobility, there must be no leaning forward onto the toes or sitting back lazily upon the heels. Let the balls of your feet carry most of the weight, using your heels for what they were intended, to improve your balance.

This much is easy, and few players, if they think about what they are doing, will have any trouble making a reasonably good start. The foot action during the swing is not so simple, yet it supplies a means of directing the correct handling of the weight.

Assuming that the feet have been placed properly, with the toes of both feet turned slightly outward to make the turning of the body in either direction equally easy, a common and fatal mistake in starting the backswing is to move the weight directly out over the toes of the left foot. This means that at the top of the swing most of the body weight will rest upon the left foot, and be thrown back upon the right as the swing comes down.

It is entirely practical to control the handling of the body, both turning and shifting, by giving attention to the heel-and-toe balance of the feet; in other words, by consciously directing the changes in support points throughout the swing.

Starting with the weight about equally divided between the two feet, and supported mainly upon the balls of the feet, the first change is made by rolling the weight supported by the left foot over onto the inside of the great toe. At the same time, the weight upon the right foot moves back upon the outside of the heel, often so completely that the toe is pulled off the ground. To make these changes the player will have to twist his hips and handle his body in approximately the correct manner. I am saying nothing about whether, at the top, the right foot bears more weight or not, because I do not believe the backward shift is necessary, if the ball at address has been placed sufficiently forward.

In the downswing the process is reversed, and the weight on the left foot moves back to the heel, while that on the right foot comes forward to the toe. And this is the correct order in spite of the fact that pictures of many expert golfers have been snapped when the left heel was off the ground immediately prior to contact. In such cases, it had already returned to earth and been lifted again by the straightening of the left leg in the effort of hitting.

As he nears his backswing, Lawson Little displays complete balance he achieves through heels and toes.

Balance permits Little to make contact with the ball with extraordinary power.

Stylist of the Stylists BY TOMMY ARMOUR

The Game's Supreme Shotmaker Has
Never Won a National Title

GENIUS, SCORNED, SHIVERING AND EMPTY-BELLIED in an attic; Pagliacci bellowing a laugh from his heavy heart; Mac Smith splitting ten thousand fairways and never winning a National Open Championship.

Art mocks the artist.

Macdonald Smith is the master artist of golf and the art of golf has denied him national championships. This fickle and utterly irrational art has crowned as its rulers men who, as the game's artists, are merely caddies compared to the master.

I can't explain it. Mac has a remarkable competitive record. But when he wins fifty tournaments with rounds of golf played as perfectly as a tranquil dream, some fellow slugs, pats and bounces the ball for seventy-two holes to win just one championship and fame, because that one championship is a national open which defies Smith.

Don't tell me that Mac hasn't golfing temperament. He has the most ideal golfing temperament providence ever put in a man's bosom.

Mac, who has seen and felt and heard open title after open title snatched right out of his grasp, and walked into the clubhouse calm and uncomplaining, is not the fellow to be upset when a few shots along a seventy-two-hole route go wrong.

You can't explain the mystery of Mac Smith to me by pointing out any deficiency in his game, because there simply isn't any.

Macdonald Smith's career has spanned that of three brilliant reigns in golf. When the Vardon sun was shining bright and high, Mac was great. When the blaze of Hagen was in the skies, Mac was great. When the radiance of Jones shone over the game, Mac was great. Macdonald Smith still is great.

Until he is sixty I will believe Mac Smith has an excellent chance to overcome the impudence of destiny and win a national title. Until Mac is ninety I'll be hoping that he wins the United States or British Open Championship. I've had a bet on Mac Smith in every national open championship he's played in. Recall, please, that the Scots wager on judgment rather than on sentiment.

In my judgment Mac is the game's supreme shot-making artist.

In my heart Mac is perennial American and British national open monarch and I know, from a very uncomfortable recollection, when frustration again put its finger on him to take a title away from him and hand it to me.

It was at Carnoustie when Mac finished 5-6-5 and the British Open Championship went to me.

I didn't know which way to look when Mac came up to me. I knew deep in me that the title belonged to Mac. I felt very humble myself and that's not a frequent experience with me. All I could get out was, "Tough luck, Mac."

Mac took my hand and pressed it until the fingers flattened. He smiled philosophically. "It wasn't meant this time. Tommy m' lad, ye deserved to win."

I felt like screaming out, "Don't give it to me, Mac won it." At no other moment in all the time I've played and won in golf tournaments, was I so depressed as when I saw Mac Smith walk into the clubhouse at Carnoustie, again the patient victim of the unkind gods of golf.

Never before—or since—in golf has there been such a gallery as there was the last day at Prestwick in the 1925 British Open. Estimates of the crowd varied. Some experts guessed it at twenty thousand; others as high as thirty thousand. Mac was due to be crowned. It was a stampeding, shoving, frantically partisan throng that came to help and witness Mac achieve his life's ambition. Instead it saw and sensed the drama of a noble man with the hand of fate tearing out his heart.

Macdonald Smith, the master, took an 82. It's still unbelievable to me, that horrifying last round of Mac's.

But here I am, sympathizing with Mac Smith when he's really one of mankind most to be envied. Mac has peace in his heart. He has triumphed over ill-health and over Mac Smith. He has won more all by himself than he ever could win—or any other man could win—on any golf course.

Smith is no Caledonian tragedy even though he often has been batted back a step away from golf's heights. When you look at Mac, or at pictures of him, you may be fooled. He has the firm, dour features of an Inquisition fanatic. Inside, he's gentler and kinder than Santa Claus.

Mac Smith with his inseparable friend Sandy.

He is no glad-hander. He's shy. But he is the most courteous of hosts and listeners. He has been trapped and bounced around by fate so often himself that he is considerate and forgiving when others fall short, even though their failure may be due to causes that others consider unforgivable.

The crowd means nothing to Mac; the man, everything. Maybe it was the crowd that beat him that time at Carnoustie. It probably was the crowd that beat him out of a title at Prestwick. You'll never hear explanations or alibis for defeat from Mac. His nerves may be fighting him, but you'll never know it. He is a self-contained, high-hearted and unsurrendering fatalist.

Mac's comeback is something unique in sports. At one time he was through—through as completely and as conclusively as an athlete can be. The jitters had him. There was hopelessness in his carriage and in his eyes. He pulled himself together and thought and fought. Mac Smith won. He won something far more important than a dozen National Open Championships. He won Mac Smith.

A strange thing about it to me is that religion is said to have had a lot to do with it. Mac should be an agnostic by all the rules of human conduct. The gods have thumbed their noses at him so often he could be pardoned for thinking that he owes them no respect.

If getting religion had something to do with it, you'll never know it by hearing Mac talk about salvation. He minds his own business and lets you mind yours.

Perhaps that's why Macdonald Smith, stylist of all stylists, hasn't had the effect he should have on the technique of the game. He is too retiring to be a missionary for his own ideas. Other good golfers marvel at his style and deliberately or unconsciously try to imitate it, but he never gets loquacious about how he plays, so golf writers find it easy to write about his methods. Only his intimate friend and brother Scot, D. Scott Chisholm, among all the golf writers, has much close-up material on Mac.

The Smith swing is as bonnie as Maxwelton's braes. It's as graceful, as smooth and as apparently effortless as the swooping glide of a gull through the blue sky.

Only Mac Smith can play a shot the Mac Smith way. I've not thought of it before, but that may be the reason why Mac hasn't been the author or interviewee on many golf instruction tracts.

If we all played golf like Mac, the National Open Championship could be played on one course every day in the year and never a divot mark would scar a beautiful fairway. He has the cleanest twenty-one-jewel stroke in golf. He treats the grass of a golf course as though it were an altar cloth.

So here you have my Mac Smith, a great character who, but for the force and clarity of his own mind, might have been forgotten as a genius born to swing unsung or in contempt as a crying specimen of a frustrated man.

Open Champion or not, Mac has the dignity of a true champion, the mien of a monarch and the deepest respect of all who know him. There is no luck to that and there is luck— plenty of it—in winning national opens.

Katharine Hepburn doesn't take club in hand just for publicity's sake. She is a fine enough golfer to reach the final of the Bel-Air Women's Championship.

Jean Harlow has begun to initiate herself into the mysteries of the game at the Agua Caliente Golf Club at Tijuana, Mexico.

How Little Won at St. Annes

BY BERNARD DARWIN

A Rare Defense of the British Amateur

IN THE ORDINARY WAY I SHOULD TRY TO MAKE this article cover the whole of our Amateur Championship at St. Annes and trace the various careers of all the various American competitors and in particular of Dan Topping and Dick Chapman, who went a good long way through. Now, I shall do nothing of the sort, because the final between Lawson Little and Dr. Tweddell was so memorable, so exciting, so packed with incident, and my mind is so full of it, that I really cannot write about anything else.

Lawson Little won by a hole. He entirely deserved to win because he was the best golfer in the field. He played like a champion and it was as well for him that he did. If he had fallen at all below his proper standard, Tweddell would have had him for certain, for such a relentless pursuit has seldom been seen. And it was infinitely to Little's credit that he never let himself be flustered by it and beat off that heroic spurt at last.

Everybody thought—or nearly everybody—that Little would win comfortably. There we were all wrong. Everybody also thought that, of all the golfers in this country, we could not have had a better man to play the part of Da-

vid to Little's Goliath than Dr. William Tweddell, and there we were perfectly right. Little's golf at times had been a little patchy and he had palpably not been in love with keen greens in a cross wind. He had been frightened of his first fence—a match against an unknown local player—and had only just got over it. He had also, I fancy, been just a little frightened of this last fence—his match against Robert Sweeney—which divided him from his haven, the final. But in between whiles he had played much magnificent golf and he had invariably shown that he had the power of finishing in style, when he had his back to the wall.

Now that he was safely through into the final, there was a general impression that he would give a pyrotechnic display such as he had against the luckless Jimmy Wallace at Prestwick last year. I think he was all set for it and might have done so, but even a champion plays only as well as the other man allows him. Tweddell could not stop him from playing very fine golf, but he would not allow him to go gloriously mad as he did at Prestwick.

At the start it seemed as if there would be no match. I never saw such an impertinently

Lawson Little is shown putting on the sixth green in the final against William Twedd

brilliant beginning as Little's. Any other man would have run his second over a low bank. Little cut the legs from under the ball, made it literally squirm as it pitched, run backward rather than forward and end two inches from the hole. He followed this by quite a terrific iron shot through the wind at the second and behold! poor Tweddell who had done no harm was two down. He was three down at the fourth and he ought to have been four down at the fifth.

Little missed a very short putt to win the hole, and, though if's are essentially futile, I cannot help thinking that *if* he had holed that putt, he would have gone away like a streak of lightning and holed the course in about 69. As it was, he gave Tweddell space to breathe; three down is not nearly as bad as four down and Tweddell settled down to splendid and resolute golf. Twice Little did get four up, twice Tweddell pulled him back by a good putt with his old wooden putter. Little finished that round in 73, a very fine score indeed in a heavy wind, but not one hole could he add to his original lead of three and he must have been very tired of Tweddell hanging on to him.

If the match was to be a match, it was essential for Tweddell to get a good start after lunch. He got it, and Little got a bad one. Tweddell won the first two holes and he seemed absolutely certain to win the third as well, but he made a terrible mess of the putting and let his man escape. That was just as vital a slip as Little's short putt in the first round had been. Tweddell was shaken for a while and Little got back two holes in the next three. He was three up again and, though he himself had had a bad jolt, his position still seemed almost impregnable.

It looked still more so when he was still three up at the eighth. Then Tweddell made his really terrible onslaught. He won the ninth in 2 against Little's par 3. The tenth was a commonplace half in 4's but Tweddell had a 3 at a very good four hole—the eleventh—and another 3 at a long and difficult one-shotter, the twelfth. The incredible and impossible had happened. The match was all even and the crowd was wrought up to a leaping, dancing excitement.

At the thirteenth, Tweddell had a putt to be one up and he ended one inch short of the hole. All this time Little had never flinched; he had played sound golf and lost holes only because his enemy had played crushingly brilliant golf. Now he sprinted in his turn and with two perfect 4's made himself two up with three to go. For about the sixth time we said regretfully that it was all over. Tweddell did not think so.

He got a perfect 4 at the sixteenth and Little saved himself by ploughing the ball out of a deep bunker and holing a six-yard putt. At the next hole it was tit for tat. Little was near the green in two, sure of his 5, like to have a 4. He played a steady enough shot to within nine feet and Tweddell was in a bunker. Tweddell chipped out, hit the hole and lay nearly dead. Little missed, Tweddell holed and we were rushing to the last hole in a state of bewildered hope.

That last hole is not a very hard 4, but anything might happen and something very nearly did happen, for Little pushed out his tee shot over the spectators' heads and over a thick patch of gorse. He was left with a horrid pitch to the green with very little room "to come and go on," but he is never found wanting when he has to make the ball stop quickly. He played the pitch to perfection and he ran up his third stone dead. Tweddell had a six-yard putt to save his neck. He hit the ball cleanly but it was never quite on the line. A half in 4 and one of the really historic battles of golf was over. What a match!

Little and Tweddell are shown walking the fairway with, to their left, Eric Fiddian, and, to their right, Johnny DeForest and Dan Topping.

A promising young professional is Byron Nelson, an assistant at the Ridgewood Country Club, New Jersey; he is shown here playing a bunker shot.

Mildred "Babe" Didrikson has proved a clear claim to the title of Longest Woman Driver. Gene Sarazen, who is now touring the country playing exhibition matches with her, admits that it is not unusual for the "Babe" to pass him three or four times from the tee during a round.

The new P.G.A. Champion is Johnny Revolta, whose rise in professional golf has been meteoric.

The longest driver in American golf is fast proving to be young Jimmy Thomson, who came to the United States from Scotland while still a youngster and who is now making his home in Southern California.

Concentration BY ROBERT T. JONES, JR.

The Difference Between Bearing
Down and Simply Worrying

THERE IS NO MORE IMPORTANT CONSIDERATION in playing one's best golf than the right kind of concentration; this applies no matter how good or how bad the mechanics of the player's stroke. And there is possibly no more fascinating side of the game than an examination of what players conceive to be concentration or how to go about concentrating.

I had a very interesting talk not so long ago with a player who plays consistently in the middle 80's. He opened the subject by asking why the fellows who write about golf do not place more emphasis on the importance of concentration. I reminded him that quite a lot had been written on the subject, and that I had from time to time taken occasion to urge the necessity of concentrating keenly on the shot to be played and the manner of playing it until the thing is done.

Then he wanted to know why there were not some one or two or three things that one might suggest for players to think about. In his own case, he said, thinking of getting the left heel back on the ground as soon as he started the downswing had helped his game greatly. I have no doubt that it did, and that it will continue to do so, as long as he feels that it is a safe guide and remembers to bear it in mind.

One may safely say that there have been thousands of such devices that have been very helpful to golfers in bringing about proper concentration. Some years ago, quite a little publicity was given to the fact that Miss Helen Hicks used wood clubs with the word "Oompah" stamped on the head. She explained that she allowed this word, with the first syllable dwelt upon, to run through her mind as she was getting ready to play a stroke to improve her sense of timing.

Some time ago I wrote that ordinarily I could take care of my swing quite well by thinking of three things, to swing the club back slowly, to make certain that my hips made a complete wind-up during the backswing, and to see that my wrists were fully cocked as I started down. Later on a correspondent wrote me that he had simplified this formula even further. He thought, he said, of ease, turn and cock, the initials of the three words being e-t-c. He kept running over in his mind the words et cetera, and found that it helped him a lot.

If various devices of this kind are found helpful, as they well may, that's fine, but one must not get the idea that any "magic" of this kind will always prove adequate in itself. For me, golf always has its ups and downs. My game is "up" when I hit on some conception which, when kept in mind as I swing the club, enables me to play well. But when, for some unaccountable reason, thinking of this one thing no longer is enough, I have my "downs." This doesn't mean that the idea was wrong or valueless, but that something that I haven't been able to account for has slipped a cog. Then I have to set about finding some new object of concentration, which will get me back to playing well again.

One very interesting angle in the comments of the middle-80's man mentioned above was his statement that he did not realize for a long time that the expert players made any special effort at concentration. I am able to tell him that any competitor in an important tournament, an Open Championship, for instance, finds that his most difficult task is to keep up his concentration uninterruptedly through seventy-two holes of play.

I can also tell him that many of the fine players in practice or informal rounds, who fail so badly in important tournament play, do so because their sense of responsibility or anxiety in the face of the importance of the occasion entirely overwhelms their concentration on the routine task of swinging the club.

A leading difficulty with the average player is that he totally misunderstands what is meant by concentration. He may think he is concentrating hard, when he is merely worrying. As he stands up to the ball, he is thinking of a cavernous bunker that lies ahead. And while his thoughts are of nothing but golf, and of the playing of this next stroke, his mental processes have to do mainly with what is likely to happen to the ball, when he hits it, rather than with what he has to do to hit it correctly.

The degree of skill that one may acquire in the game is dependent largely on the measure of good form he develops in swinging the club. But that form must be carried into the actual hitting of the ball. We are all familiar with the great army of players who have a well-nigh faultless practice swing, which vanishes completely when they step up to hit the ball. The

practice swing is not repeated because the player is thinking of too many other things when he comes down to playing the stroke.

Then there is the other great group of players who swing awkwardly, but who manage to swing in pretty much the same way each time. They lack the benefit that comes from good mechanical form, but they are free from the entanglements of confusion as to what they are going to do and how they are going to do it, when they step up to hit the ball. They are able to concentrate properly on what they are doing, without disturbing thoughts on what the result is likely to be.

In golf, as in everything else, one reaches a certain stage simply through a given amount of repetition. When the stage has been attained where he can do the thing over and over pretty nearly the same way each time, he has acquired form. It may be good form or bad. He can be led or prompted to improve this form, given proper tutelage and the patience to practice.

The real road to improvement lies in gaining a working understanding of the correct swing in general, and of his own swing in particular. When he has done this, there will then be something on which to hang his concentration. Then he will have some chance of learning what to think about, instead of finding himself in utter confusion over half a hundred details as he stands up to start his stroke.

You can give the general advice to leave off thinking of everything except swinging and hitting the ball. You can recommend a procedure of sizing up the shot in advance, selecting the proper club and deciding just how the stroke should be played, and then forgetting everything except hitting the ball. You can, in individual cases, suggest one or two pointers for the player's consideration, after watching him swing. But no one will ever be able to name one or two subjects for attention with the idea that these will provide every golfer with the secret key to success. It will never be that simple.

They Made a Great Match BY O. B. KEELER

Miss Wethered and Bob Jones Put
on a Brilliant Atlanta Show

MISS JOYCE WETHERED, ON HER FIRST VISIT TO America, has played in a dozen noteworthy exhibition matches at golf as these lines are written, and before they appear in print she will have played in many more. And she may have scored more brilliantly than even her beautiful 74 on the old course at East Lake, Atlanta, where, the afternoon of June 18, Miss Wethered and Charlie Yates halved the match with Miss Dorothy Kirby and Bobby Jones. But of one thing I am sure—Miss Wethered will not have played, and perhaps will never play, in a match with so pretty a background, and affording so vivid an inspiration for the two greatest golfers of their times.

You see, it was Bobby Jones who arranged the Atlanta match, which he requested the Atlanta Women's Golf Association to sponsor for charity. And Bobby had been invited to play as Miss Wethered's partner in her first appearance in this country—the match May 30, at the Women's National Golf and Tennis Club on Long Island. Shortly before that date Bobby was taken ill; an attack of appendicitis, an old enemy concerning his previous bouts with which few persons were aware.

It never leaked out, for instance, that Bobby was quite ill a week before the last championship competition in which he engaged—the National Amateur at Merion; the last trick in the Grand Slam of 1930. It was rumored that he had suffered a slight attack of ptomaine poisoning; but only a few heard even that rumor—though an Atlanta surgeon, Dr. Lon Grove, accompanied Bobby to Philadelphia when he went to the tournament, in which he played well, though erratically.

At any rate, a week before the match in which he was scheduled to appear with Miss Wethered on May 30, Bobby went under again; and at the last was compelled to cancel the engagement—the only golfing engagement he ever had cancelled for any cause in his long career. Johnny Dawson took his place and a great match, ending all square, ensued with Mrs. Glenna Collett Vare and Gene Sarazen as the other side.

In the next week Bobby recovered sufficiently to make a business trip to Massachusetts, and to attend the Open Championship at Oakmont, which he was covering for a syndicate. He steadily insisted that he was feeling all right, though obviously he had lost much weight; and he declined to consider suggestions that he might not be in shape to play the match at East Lake on June 18.

In New York following the Open, Bobby suffered two more attacks, slighter than the preceding one, but sufficient to keep him in bed several days at the Vanderbilt Hotel, where his father joined him. And there was never a word said, that I am aware of, concerning a cancellation or a substitution in the approaching Atlanta match. The last word I had from Bobby was a telegram with the information that Miss Wethered and her companion, Miss Dorothy Shaw, would arrive by plane after her match at Baltimore June 16. And presently Bobby himself turned up, having returned by train, announcing that he was feeling fine and was certain to go through with the match, unless he broke a leg, as he inelegantly expressed it.

And at that time he had already reserved a room in an Atlanta hospital and had got the operation scheduled for the next day but one after the match on Tuesday. But that was not generally known, of course.

So Bobby and his party met Miss Wethered and Miss Shaw at the airport—it was the English girls' first journey by plane, and they liked it so well they would have said they were crazy about it, had they been American girls—and at dinner that evening Miss Wethered and Bobby talked golf incessantly and she told him how Bobby Cruickshank had suggested a change in her putting grip for the American greens—the reverse-overlap; it appeared to me almost identical with that suggested to Bobby so long ago by the late Walter Travis; and Tuesday was fair, and a fine gallery turned out to see the match at old East Lake.

From the start it was easy to see that the two principal figures were "putting out"—to employ the vernacular. I have watched many exhibition matches, but none like this one. Miraculously, Bobby's putting touch, deplorably off-color these later years, had returned, as he laid a long one dead over the tricky Bermuda at the first green and holed a thirty-footer for a deuce at the second, to put his side two up.

And Miss Wethered, hitting two hundred and forty yards into a light headwind, laid her pitch four feet from the flag at the third and holed the putt for a 3, while at the five-hundred-sixty-five-yard fifth, down the wind, she was level with Bobby in two great wood shots, just in front of the green, and squared with another fine wee pitch and a seven-footer, for a birdie 4. Then it was Bobby again, who holed a fifteen-footer for a birdie 3 at the seventh, and pitched dead for another birdie 3 at the eighth; and then Miss Wethered, just short of the green with two wood shots at the five-hundred-and-six-yard ninth, gained back a hole with an exquisite little approach that left her no putt at all.

Bobby was out in 34. Miss Wethered was out in par 36. And in the popeyed gallery people hammered each other on the back, and called attention to the fact that Bobby Jones with a 34 was just one up on the English girl. Between them they had a best-ball of 31, and while Dorothy Kirby and Charlie Yates were playing admirable golf—the fifteen-year-old Atlanta girl did a 41 from the back tees—the combat was between the two greatest golfers, and that was what all the gallery had come out to see, though never expecting anything so utterly dazzling as this.

And Miss Wethered, driving level with Bobby across the lake and up the long hill of the tenth fairway, squared the match for her side, and with Bobby, at the tenth. And she was square also with par of the East Lake course from the back tees, through the thirteenth, where the little Dorothy, with an exquisitely placed wood second, catching the run of the narrow apron to the bunker-surrounded green missed a four-foot putt for a birdie 3 that would have been a hole won all by herself, in that company!

Miss Wethered's driving was simply tremendous. The wind was coming up, and when facing it she was hitting a low, raking drive of great carry and astonishing run. And at the fourteenth, a hole of four hundred and forty-eight yards, there was, for the moment, a half-gale coming out of the west, straight in her face. And there—well, Bobby and Charlie Yates struck off two of their best, and Miss

Wethered's ball was well in front.

Against the sweeping wind Miss Wethered was flag-high with her second shot, the ball curling off to the left into a bunker. And here ensued the most whimsical play of all the afternoon.

Miss Wethered, of course, was unfamiliar with East Lake bunkers in summer, or at any other time. This was her first recovery off what looked to her as if it might be sand. She essayed a good, substantial half-blast with the niblick, and the blade, ricocheting from the sun-baked surface under a thin layer of sand, clipped the ball fairly in the back and sent it flying fifty yards over the green and the gallery, to the frank amazement of the latter and no less of Miss Wethered herself.

But she trotted down into a little valley, found the ball in a difficult place, pitched back beautifully, almost hitting the flag—and holed a twenty-foot putt for a 5, to be a stroke above par, while Bobby won the hole with a 4.

Charlie mopped his brow.

"This is the first time," he said, puzzled, "I ever played fourteen holes as a lady's partner before I ever figured in one."

He reflected further, and added:

"Well, as long as she's carrying me around on her back, I'll just try not to let my feet drag!"

They halved the four-hundred-and-thirteen-yard sixteenth with 4 all around, Miss Wethered nearly holing a five-yard putt for a 3, and Charlie, in pursuance of his announced policy, squared at the seventeenth, when Bobby's long drive was hooked to a ditch by the roadway, and Miss Wethered, for the second time on the strange Bermuda greens, took three putts.

And then came the climax of a great match.

The eighteenth hole at East Lake is two hundred yards, across the lake, from a hillside tee to a hilltop green.

"I know a one-shot finishing hole is not usually well regarded," Big Bob Jones, Bobby's father, once said to me. "But when a player stands on that tee at East Lake, with the match square, or dormie—that drive calls for all there is, in the delicatessen department."

Miss Wethered drove first, a spoon into the wind, and her ball was dead on the line, stopping twenty feet in front of the flag. Yates' shot was the same distance beyond the pin. Dorothy's was short and to the right. Bobby's was shoved a bit, and his wee pitch from the side of the hill caught the slope and trickled down five yards below the hole. Dorothy came on for a 4. Miss Wethered putted, and just missed a 2. Charlie likewise. And the gallery pressed closer, for it was up to Bobby.

Odd, how the film spins back on the reel of memory to a certain scene, at a certain time. As I stood there watching Bobby line up that putt, I saw him again on the same green, and in the same spot, at the close of a round in the famous Southern Open, eight years before— the tournament he won from a great field, with eight strokes to spare, on his home course. And I saw him sink that putt, eight years ago, and then—well, then the roar of that faraway gallery went out under the roar of the gallery that stood all about me. For Bobby sank this putt, too. And the match was square.

Nothing devised in a scenarist's shop at Hollywood could have helped that climax. Bobby had done a par 71, on his home course. Miss Wethered, a 74. The little Dorothy, in the most distinguished company in which she will ever play, an 84. And Charlie Yates, at last traveling on his own feet in the pinch, a 76.

Miss Wethered's play was beyond praise. On Bermuda greens—more than a score of years ago characterized by one of her countrymen, Ted Ray, as "not grawss but grapevines" —which she then saw for the first time, she had needed three putts twice, and she had been a trifle off-line with two drives. And that was all that stood between Joyce Wethered and a level 70, the first afternoon she had seen the 6600-yard East Lake course. The individual match with Bobby—the gallery of course kept that in mind—was won by Bobby, two and one. As between Miss Wethered and Charlie Yates, intercollegiate champion, she was one up.

Going down the fairway toward the sixteenth green, I was walking momentarily with Miss Wethered, and, naturally, I was complimenting her on her brilliant play.

She smiled and then became suddenly grave.

"I had to play well here," she said, simply. "Bobby arranged the match, you know. And he's said and written so many kind things about my game. And then he was ill, and then he insisted on playing. . . . I wish I were sure he *should* be playing, now. . . . It's—it's the most sporting thing I've ever known. I had to play well, at East Lake. I couldn't let Bobby down, you know."

Yes—I knew. And I know too that I saw something that afternoon at East Lake that will stand out as the prettiest picture of a lifetime in sport—the two greatest golfers, playing all they knew in every shot, in generous and gallant complement to one another, in the greatest match I ever witnessed.

Dr. Robert A. Millikan was located by the cameraman while playing golf at Pasadena, California.

One of the country's great industrial leaders and also one of its keenest golfers is Mr. Charles M. Schwab, who appears here while playing at White Sulphur Springs.

The Matter of Control BY ROBERT T. JONES, JR.

The Contest of Hand Action

Against Body Action

THE AVERAGE GOLFER OF TWENTY YEARS AGO had to take a lot of punishment. If he happened to be seriously concerned with his progress in the game, and made any special effort to keep informed of the latest theories of the leading players and writers, he might reasonably have come to believe almost anything. The idea of throwing the clubhead from the top of the swing was only the most absurd of the conceptions prevalent among players who had never seen their swings in slow motion.

Today there is very little excuse left for argument about what actually happens during any particular swing. And because so many of these swings have been found to include similar movements, we are justified in asserting that the fundamentals of a correct swing have been established. But the battle has only been transferred to another sector. The question now is one of control. Upon what does one direct one's thought in order best to cause one's muscles to accomplish a correct swing?

In brief, the contest is one of hand action against what we call body action. One side of the argument is that if the hands swing freely and are used correctly all else will follow; that if one swings the club with the hands the winding and unwinding of the body will take care of itself. The other side is that the action of the swing should originate in the center of the body, initiated by the muscles in the waist and back, that it is in this way that the average golfer will have the best chance of building up a sound and complete method.

Upon each side there is eminent authority of both players and instructors. A perfectly reasonable difference of opinion exists upon a question which is wide open to argument. The only unfortunate aspect has been supplied by certain extravagant and patently thoughtless statements to the effect that hand action or hip action accounted for seventy percent or eighty percent of the golf swing. Such statements have confused the real issue, and made it appear one of mechanics when it is not so at all. Whether a person may learn more rapidly in one way or the other to accomplish a swing that is correct according to standards accepted by both sides depends in great measure upon the pupil.

There is no conceivable way in which the relative importance of two functions, both essential parts of a correct swing, can be evaluated. For purpose of study we sometimes find it to advantage to consider the hands or the hips alone, but even then, in any discussion, it is always assumed that the action of either must always be in proper relation to the movement of the other parts of the body. Obviously if the rest of the body is held immovable, the hands and arms, in order to bring the club against the ball, must do something different from the performance which would be correct when supplementing an ample body turn.

Gene Sarazen is one of those who place great emphasis upon the hands. Gene has made the statement that the grip is the most important thing in the golf swing. That it is a first essential without which a correct swing is utterly impossible there can be no doubt. Until the hands are placed on the club in something like correct positions there is no need to go on.

But when one begins to talk of hands and body in the swing one runs up against something like this. In describing the familiar swing which hits up at the ball by means of an awkward lift of the body, it can be said correctly that the faulty body movement was induced by incorrect hand action. In other words the shovelling action of the shoulders was made necessary because the hands straightened out too soon and put the swing so out of gear that the body chose the only means of completing the stroke. But it could have happened just as well that the hips by refusing to lead the unwinding from the top of the swing had made it necessary for the hands and arms themselves to begin the movement.

Sarazen, of course, recognizes the question as one of where to apply the control. Apparently he believes in following his hands, for he says that he starts his backswing with them. Even though to make a similar effort would destroy my swing, as long as Gene accomplishes a sound swing in this way I agree that he applies control in the best way for him.

One cannot say that the average golfer is deficient in either hand action or body action. He is deficient in both, or he would not be an average golfer. But in most cases his hands are at least active. The player tries to use them and it seems to me would be likely to succeed fairly well if his body movement gave him a chance.

On the other hand one finds any number of players who are so tied up that they cannot make use of their hips and legs. Having started the swing by picking the club up with the hands, no suggestion is ever received that an important source of power is being neglected. Only among really expert players does one find even an apparent attempt to assure an ample use of the muscles in the waist and back.

It is for this reason that I prefer a control that will start the hips to moving. The power available from a full wind up of the hips is the cheapest power in terms of effort that a golfer may come by. As Abe Mitchell puts it, a good golfer plays a lot of golf "beneath himself," that is, with his hips and legs. The average golfer can afford to run no risk of leaving these important members on the side lines.

Gene Sarazen's face is a study in concentration as he lashes out a drive.

Little Sees It Through BY GRANTLAND RICE

Wins Thirty-One Straight Matches

IT HAS REMAINED FOR LAWSON LITTLE OF STANford University to kill off the roulette feature of golf. In his last four Amateur Championships, British and American, there have been twelve different survivors for the four semifinal rounds, but it was Lawson Little who came marching on to his thirty-first match-play victory.

When anyone can pick up thirty-one consecutive championship matches, twenty-five of these at eighteen holes, the killing route, there is little to be said about the part that luck can play.

There was something more important than the mere record of these thirty-one victories from Prestwick to Cleveland. There were the manner and method of his two finishing thrusts against his two hottest challengers, Johnny Goodman of Omaha and Walter Emery of Oklahoma City.

Here were two rivals who fought him tooth, nail and scalp. They nailed him at the time when the long strain must have been at its tautest point. Yet the answer is this: in the face of high class challenging golf, Little played the last eleven holes of these two rounds eight strokes under par. He played these last eleven holes in nine under even 4's—or just two over even 3's—through a stretch that included three par-5 holes.

And with the faraway goal at last in sight, where he might have been expected to waver

a bit or start slipping, he finished off the big job with a birdie and an eagle. His closing salute against Emery at the 520-yard sixteenth hole was a long drive into the face of a head wind, and then a 240-yard spoon shot through a cross wind that dropped the ball just twelve feet from the cup. To polish up every closing detail, he then rolled this putt in for an eagle 3 as Emery lay stone dead for his birdie 4.

Seven times in this Amateur Championship test at Cleveland, Lawson Little found himself struggling in the rear, facing quick starters who got the jump. Young Rufus King jumped him three holes the first day by opening up with 4-4-3-3-2. These quick starters can be deadly poison over an eighteen-hole route, but in each case the long-hitting Californian soon hammered his way to the lead again, and he kept on hammering until the match was over.

What feature of golf gave Lawson Little his fourth consecutive championship? The peculiar part is that no single feature, but a blend of several essentials, left him master of the field.

One. Long, straight hitting, despite several narrow fairways guarded by trees and ravines. His length from the tee was amazing enough, but not as amazing as his uncanny accuracy.

Two. His fine iron play, from an eight-iron pitch to a two-iron, where the ball usually landed almost directly on the line, and rarely missed the green.

Three. His consistent putting that reached a

Lawson Little, in winning the Amateur Championship for the second year in succession, not only confirmed the claim that he is one of golf's mightiest hitters and entitled to rank with the best of putters; he also proved that he is a master as well in negotiating the short stroke-savers, those little teasers from just off the putting green.

brilliant peak the last day with a smooth, even stroke under perfect control.

Four. His cool, unruffled, determined match-play temperament that considered nothing except the next shot to be played; that allowed no discouragement to wander in; that permitted no break in his all-week concentration.

No amateur living has guns enough to blow away this quadruple fortress that embraces power, skill and all that is needed on the mental side to complete the picture.

The recent championship at Cleveland was replete with thrills. There was the showing of Chandler Egan and Ellis Knowles, the two veteran entries who were on golf's firing line thirty years ago. Both won extra-hole matches against stout competition and both were around par when they finally slipped out.

There was the early downfall of Francis Ouimet and Chick Evans, who were caught on somewhat struggling rounds.

There was the high class of Charley Yates of Atlanta, Western Champion, Maurice McCarthy of Cleveland, Reynolds Smith of Dallas, George Voigt of New York, and Ross Somerville of Canada. Somerville, as usual, stuck grimly to the finish where a birdie 3 from Emery caught him on the nineteenth green.

But it was the shadow of Lawson Little that dominated the scene from start to finish. It was soon evident that the Californian was riding the crest of his best game, and that he was getting better day by day. With Scotty Campbell eliminated in a sub-par war, it was also evident that if the field ever let Little loose into the thirty-six-hole pasture there was small hope left of turning him back.

No two better men in the tournament could have been chosen for the job than Johnny

Goodman and Walter Emery, not only fine golfers, but also game, cool, seasoned competitors, who had no intention of beating themselves. In this semifinal group, Joe Lynch of Boston and Georgetown was the only stranger, but Lynch had earned his place by some heavy hitting and hard fighting in the tougher spots.

It was felt as the week's play moved along that, if anyone could take Little's measure, it would have to be Goodman or Emery. Goodman held his match all square at twenty-seven holes by turning in a 32 to start the afternoon round—just 4 under par. But down the stretch Goodman suddenly ran into a heavy blast that included five birdies in the last seven holes, a pace too fast for anyone to meet.

It was a pace where pars might as well have been 7's or 8's. "Can Little keep this up?" was the prevailing question. Emery, after winning the first three holes, was still all square at the eighteenth. Three down at the twenty-eighth, and apparently on his way out, the Oklahoma law student suddenly turned, won the next two holes, and forced Little once more into a

hot corner. How would Little meet this new challenge? His answer was 4-3-3-3, with a birdie and an eagle on the finishing two holes.

There were two hundred and four matches fought out through the week, so you can imagine the picture. For the first three days it was like being in the middle of four beehives. But the galleries were enthusiastic and well-mannered all the way, and there were enough thrills to last a season. For example, Walter Emery handed the crowd no less than eleven 2's, a record for any championship count.

All in all, the four-time champion within two years had too much in the way of power, control, timing, touch and concentrative determination to be stopped. He kept on hitting the ball too consistently with every club, he made too few mistakes, to be caught and held.

He was nineteen under par for the week in spite of several stymies that blocked out other birdies, and he was ten under par the last two days when the pressure was greatest. These are figures that tell the story far more eloquently than any set of words could ever hope to do.

Walter Emery is shown making a recovery shot.

Lawson Little's winning of the British Amateur Championship at St. Annes for the second time in as many years is a duplication of a feat achieved only twice before in the history of the Championship.

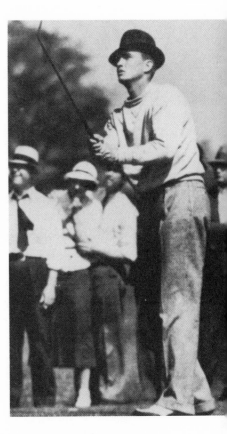

Three Seats of Tension BY ROBERT T. JONES, JR.

An Analysis of When Tenseness Begins

"ONE OF THE MOST EFFECTIVE GOLF LESSONS I ever had," said a friend of mine one day, "I got at the zoo."

"That's queer," said I. "How come?"

"Well," he replied, "I was watching an old elephant shifting from side to side in a sort of lazy rhythm. After a while, as I felt inclined to fall in with him, it occurred to me that here was a fine way to keep relaxed as I addressed a golf ball. So from then on whenever I have stepped up to a shot, I have said to myself 'Remember the old elephant.' "

"Silly," say you? "Not a bit," say I. For you must be relaxed in order to swing smoothly, and you must swing smoothly in order to play golf well. And there is no better way to keep your muscles relaxed and responsive as you address the ball than to maintain some sort of leisurely movement.

I have watched beginners, most commonly lady beginners, freeze over a golf ball until I thought I would yank out a handful of hair if they didn't do something. The customary attitude, with knee joints thrown back and locked securely, and with arms extended with perfect rigidity, represents the last word in tenseness. If it makes your flesh crawl merely to watch, what must be the state of mind of the person who is up there hoping to hit the ball? As he grows more and more taut he loses whatever

chance he might have had to get off a respectable shot. To "remember the old elephant" would surely do this player a lot of good.

To learn to relax one must only learn to recognize and locate tension, and then, by practice, learn to eliminate it. Sounds simple enough. Working along the same line, a golfer should be benefited by a knowledge of where and when he should feel this much-talked-of relaxation.

To begin with, no one expects him to continue in a state of complete relaxation throughout the swing. He is not to emulate Fred Stone's scare-crow dance with a golf club in his hands. Once his swing is under way, what he wants is control of tension. But while addressing the ball he may consider that relaxation cannot be too complete.

The three most formidable enemies of relaxation in the address are a hard grip; any undue extension of the arms made necessary because the player stands too far from the ball; and a too-wide separation of the feet. Combine the three, as the beginner does, and you will find that you are tied up as effectively as if by chains. With all this tension to overcome, is it any wonder that his effort to swing is full of jerks?

Dealing with the three enemies in order, the

first is the grip—always, incidentally, a good place to start. If your grip is hard you must recognize its character, if you only think of it. Relax it. Make it as light as you can. Grip the club in your fingers and hold it out before you. Now toss the head up and let the clubhead fall, holding the handle only enough to keep it in your hands. Get the feel of the clubhead against your relaxed wrists. Have someone grasp the head of the club and try to jerk it suddenly from your hands. See—you have no need to fear that it will escape. Even with a grip as light as you can make it, instinctively you take hold as you need to. So in the swing, no matter how relaxed your hands may be at address, your grip will be tight enough as your hands begin to move the club.

To avoid introducing tension by reaching for the ball, determine to relax the muscles of the upper arms and shoulders. Then get close enough to the ball so that, with only a slight bend at the waist, the arms may *hang* without need of extension. If the ball seems to be brought too close by this maneuver, remember that it does not have to be located opposite the center of the club-face. Off the toe is just as good, or perhaps better, to allow for some stretching in the actual hitting. You may learn to hit the ball from its new position, but you can never learn to swing until you relax.

The third seat of tension which must be elminated is in the legs. I always like to repeat Abe Mitchell's expression that a golfer must "move freely beneath himself." It describes graphically the mobility which must be felt in the legs, and which can be had only when these members are free of tension. The player who spreads his feet far apart in an effort to strengthen his foundation, or who otherwise puts his legs out of commission, has thereby invalidated the greatest source of effortless power at his command. He can't use his hips or his back and so he has become a weakling.

The keys to the proper functioning of these parts of a player's anatomy are his knees. He must keep them relaxed and responsive. A wide stance is seldom excusable. A separation equal to the width of the shoulders is nearly always sufficient. Upon such a base, with both knees slightly bent, and the whole body in an alert attitude, it becomes easy to turn the hips and to make some use of the muscles in the waist and back.

Relaxation in the address posture means so much in making a smooth start of the backswing possible. Emulating the old elephant, swinging from such a position into unhurried movement, should not be difficult.

Notice the utter relaxation at the end of the author's follow-through.

Number Six for Great Glenna

BY BERNARD E. SWANSON

Mrs. Vare Wins Sixth National Title in Fourteen Tries

THE NATIONAL WOMEN'S CHAMPIONSHIP, concluded with a sentimental wave upon which Mrs. Glenna Collett Vare, Jr., of Philadelphia rocketed to her sixth title, may be concentrated into one antithetical statement: Mrs. Vare won the title, but youth, in all its vigor and impulsive recklessness, stole the show.

If ever the correspondents had something to write home about, it was consolidated into the space of that one week of variable weather at Interlachen Country Club, Minneapolis, the week of August twenty-sixth to thirty-first. There was the throaty rejection of the challenge that "they never come back." There was the unprecedented turnout of more than 15,-000 spectators, in the face of morbid weather conditions. But more significantly, there was the continued defiance of youth, rising to the greatest crescendo in the thirty-nine-year history of the event.

Mrs. Vare, representing that older line of big name golfers, did win the championship. But to do it she had to play the greatest golf of her long and conspicuous career. She had to clamp down on the rising tide that insisted on being beaten only by the best.

That represents the outstanding achievement of the National Women's Championship of 1935. Veterans have held a monopoly on the titles for more than a decade, much more so, for instance, than in the men's field. There have been the Vares, the Hicks, the Van Wies, the Orcutt-Crews, the Hills, the Cheneys and others. Strong contenders they still are, but at least they are being given more of a tussle than has been their experience before.

In recapitulation, Mrs. Vare won her sixth championship for as sentimental a triumph as you would care to observe. She has been in national tournament golf for fully fifteen years. She won her first title in 1922 and she repeated in 1925. She equalled the all-time performance of three in a row starting with 1928. In her last thirty-eight National tournament matches, she had lost only three, and each of those losses was either in the finals or to the player who finally finished out the championship string.

If there is something a doting public loves to witness, it is to see a noble figure emerge from the shadows of the past and return to head the parade. Mrs. Vare was not very far back in those shadows. But she did come out of the past to win a title which had evaded her for three years. In 1933 she retired from competition in order to attend to the mothering of her little brood. Last year she went to the semifinal, where she saw Virginia Van Wie and another of those golfing youngsters, Dorothy Traung, survive to the final. And so it must be recorded that Mrs. Vare was in the throes of a progressive comeback.

Mrs. Vare admitted that her present game compared favorably with the one of her peak days and she declared herself steadier and more consistent than in those halcyon days when she was the unchallenged leader of all American women's golf. She was of the opinion that she was not quite as long off the tee, but her friends, friends who attended her in her latest triumph at Interlachen, quickly argued the point. Said one: "Glenna, you have been hitting the ball with greater distance this week than you ever did. You never gained such length with your tee shots as you did today against Patty Berg."

That tells the whole story. It took Glenna Collett Vare at her best to stand off the challenge of a youngster, in fact, to stand off a coterie of youngsters virtually new to national tournament play.

After the final match Mrs. Vare was asked to rate the youngsters who had been such a wholesome part of the title picture. She had just stood off snub-nosed, freckle-faced, red-haired Patty Jane Berg of the host club, winning by three and two with a birdie on the thirty-fourth green. She had been forced to fight off one challenge of youth after another, so her observations were most interesting.

"By all means, Patty Berg first," explained Mrs. Vare. "In fact, quite a distance ahead of the rest, and they all were good. Then would come Elizabeth Abbott of Los Angeles and Beatrice Barrett of Minneapolis, with not much to choose between them."

Seventeen years old and weighing only 115 pounds, Patty Berg hits a surprisingly long ball. Having played golf only three years, she has not the perfect iron play, especially with her run-up shots, that she will have later. But she handles her putter as Bobby Jones stroked Calamity Jane at his best. With a spectacular forty-five-foot putt, from identically the same spot Bobby Jones had dropped his "pinch putt" to clinch the National Open of 1930, she had beaten Mrs. Dan Chandler. With a 25-footer on the same eighteenth green, she had caught Charlotte Glutting, playing the finest golf of her life, to square the match and give the tiny Minneapolis girl the moral strength to defeat the West Orange registerite on the third extra hole of the semifinal match. And with a 12-footer on the same green again she had prevented Mrs. Vare from being five up with their 36-hole match half completed, thereby setting the stage for the fight to the finish that attracted fully 7000 spectators to the tournament course on the final afternoon.

Those miraculous saves fanned the ardor of her home-town admirers. They kicked up the attendance figures to fully fifteen thousand for the week and for the first time really poured money into the women's coffers of the United States Golf Association. It marked the second smashing success for the Interlachen club, which in 1930 accommodated forty thousand dollars worth of customers for an all-time record. And it was largely because of the achievement of this extremely modest, boyish youngster.

Patty Berg is an honor student in high school and she spends most of her summer playing golf. She isn't satisfied only to go round and round the course; she spends fully as much time on the practice grounds as on the fairways. With the ordeal of the championship final over, she was back at her own course only a day or two later in order to practice the things she had learned in the National tournament.

Miss Berg gained her competitive flair from engaging in boys' games. When fourteen years old, she coached a boys' football team, because her parents refused to allow her to play any more and she just had to have a hand in it. Three years ago she was interested in golf by an admirer from her home course, Patricia

Stephenson, a former State champion. Urged to play in the Minneapolis City tournament of 1932, she gathered together a makeshift set of clubs from her broker father's collection, made up her own lunch and thumbed a ride to the course. There she shot a 122 total for her first venture, and decided right there that she liked the game and wanted to master it. Two years later she won the championship of that particular tournament.

But the Misses Berg, Abbott and Barrett do not stand alone as youth's sole contribution to the National women's tournament of 1935. There was a circle of others who could shape up quite a respectable championship field by themselves. There was Marion McDougall, twenty-one-year-old Portland girl who had won the Oregon State, the Women's Western Open and the Pacific Northwest. There was twenty-one-year-old Marion Miley, who had won five straight titles, including the Trans-Mississippi, Western and Kentucky State before losing to Miss Glutting at Minneapolis. There was seventeen-year-old Betty Jameson, who won the Southern title when only sixteen and qualified for the National. And many others.

It isn't everyone who, playing in their fourteenth National championship, is still good enough to cope with the next generation on their own field of sports. And fewer still could win.

Seventeen-year-old Patty Berg sinks a long putt in her match against Charlotte Glutting.

A syndicated columnist for *The New York Herald-Tribune*, RED SMITH is one of that gifted breed—a sportswriter whose work frequently ends up in textbooks.

In 1921 JOCK HUTCHISON became the first American citizen to win the British Open, which he accomplished at his native St. Andrews.

Beyond all dispute Great Britain's greatest golfer, HARRY VARDON won a record total of six British Opens. In 1900 he also won the United States Open.

A syndicated columnist for *The Chicago Sun*, RING LARDNER also wrote widely anthologized stories which moved some critics to refer to him as the most trenchant satirist since Jonathan Swift.

A sportswriter who could quote Ovid by the hour (and limericks by the day) O. B. KEELER covered for *The Atlanta Journal* all twenty-seven of the major national championships in which Bobby Jones competed.

Grandson of the famous evolutionist, BERNARD DARWIN was a first-hand observer of British and American golf for more than seventy years. His essays on the game are considered the classic examples of golf eloquence.

Born in Cornwall, England, JIM BARNES emigrated to the United States at the age of nineteen. During a long career, he won the United States Open, the British Open, and two P.G.A. Championships, including the initial event in 1916.

A Boston newspaperman, ROBERT E. HARLOW was for many years the personal manager of Walter Hagen. He then became Tournament Director for the P.G.A. and later founded *Golf World*, the weekly international newspaper.

EDDIE LOOS was one of the few American professionals who has been able to combine an eminent teaching career with a conspicuous record on the tournament circuit.

Scotland's ALEXANDER "SANDY" HERD won the British Open in 1902 and came in second on three different occasions during a period that spanned twenty-five years.

In 1913, at the age of twenty, FRANCIS OUIMET stamped his name indelibly on golf history by winning the United States Open in a play-off at Brookline, Massachusetts, against Harry Vardon and Ted Ray, thus becoming the first amateur and the second native-born American to win the championship. The following year he won the United States Amateur, a title he won again in 1931. In 1951 he became the only American ever to be elected Captain of the Royal and Ancient Golf Club of St. Andrews.

At forty-three, the oldest age at which the championship has ever been won, EDWARD "TED" RAY, of England, won the United States Open in 1920. This occasion marked the second and last time the trophy has ever been taken abroad. Ray had won the British Open in 1912. For years he was widely acclaimed as the game's longest hitter, and he was perhaps its most underrated putter.

RUBE GOLDBERG, an occasional and invariably witty writer, is the veteran cartoonist of surrealistic inventions that accomplish nothing.

After losing a limb during World War One, professional ERNEST JONES emigrated to the United States from England to become one of the game's most dedicated teachers and easily its most debated theorist.

WALTER R. MC CALLUM was for many years a sportswriter and the golf editor of *The Evening Star* in Washington, D.C.

HAL SHARKEY, a former sports editor for the *Newark News*, was the first manager of the "pro tour" during its embryonic circuit of the mid-1920s.

W. D. RICHARDSON was a veteran golf reporter for *The New York Times*.

No American professional yet has equaled WALTER HAGEN's record of eleven major national titles: two United States Opens, four British Opens, and five P.G.A. Championships. He won four of the last in a row when played at match.

A magnificently graceful stylist, CHARLES "CHICK" EVANS, JR., has played in the almost incredible total of fifty United States Amateur Championships. He won the first of his two titles in this event in 1916, the same year in which he had also won the United States Open, establishing a scoring record, while using only seven clubs, that stood for twenty years. Evans also won the Western Open once and the Western Amateur eight times.

ROBERT T. JONES, JR., is the only golfer in the history of the game to have won thirteen major national championships: five United States Amateurs, four United States Opens—both record totals—three British Opens, and one British Amateur. All of these were won during a span of a scant eight years—1923 to 1930 inclusive. He retired after winning each of the four titles during the 1930 season.

During an active career that stretched almost thirty years, MACDONALD SMITH was regarded as the most graceful swinger in modern golf, not excluding even Harry Vardon, Bobby Jones, or Sam Snead. It became something of a mystery, therefore, why he was able to win more than sixty tournaments without winning one of the internationally recognized championships.

JOYCE WETHERED, who became Lady Heathcote-Amory, was once ranked by many knowledgeable golfers as one of the three best amateurs in Great Britain—male or female.

GEORGE T. HAMMOND began writing about sports for *The New York Sun* during his high school days in the 1920s. In 1932 he left *The Sun* to join Carl Byoir Associates, the public relations firm of which he is now president.

A good amateur golfer since boyhood, JAMES "SCOTTY" RESTON has been for many years the distinguished analyst of national and international affairs for *The New York Times*.

Thought by many to have been the most brilliant putter in American golf, JERRY TRAVERS won four United States Amateur Championships between 1907 and 1913. In 1915 he also won the United States Open.

MAXWELL STYLES is a veteran sportswriter and editor in Southern California.

A golf fan during almost all of the sixty-one years he was a professional writer, CLARENCE BUDINGTON KELLAND was perhaps the most prolific author since Balzac.

Born in Edinburgh, TOMMY ARMOUR came to the United States as a member of the British Walker Cup team. Soon afterwards he secured the position of secretary to the Westchester-Biltmore Country Club, and then turned professional in 1924. Between 1927 and 1931 he was able to win the United States Open, the P.G.A. Championship, and the British Open.

With the *Minneapolis Star* and *Tribune* newspapers for thirty years, BERNARD E. SWANSON was a former sports editor of the *Star*. In addition to covering sports for the twin-city area, he often wrote articles for national publications.

[Despite exhaustive checking, the editor has been unable to obtain information regarding the following contributors: OWEN BROWN, ALEXIS J. COLMAN and HUMPHREY L. G. FRY.]

A NOTE ON THE EDITOR

CHARLES PRICE is the author of *The World of Golf*, which appeared in 1962 and is, in fact, the only complete and fully illustrated history of the game ever published. In his eloquent foreword to that work, Bobby Jones said, "The whole book is testimony to an ardent love of the game and a thorough understanding of its nature." This understanding of golf comes from an intensive career devoted to playing the game and writing about it.

On graduation from college, at age twenty-two, he played as an amateur in the winter of 1947–48 on the coast-to-coast tournament circuit of the Professional Golfers Association. A year later he published his first article on golf, which appeared in *The Saturday Evening Post*. Since then he has written more than three hundred magazine articles on a variety of subjects. He was the original editor of *Golf* magazine, a position he held for three years before writing *The World of Golf*. Mr. Price is one of the rare golf writers who has serious tournament qualifications to his credit. He lives in New York City.

Afterword
by
Robert Cromie

The American Golfer *was a maga-*
zine which delighted and instructed
devotees of the royal and ancient
game for some three decades prior to
its demise during the depression of
the 1930s. This collection of writings
from that magazine is preceded by a
scene-setting preface by Charles
Price, who put this book together, and
brief pieces about Walter J. Travis,
the publication's founder and first
editor, and Grantland Rice, the sec-
ond and last editor. Rice writes about
Travis, surely one of the most amaz-
ing golfers of all time, who was al-
most thirty-five when he took up the
game and won the United States Am-
ateur title four years later. The vi-
gnette on Rice is by the late Red
Smith, one of the most stylish of
sportswriters, who begins, "Grant-
land Rice was the greatest man I have
known, the greatest talent, the great-
est gentleman . . ."

The seventy-five selections cover the
period from 1920 through 1935
(Rice's tenure as editor ran from 1919
to 1936). There are twenty-eight by-
lines (Bobby Jones, Bernard Darwin,
O.B. Keeler, and Rice account for
thirty-nine articles). The pleasurable
task of reading the text and poring
over contemporary photographs
leaves one with the certain conviction
that the top players of that era were
superb and their scores often sensa-
tional—especially when you realize
that they were playing with un-
matched sets of clubs with wooden
shafts and that the rough they en-
countered was often horrendous. The
stymie was no help either.

The collection makes you think
wistfully of what an entrancing spec-
tacle it would be if an Impossible
Open tournament could be arranged
in which Bobby Jones, Walter Hagen,
John Ball, Harry Vardon, Ted Ray,
Chick Evans, Tommy Armour,
Lawson Little, Jerry Travers, Walter
Travis, Byron Nelson, Sam Snead,
Ben Hogan, and all the rest could
match swings with Arnold Palmer,
Jack Nicklaus, Gary Player, Lee
Trevino, Tom Watson, Seve Bal-
lesteros, Bernhard Langer, Fuzzy
Zoeller, and Greg Norman—with all
of them at the top of their games.

There would be a women's division,
also, with today's top-notchers meet-
ing the stars of yesterday and the day
before: the Babe, Louise Suggs, Betty
Jameson, Patty Berg, who at seven-
teen competed in the 1935 United
States Women's Championship at the
Interlachen Golf Club in Hopkins,
Minnesota, which was won for the
sixth time by Glenna Collett Vare.
This field would be incomplete, of
course, without Mickey Wright and
some of the other leading players of
the last three decades. Nor can we
neglect an English player almost for-
gotten by all but the most ardent
golfing historians, Miss Joyce
Wethered, who, half a century ago,
could worry the best men players,
even when she was hitting from the
tiger tees.

Bobby Jones played at least two
rounds with Miss Wethered, both of
which are described in this collection.
They played in 1930 at St. Andrews
and, five years later, at Jones's home
club, East Lake, in Atlanta. This was
his reaction after the round on the
Old Course:

"Miss Wethered holed only one putt
of more than five feet, took three putts,
rather half-heartedly, from four
yards at the seventeenth after the
match was over, and yet she was

around St. Andrews in 75. She did not miss one shot; she did not even half-miss one shot; and when we finished I could not help saying that I had never played golf with anyone, man or woman, amateur or professional, who made me feel so utterly outclassed . . . I have no hesitation in saying that, accounting for the unavoidable handicap of a woman's lesser physical strength, she is the finest golfer I have ever seen."

Play was from the championship tees, and Jones said that when he hit his best drives, he was in front of Miss Wethered by only twenty yards or so.

In case you imagine Miss Wethered was playing above her usual form, look at the account of the charity match at the East Lake course, in Atlanta, in which she, Dorothy Kirby (then a fifteen-year-old Atlanta sensation), Jones, and Charlie Yates, the intercollegiate champion, took part. Miss Wethered had never seen East Lake and had never before putted on Bermuda greens, but she had a sparkling 74 from the back tees despite three-putting two greens. She outdrove both men on the 448-yard fourteenth, and, although hitting into a half-gale, was in the bunker, pin-high, with her second. Not realizing that the bunker had only a thin sun-baked layer of sand, she exploded some fifty yards over the green, pitched back, and ran in a 20-footer for a five. When the match ended, with Miss Kirby and Jones 1 up, the young lady had an 84, Jones a 71, Miss Wethered an unlucky 74, and Yates a 76. When O.B. Keeler complimented the English star on her performance, she replied simply, "I had to play well here, Bobby arranged the match . . . I couldn't let Bobby down, you know."

There are some excellent pieces about these great golfers of long ago, and dozens of photos of the players and of golf-loving celebrities, including Ring Lardner, the humorist. Lardner is shown with Grantland Rice, President Harding, and Henry Fletcher, Secretary of State, leaving the White House for a round at Chevy Chase. As they were playing, President Harding asked Lardner how he came to be included in the foursome. Lardner told the President it was because he wanted to be named Ambassador to Greece. The President wanted to know why Greece. Lardner explained that his wife didn't like Long Island!

My own knowldege and pleasure were increased by learning that Jones won more than sixty percent of the twenty-three major tournaments he entered, and in only four finished worse than second . . . that Macdonald Smith, in winning the 1933 Western Open at Olympia Fields, hit all seventy-two greens in regulation and was off the fairway only once . . . and that Stewart Maiden, Jones' famed teacher, anticipated one of Yogi Berra's remarks by many years. Asked what a golfer should be thinking during the swing, Maiden said: "That's a common fault . . . trying to think after the swing is started."

What a cast is gathered between these covers! Walter Hagen, who was 55th at Deal in 1920 in his first try for the British Open crown, and then crossed the English Channel almost immediately and won the French Open. Hagen returned the following year, 1921, and was sixth in the Open at St. Andrews. He came again the *next year, and this time he won the Open at Sandwich.*

Hagen's manager, Bob Harlow, has a moving piece in this collection on Hagen's ill-fated first try at the Open at Deal, with Hagen pluckily continuing to try after skill and luck both had deserted him, "playing every dreadful shot until the last putt was holed." Hagen was legendary for two traits: his urge to win and his ability to scramble. Harlow once said, "I believe that if Walter got in a game of tiddledy-winks with a couple of kids on the nursery floor, he would try as hard to beat them as he did to win the British Open." And the usually unruffled Bobby Jones, asked about the Haig's marvelous gift for the nearly impossible recovery, said he didn't mind playing those who hit the ball straight, no matter how good they were. "But when a man misses his drive, and then misses his second shot, and then wins the hole with a birdie—it gets my goat!"

You will meet in this splendid book such lovely folks as Freddie Tait of Scotland, who was killed when still a young man in 1901 during the Boer War. Darwin ends his panegyric on Tait with the words of the late Andrew Lang, another Tait admirer: "I never heard a word said against him except a solitary complaint that, in the lightness of his heart, he played pibrochs round the drowsy town at the midnight hour. What would we not give to hear his pipes again?"

Robert Cromie